D0427439

A Practitioner's Guide to Public Sector Productivity Improvement

A Practitioner's Guide to Public Sector Productivity Improvement

Elaine Morley

VNR VAN NOSTRAND REINHOLD COMPANY
New York

Library of Congress Catalog Card Number: 85-3188
ISBN: 0-442-26323-6

Manufactured in the United States of America

Published by Van Nostrand Reinhold Company Inc.
135 West 50th Street
New York, New York 10020

Van Nostrand Reinhold Company Limited
Molly Millars Lane
Wokingham, Berkshire RG11 2PY, England

Van Nostrand Reinhold
480 LaTrobe Street
Melbourne, Victoria 3000, Australia

Macmillan of Canada
Division of Gage Publishing Limited
164 Commander Boulevard
Agincourt, Ontario M1S 3C7, Canada

16 15 14 13 12 11 10 9 8 7 6 5 4 3 2 1

Library of Congress Cataloging in Publication Data
Morley, Elaine.
A practitioner's guide to public sector productivity improvement.

Includes index.
1. Government productivity. I. Title.
JF1525.P67M67 1985 351.007 85-3188
ISBN 0-442-26323-6

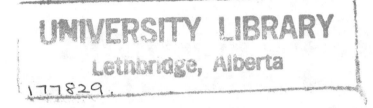

Preface

The public sector in the United States, particularly at the local government level, has been experiencing fiscal stress since the 1970s. While this problem may have diminished, or even disappeared in some locations, there is no assurance that fiscal stress is a thing of the past. Fiscal constraints arise not just from economic conditions, but from taxpayer willingness to support public services. Thus improvement of the former which is accompanied by reduction in the latter (which can and does occur), may still result in fiscal stress.

This book is intended to help public sector practitioners use productivity improvement to cope with fiscal stress. There has been growing interest in doing this since the 1970s. However, it appears that information on productivity improvement has not been organized in a way that makes it easy for practitioners to learn about the various ways to improve productivity and how to go about applying them in the public sector. Relatively few books on productivity are written with a public sector perspective. Most books on improvement methods are limited to describing, and promoting, use of a particular method. Such works often do not deal with all aspects of productivity improvement. Some books are collections of essays or articles, and may not always be cohesive, or may cover only selected aspects of productivity improvement.

This book represents an effort to make it easier for public sector practitioners to learn about, and use, productivity improvement. It is meant to be a comprehensive guide or resource that is not overwhelming in size or detail. It is comprehensive in the sense that it deals with the major aspects of productivity improvement in the public sector: its meaning, measurement, introduction, implementation, and maintenance. Material is presented in a clear and direct way that is intended to facilitate, and encourage, taking action.

Several themes underlie this book's approach to productivity improvement. One of these is its focus on efficiency. Productivity improvement is defined and measured in terms of efficiency here, and the techniques that are explained work to improve productivity by increasing staff efficiency. Another theme is the need for, and use of, a Productivity Improvement Program (PIP) to help plan for, introduce, and implement, productivity improvement in the public sector.

The final theme is use of a tailor-made, or individualized, approach to productivity improvement. This means that the improvement method used should be determined by individual circumstances, and that the practitioner should decide which method, or combination of methods, to use in a particular location. Thus a variety of improvement methods are described here to provide information needed to make such a choice, but no method is singled out as "the" way to improve productivity.

It is hoped that the presentation of these ideas will prove useful to government and nonprofit sector practitioners who are trying to grapple with the problems of providing services under conditions of fiscal constraint.

ELAINE MORLEY

Acknowledgments

As is usually the case, this book would not have reached publication in its present form without the direct and indirect contributions of many people. Therefore, as is usually the case, the author would like to acknowledge this help, while accepting responsibility for any errors remaining herein. Thanks are extended to: Alan Walter Steiss, for initiating this endeavor; Stephen Keeble, for keeping it alive and offering helpful advice; Gerald R. Galbo, for bringing it to publication; several unidentified manuscript reviewers, and two who were identified—Walter L. Balk and John Tepper Marlin—for their comments and suggestions; several typists who worked on various stages of the manuscript, particularly Dolores Kohler, Brenda Branson, and Sandra Crome; numerous Urban Affairs and Policy Analysis graduate students in my productivity improvement classes, who unknowingly helped shape my ideas and presentation; Al Kahn, for providing "time off" from other projects at crucial stages of manuscript preparation; Rob Boyle and Jay McKay, for providing encouragement and support. Particular thanks are extended to Mark Drucker, for providing departmental support needed to produce the manuscript, for helping to find the right words, and for providing encouragement, advice, and support.

Contents

A Practitioner's Guide to Public Sector Productivity Improvement

Section I
What Is Public Productivity and Why Is It Important?

This section provides the foundation for understanding and employing productivity improvement methods in public sector and nonprofit organizations. The first chapter explains the importance of productivity/efficiency in the context of the fiscal climate of the 1980s. It also provides an overview of the contents and organization of the remaining chapters of the book.

The second chapter explains the meaning of public sector productivity and how it is approached in this book. The closely related topic, productivity measurement, is also explained. Understanding what public sector productivity means, and how it can be used to deal with current fiscal problems, are prerequisites for launching a successful productivity improvement program.

1
INTRODUCTION

It's no secret that public managers working in state and local governments have experienced fiscal difficulties in the early part of the 1980s. Will these problems extend through the entire decade? That remains to be seen. But we cannot wait to find out. Managers must act *now* to find ways to continue providing needed government services with limited or shrinking resources. This book describes a course of action to obtain more public services from existing resources: improving productivity through staff efficiency.

This book will serve as a guide to selecting and using techniques that can be successfully applied in the public sector to increase employee efficiency and thus improve overall productivity. It also describes a framework useful for introducing and implementing these techniques, the Productivity Improvement Program (PIP). This chapter will briefly review why productivity improvement is needed in the public sector now. It will also present an overview of the perspective and organization of the book.

WHY YOU NEED PRODUCTIVITY IMPROVEMENT

Fiscal Crisis. The service provision and fiscal climate, particularly for local governments, seems to have come full circle since the expansionist 1960s. Deteriorating tax bases and rising costs of service provision during the 1970s led some cities, most notably New York, to teeter on the brink of bankruptcy. Public sentiment in the form of the "taxpayer revolt" that began with Proposition 13 in California in 1978 complicated matters by making it politically difficult to increase taxes to offset declining revenues. Since many people who voted for such measures apparently did not want reductions in most public services, providing government services in the 1970s became increasingly challenging for many public managers.

Public reaction against the growth in taxing and spending, as well as perceptions of inefficiency and waste in government, culminated in the election of Ronald Reagan as President in 1980. While all aspects of his "new federalism" have not been enacted (and some may never be), some of its implications are fairly clear. Less federal aid will be provided to state and local governments. At the same time, increased responsibility for provision of a variety of services will be transferred to them. It is reasonable to expect that fiscal problems will continue and/or worsen under these conditions. The degree to which recession and inflation continue to plague the economy compounds the problem by increasing the need for services and raising the cost of service provision.

Given the combined effects of fiscal stress and public opinion, there are three things public managers can do to improve their situation:

1. Increase revenues, particularly nontax revenues (such as fees for services, licenses, etc.)
2. Reduce service provision
3. Increase the amount of services provided with existing resources.

The first two options are least desirable from a political perspective, since they have negative effects on citizens. Thus the most viable option for dealing with fiscal stress is to try to increase the amount of services provided with existing resources. This translates into increasing the efficiency of resource use. Since the major input in the production of most services is labor, staff efficiency is the logical focus for improvement. Increasing staff efficiency will contribute to general productivity improvement (these concepts will be explained in greater detail in chapter 2).

Government Productivity Efforts. Although improving productivity or efficiency in the public sector is particularly appropriate at this point in time, it is certainly not a new concept. Interest in this subject expanded during the late 1960s and 1970s, at least partly due to federal efforts. The federal government set an example by beginning to measure and improve its own productivity, and by creating the National Center for Productivity and the Quality of Working Life. The Center's state and local government productivity improvement efforts primarily involved supporting research and demonstration projects, distributing information, and generating support and interest.[1] Professional organizations and journals also paid increasing attention to the subject.

Although it is difficult to trace efforts by state and local governments to improve their productivity, it seems clear that they have grown considerably since 1970. A few programs have been widely publicized, such as those in New York City, Nassau County, New York, Dallas, Phoenix, Wisconsin, and Washington State. Efforts elsewhere have been cited in reports on different improvement techniques. A 1976 survey found that 400 cities were involved in improving productivity to some degree.[2] Unfortunately, the lack of consistent monitoring and/or reporting of improvement programs makes it impossible to determine the true extent of state and local involvement.

The above shows that public sector productivity/efficiency improvement is not a new concept, and it has been successfully applied at the state and local level. Interest and involvement in productivity improvement has increased in recent years, a period of deteriorating fiscal conditions. This indicates that public managers have recognized that improving productivity can be an effective tool for dealing with fiscal constraints. This, in fact, is the theme of this book. Many, if not most, state and local governments are facing some degree of fiscal constraints in the 1980s, and it is unclear when, or whether, this situation will improve. Improving productivity/efficiency can help alleviate, but not eliminate fiscal problems by increasing the amount of services produced with a limited quantity of resources.

HOW TO USE THIS BOOK

The purpose of this book is to help public managers successfully introduce and implement techniques to improve productivity by increasing staff efficiency. This book can be useful to managers at a variety of levels in local, state, and federal government and in service-providing, nonprofit agencies. Students preparing for management careers in this sector are also part of the intended audience.

Since productivity improvement must be individualized to suit prevailing conditions, this book will not prescribe *exactly* what to do. It *will* provide a solid foundation in the fundamentals of productivity improvement and improvement methods. It will describe the options available and how to use them, as well as providing guidelines for applicability. It will identify potential problem areas and how to deal with them. This will enable the reader to select the approach(es) best suited for his/her circumstances and implement them successfully.

This book provides a comprehensive perspective that views productivity improvement as a process. The framework for the process is the PIP. This framework can be used by a central governing body (city, county, or state) to establish a governmentwide productivity improvement effort. A scaled-down version of the PIP can be applied for improvement efforts confined to a department or agency. Note that the term *Productivity Improvement Program* is being used here even though the focus of improvement is staff efficiency. However, *productivity improvement* is the more conventional and familiar term. It also represents the intended goal of the program. Therefore, productivity improvement and productivity improvement program (or PIP), will be used for the sake of simplicity and familiarity.

The chapters in this book are organized to describe the actions and/or information needed once the decision is made to improve productivity. This involves a sequence of steps common to making any organizational change. These include: gathering information about the change; planning and organizing for it; implementation; and evaluation and maintenance.

Basic information about the change is required first. Section I discusses the need for improving productivity/efficiency, and explains their meaning and measurement in the public sector context. These basic concepts must be understood before undertaking an improvement program.

Planning and organizing for productivity improvement is the second stage (section II). The chapters in this section deal with a structured program for implementing change, called a Productivity Improvement Program, which is described in chapter 3. Next, organizing and staffing to implement the PIP is discussed. Introducing the program is the subject of chapter 5. Establishing a system to measure productivity is covered in chapter 6. The section concludes by discussing how to select the appropriate improvement method(s).

Implementing productivity improvement is the next step (section III). Each chapter describes a different efficiency improvement method (or group of related methods) that might be implemented at this stage. Each chapter explains how the method improves productivity and how to implement it. Examples of public sector applications are provided, and factors affecting implementation or use are noted.

Follow-up activities are the final stage in introducing change (section IV). This section deals with the ongoing aspects of the PIP. This includes continued evaluation to insure that productivity remains at satisfactory levels. It also explains steps that can be taken to maintain improvement methods in the long run. The last chapter summarizes the material covered.

The PIP is described here from the perspective of a citywide approach to provide a consistent and familiar frame of reference. As noted earlier, however, concepts and processes discussed are generally applicable to other central governments or to departments or agencies. While this book is oriented toward those involved with introducing productivity improvement at centralized or departmental levels, it should be of use and interest to those involved in productivity improvement in any way.

NOTES

1. General Accounting Office, *The Federal Role in Improving Productivity—Is the National Center for Productivity and Quality of Working Life the Proper Mechanism?* (Washington, D. C.: U.S. General Accounting Office, 1978), pp. 28-29.
2. Rackham S. Fukuhara, "Productivity Improvement in Cities" in *The Municipal Year Book* 1977 (Washington, D. C.: International City Management Association, 1977), pp. 193-200.

2
THE MEANING AND MEASUREMENT OF PUBLIC SECTOR PRODUCTIVITY

Before implementing a program to improve efficiency or productivity, it is important to know what these terms *mean.* This chapter will strengthen understanding of these concepts by:

1. describing different meanings of productivity; and
2. explaining how to measure it.

Increased familiarity with these closely related subjects will make it easier to understand what is involved in improving productivity/efficiency. The first section of this chapter will explain how productivity is defined in the public sector and how it is related to efficiency. It will also discuss the perspective that will be emphasized in this book. The second section of this chapter will explain basic terms, concepts, and methods used in measuring producitivity. (A more detailed explanation of measurement is provided in chapter 6, which describes how to establish and use a measurement system.)

WHAT IS PRODUCTIVITY?

A Simple Definition. Although it may seem surprising, a common, agreed-upon definition of public productivity does not appear to exist.[1] Productivity seems to mean different things to different people. This section will explore the various meaning of productivity to provide a clear understanding of the term.

The simplest definition of productivity is the one used in the private sector (where concerns with productivity originated):

> Productivity is the relationship between outputs and inputs, expressed as a ratio (O/I). It is a measure of efficiency.

In other words, productivity refers to how *efficiently* resources are converted into outputs. In fact, the output/input ratio is often characterized as a measure of efficiency. The above definition will be used here because of its simplicity and clarity, and because efficient resource use is one of the major concerns in the public sector during periods of fiscal constraint. (Other reasons for preferring this definition are discussed below.)

This definition can be illustrated with a simple flow chart of the production process:

PRODUCTION PROCESS

INPUTS ⟶ THROUGHPUTS ⟶ OUTPUTS

Inputs consist of labor (personnel), equipment, and (primarily in the private sector), raw materials. The throughput stage is where "production" takes place. Either service activities are performed (as is primarily the case in the public sector), or materials are transformed (as in manufacturing). Outputs are the results of the production stage. They may be completed services or finished products, for example, a filled pothole, an automobile. Only those goods or services that meet acceptable standards of quality should be counted as outputs. That is, defective or incomplete outputs should not be counted. For example, a filled pothole that must be *re*filled the next day should only be counted once, since the first job was inadequate.

Government Productivity. The simple, or narrow, definition of productivity explained above is generally used in the private sector. However, it is not as widely accepted for measuring public sector productivity. The major reason for this is that the public sector primarily provides services, not products.

Although services are the output of the government production process, they are not as "final" an output as products are in the private sector. That is, services are provided in order to reach some desired social goal or consequence. For example, streets are cleaned to maintain public health and attractiveness; police patrols are intended to reduce crime, etc. Thus for the public sector, the production process flow chart is expanded:

GOVERNMENT PRODUCTION PROCESS

INPUTS ⟶ THROUGHPUT ⟶ OUTPUTS ⟶ CONSEQUENCES

Achievement of desired consequences is viewed as *effectiveness,* which is sometimes described as a "quality" dimension of output. This differs from the concept of quality in private sector production. There, quality is often an observable part of the finished product (and is monitored in the quality control phase of production). If quality is not observable (as in most private sector service production), it is assumed to be reflected in sales.

Since neither of these methods for assessing quality are applicable to government services, consequences are generally accounted for in an expanded definition of productivity:

> Public sector productivity is often viewed as a measure of efficiency *and* effectiveness.

Arguments favoring this broad definition are usually based on the greater importance of service consequences and/or the perception that focusing on efficiency will result in deterioration of effectiveness.[2]

Emphasizing Efficiency. There is no doubt that both efficiency and effectiveness are important. However, for reasons explained below, it seems preferable to view them as reflecting different dimensions of performance[3] than to include both in an expanded definition of productivity.

This book will focus on the *efficiency* dimension, using the narrow definition of productivity. There are several reasons for this approach, which are:

1. The efficiency-oriented definition of productivity has a long tradition of use and acceptance due to its application in the private sector. It is a conceptually simple model, based on the direct relationship between inputs and outputs. Therefore, the information it provides can be readily understood as a clear indicator of the output production of specific resources. For this to be the case, direct service outputs, such as the amount of refuse collected, number of cases investigated, etc., should be used in this model.

Effectiveness measures do not fit this model as well as direct outputs because the process by which inputs are converted into *consequences* is not clear and direct. It can be strongly affected by factors outside of the production process.[4] These can include physical conditions as well as human behavior. For example, crime prevention is partly the result of Police Department inputs, but it is also affected by the behavior and cooperation of citizens. The link between inputs and service effectiveness tends to be offset or augmented by outside influences frequently. Therefore, it is more appropriate to use direct outputs in this model.

2. In addition to conceptual clarity, defining productivity in efficiency terms may be perceived as being fairer to departments. This is because departments have more control over inputs that lead to direct outputs, and thus can influence their efficiency more than their effectiveness. This may be important in gaining departmental and employee support for improvement efforts (which will be discussed in greater detail in section II).

3. Finally, from a practical perspective, it is usually easier to measure service activities than it is to measure effectiveness. Of course, it can be difficult to measure either. Service outputs are hard to measure because services are intangible; there are no physical products to count. You must

measure completed service activities instead. On the other hand, effectiveness is difficult to measure because it involves analyzing impacts on social conditions. This is particularly difficult for preventive services, where effectiveness is represented by reduction or prevention of something, such as crime or disease. As a final point, it is more difficult to construct and interpret a measure that includes *both* efficiency and effectiveness data, although it certainly is possible to do so.[5]

The above discussion is not meant to suggest effectiveness and its measurement are unimportant. It is merely intended to explain why this book is focusing on the efficiency-based definition of productivity. This does not mean effectiveness and other aspects of service quality should be ignored. They are part of the quality control monitoring aspect of the Productivity Improvement Program (PIP). Effectiveness can also be monitored apart from improvement efforts, as is often done in program evaluation or Total Performance Measurement. However, placing emphasis on efficiency seems to be clearer, as well as being more in line with current concerns about fiscal limitations.

MEASURING PRODUCTIVITY

Why Measure Productivity? Measurement plays a critical role in productivity/efficiency improvement. It is used:

- to locate areas where improvement is needed;
- to act as a feedback mechanism.

Measurement is initially used to analyze current conditions to determine where improvement is needed. After improvement methods are implemented, "before" and "after" productivity ratios are used to monitor their impact. Collecting and analyzing feedback data allows corrective action to be taken, if necessary. It can also be helpful in planning for future efforts by indicating which methods are most successful.

This section will explain how to measure productivity in terms of efficiency. The definition of productivity requires that outputs and inputs of services included in the improvement effort must be measured. The following sections explain *how* they should be measured and how productivity ratios should be constructed.

How to Measure Outputs. Because governments provide services rather than products, outputs should be measured in terms of completed service activities, such as: streets cleaned; clients served; arrests made; checks processed; and so on. Since most departments provide a number of different services, multiple output indicators are needed both to reflect the variety of functions performed and to monitor the effect of improvement methods on them. Table 2-1 provides some examples of output measures.

Just as departments require multiple indicators, some services require more than one output measure to reflect the full range of activities associated with them.[6] For example, crime prevention might be measured in

Table 2-1. Illustrative Output Measures For Municipal Services.*

SANITATION—SOLID WASTE COLLECTION AND DISPOSAL

Tons of waste collected
Tons of waste disposed (may be subdivided by disposal method)
Curb-miles of street cleaned

POLICE PROTECTION

Miles patrolled
Investigations conducted (by crime category)
Arrests made (by crime category)
Response to service calls (by type of call)
Stolen property recovered

FIRE PROTECTION

Fires extinguished (by type of fire)
Responses to nonfire emergencies
Fire prevention inspections
Fire investigations

LIBRARY SERVICE

Items circulated
Items cataloged
Number of users

PUBLIC TRANSPORTATION

Number of passengers
Number of vehicle-miles

STREET MAINTENANCE

Miles of streets/sidewalks constructed
Miles of streets/sidewalks maintained

STREET MAINTENANCE (CONTINUED)

Number of repairs made
Signs/signals installed
Signs/signals maintained or reapired

HEALTH AND WELFARE SERVICE

Clients served (by service category)
Applications processed
Health care services performed (by type)
Counseling sessions held (by type)

RECREATION SERVICES

Hours of operation (by type of facility)
Acres (or feet) maintained (by type of maintenance task)

ADMINISTRATIVE AND SUPPORT SERVICES

Cleaning and maintenance:
- Number of repair or maintenance operations (by type)
- Square feet cleaned
- Number of other cleaning activities performed (by type)

Office and personnel functions:
- Number of forms/reports prepared (by type)
- Number of forms/reports processed (by type)
- Number of employees trained (by job category)
- Hours of training (by job category)
- Licenses/permits issued

*Outputs mentioned here are intended to represent typical services performed by the departments indicated. The source for a number of outputs included here is: Harry P. Hatry et al., *How Effective Are Your Community Services?* (Washington, D.C.: The Urban Institute, 1977), pp. 241-244.

terms of patrols, investigations, and arrests. Using only one output indicator for a complex service will not fully reflect the work performed or the level of productivity associated with it. However, it may be sufficient to use one output measure for less complex services. For example, tons of refuse collected would be an adequate output indicator for refuse collection service. If a single measure is used, the one chosen should reflect the primary purpose of that service.

Each output measure selected should reflect a fairly uniform degree of employee effort to provide the service. In other words, outputs should be basically homogeneous. Therefore, output measures should be subdivided into categories that represent similar levels of difficulty, where applicable.[7]

Although improving provision of direct services is usually the focus of attention, efforts should also be directed toward administrative and support services. Considerable gains in overall productivity and/or cost savings can frequently be made in these areas. Therefore, their outputs will have to be measured just as any other activity subject to improvement efforts. Maintenance outputs can be measured in terms of area cleaned, items repaired or maintained, or similar measures of activity. Office outputs can also be measured. The number of forms processed, pages typed, items filed, cards keypunched, and so on, can be counted in order to monitor productivity in the office. As in the case of direct services, supporting service outputs should also be grouped into homogeneous categories.

How to Measure Inputs. Once you have measured service output, the next step is to measure input. Ideally, this would include all inputs (labor, capital, supplies, etc.), used to provide a particular output. This type of "global" measure is primarily of interest to higher-level officials. They are more likely to be concerned with efficiency of all resources because they are responsible for policies affecting patterns of use and/or allocation of different types of resources.[8] However, this form of input measurement is not often used in the public sector because of its complexity. For example, much capital is in the form of buildings and infrastructure (e.g., streets, roads, sewers), that cannot be allocated among services. Other resources are also frequently shared among services.

In practice, direct labor alone is typically used as the input measure. Since services are labor intensive, this approach is a reasonable one because it highlights the major input in the productivity ratio. It is also common practice to measure private sector productivity in terms of labor only. This type of measure is of primary importance to lower-level administrators who have major responsibility for monitoring, (and improving), staff performance. Labor efficiency is also of interest to policymakers because it represents a major portion of overall productivity.[9]

Labor inputs are typically expressed in terms of labor, (or staff), hours (although different units of time, e.g., days, weeks, or months, are sometimes used). Only hours that are considered part of the workday should be counted. That is, lunches and breaks should be omitted. However, idle time (time spent waiting, for example), should be included among hours worked. Thus most labor days will be between seven and eight hours long. Since most employees divide their time among different service activities, some effort should be made to correctly allocate employee work hours when measuring productivity. (How to allocate staff time will be discussed in chapter 6.) If this is not done, actual productivity will be understated. An example will illustrate this problem:

Time Allocation Example

> Assume a secretary spends 3 hours typing a 24-page report and devotes the rest of an 8-hour workday to other functions. Typing productivity in this case is actually 8 pages per labor hour. However, if the allocation of hours is not known and output (the number of pages typed), is divided by total labor hours (8), productivity would be understated as being 3 pages per hour.

This example really illustrates two points: the need to use multiple output measures to correctly reflect service or job outputs; and the need to allocate employee time among activities.

In addition to labor hours, another common approach to input measurement is to add up the costs of all inputs (labor, supplies, equipment, etc.), used to produce output. This approach is not used here because it can lead to overemphasizing cost reduction as an approach to improving productivity. For example, buying less expensive supplies or reducing employee salaries would be counted as an improvement in productivity if inputs were measured in this way. Although cost cutting is desirable, it is not included in the focus of this book (increasing staff efficiency). Labor hours are the more appropriate input measure for the latter, and will be used here.

The Productivity Ratio. The final aspect of measurement requires putting the output and input measures together in ratio form in order to measure productivity (see example in table 2-2). Dividing outputs by inputs shows the hourly production rate for a specific point in time. However, it does not indicate whether productivity is better or worse than before.

Because productivity improvement implies a comparative process, *two* ratios are needed. Returning to the example in Table 2-2, assume that 80 clients were interviewed the prior week, using the same amount of labor

Table 2-2. Example of Productivity Ratio Calculation

MEASURING OUTPUTS

In a particular social service agency office, 100 clients were interviewed to determine eligibility during one week. Thus total output in the activity category, client eligibility interviews, was 100.

MEASURING INPUTS

In this office there are three employees who have responsibility for conducting interviews. Each works 40 hours a week, a total of 120 labor hours. However, they each spend only half their time conducting interviews, for a total of 60 labor hours.

MEASURING PRODUCTIVITY

Outputs must be divided by inputs:

$$\frac{100}{60} = 1.7 \text{ interviews/labor hour}$$

input. The productivity ratio for that week would be 1.3 interviews/labor hour. The *change* in productivity would be shown in a productivity index as:

$$\begin{matrix}\text{Week 2} \\ \text{Week 1}\end{matrix} \quad \frac{1.7 \text{ interviews/labor hour}}{1.3 \text{ interviews/labor hour}} = 1.31$$

In this case, productivity increased 31 percent in the second week.

Any productivity index greater than one indicates an increase in productivity. An increase can occur for several reasons:

More output is produced with the same level of input.

The same level of output is produced with fewer inputs.

More output is produced with fewer inputs.

More output is produced with more inputs, but output increased more than input.

In order to monitor the impact of productivity improvement methods, efficiency ratios for different points in time are generally used. Sometimes other comparisons are desirable. These include comparisons of:

Different levels of productivity among work crews (e.g., maintenance crews, refuse collectors).

Productivity differences in different offices (e.g., social service caseworkers in different neighborhoods; typists in different departments).

Productivity differences between units of government (employees performing the same kind of work in other, comparable locations).

Any of these comparisons is valid if the service activity is performed in essentially the same way and in similar settings (i.e., in areas of comparable size, with similar social and environmental characteristics). Such comparisons can be used to indicate where improvement may be needed. Comparisons over time indicate whether or not improvement has occurred.

SUMMARY

A thorough understanding of the concept of productivity is necessary before beginning an improvement program. This chapter has explained the meaning of productivity/efficiency in the public sector and how to measure it. This chapter, and the previous one, have provided the fundamentals needed before launching a productivity improvement program. The next section explains the functions of the program and how to operate it.

NOTES

1. For discussions of the definition of public productivity, see, for example: Walter L. Balk, "Toward a Government Productivity Ethic," *Public Administration Review,* 38 (January/February 1978): 46; Jesse Burkhead and Patrick J. Hennigan, "Productivity Analysis: A Search for Definition and Order," *Public Administration Review* 38 (January/February 1978): 34; C. Gregory Buntz, "Problems and Issues in Human Service Productivity Improvement," *Public Productivity Review* 5 (December 1981): 300-302; Osbin L. Ervin, "A Conceptual Niche For Municipal Productivity," *Public Productivity Review* 3 (Summer/Fall 1978): 15-22; Harry P. Hatry, "The Status of Productivity Measurement in the Public Sector," *Public Administration Review* 38 (January/February 1978): 28-29.
2. See, for example, Balk, "Productivity Ethic," p. 46; Hatry, "Status of Productivity Measurement," p. 28; Ellen Doree Rosen, "O·K Work," *Public Productivity Review* 5 (September 1981): 208-211.
3. Jacob B. Ukeles, *Doing More With Less* (New York: AMACOM, 1982), p. 232.
4. Ross and Burkhead, *Productivity in the Local Government Sector* (Lexington, Ma.: Lexington Books, 1974), pp. 48-49.
5. For one example of a combined measure, see: Rosen, O·K Work": 211-215.
6. Harry P. Hatry et al., *Efficiency Measurement for Local Government Services* (Washington, D.C.: The Urban Institute, 1979), pp. 5-6.
7. Ibid., p. viii.
8. Ibid., p. 5.
9. Ibid., p. 15.

Section II
Establishing a Productivity Improvement Program

The chapters in this section deal with one of the most critical parts of any program—its implementation. While there is a natural tendency to concentrate attention and activity on the actual efforts to improve productivity, it is a serious mistake to overlook the steps involved in launching a new program. Insufficient attention to these factors could lead to suboptimal results and, possibly, to program failure.

The chapters to follow explain the steps necessary to successfully establish a Productivity Improvement Program (PIP). Chapter 3 begins by explaining what a PIP is and why it is needed. Chapter 4 discusses organization and staffing matters. Goals and strategies for introducing the PIP on a citywide basis are presented in chapter 5, along with a model for the introductory process. Chapter 6 describes how to establish a productivity measurement system. The process of selecting improvement strategies and factors that influence the choice of methods are covered in chapter 7. These chapters will provide the information needed to operationalize the PIP, a vital first step before improvement efforts can successfully be undertaken.

3
THE PRODUCTIVITY IMPROVEMENT PROGRAM

Productivity Improvement Program (PIP), is the name being used for the particular framework or organization recommended here for introducing and implementing improvement methods. This chapter will explain the scope, structure, and functions of this PIP. This will help you understand and take the necessary steps to operationalize the PIP, which will be described in the rest of section II. Before examining the PIP in greater detail, an explanation of why it is needed will help clarify its purpose and functions.

WHY YOU NEED A PIP

There are two major reasons why the framework of a PIP is needed. First, failure to establish some kind of program or structure leaves productivity improvement to chance. Productivity can, and often does, improve without an organized improvement program. It might occur because the management of a specific agency or department is particularly interested in seeking out and implementing improvement methods. It might occur because someone —an employee, supervisor, or manager—suggests a way to "do things better." It often occurs when equipment is replaced with new models designed to enhance productivity. The gradual transition from manual to electric typewriters to word processors provides ample illustration of this.

All of these are acceptable ways of improving productivity. The problem is that without some kind of organized effort, they will occur at random. Given the fiscal problems besetting the public sector, we cannot wait for productivity improvement to happen by chance. A more structured approach, such as the PIP described here, will greatly increase the likelihood that appropriate methods will be employed where and when they are needed.

The second reason for needing a PIP is that improving government productivity is a fairly complicated and extensive process. Governments encompass a variety of agencies and/or departments. The appropriate improvement method(s) for each service or type of work involved must be selected and implemented. This is a substantial task, and requires a system for planning and organizing the actions necessary to carry it out. The need for such a system can best be demonstrated by describing what the PIP does, which is the objective of the following section.

WHAT IS A PIP?

The PIP recommended here performs the functions necessary for planning, organizing, and guiding the introduction and implementation of improvement efforts. The functions are needed partly because of the scope of the program. The scope also affects the structure of the PIP. Therefore, both scope and structure will be briefly described before moving on to an explanation of PIP functions.

Scope. This book is using a governmentwide PIP as its model. This will be referred to as a citywide PIP, although material presented here will generally be applicable to other units of government.

The citywide PIP is a centralized effort to introduce productivity improvement to all city agencies and departments. The impetus for the program is most likely to come from the office of the mayor (or city manager), or from the budget office. There are three reasons for this: Personnel in these offices are most keenly aware of fiscal problems; they are also likely to be familiar with the benefits of productivity improvement; finally, they are in a position to require or urge city departments to participate in productivity improvement.

Although governmentwide PIPs are common, it is also possible for a PIP to be confined to an agency or department. This also fits the model of a centralized effort. In this case, however, improvement would be introduced to various units within the agency. Although a smaller scope would be involved, the top-down approach of the citywide PIP would still apply. Thus most of the points made regarding a citywide PIP are applicable to agency or departmental programs.

Structure. The structure of the PIP is determined by its centralized perspective. There are two basic components. The major component is a central unit that introduces the program to city agencies and departments and guides their productivity improvement efforts. The other component is a counterpart to the central unit that is formed in each agency and department. These decentralized units act as liaisons with the central PIP office. They also work with the central office to help it carry out its functions at the agency or department level.

Functions. The central PIP unit acts as a project management office or "command center." To do this, it initially works with central administrative offices (such as budgeting, personnel, and the mayor or city manager's office) in setting overall policy. It also performs a continuing coordinating role with these offices, reviewing PIP plans and activities to insure they do not violate existing policies or create problems. The central unit's primary responsibility, however, is introducing productivity improvement concepts to agencies and departments and helping them implement improvement methods. The steps involved in this process are shown in chronological order in Table 3-1. These steps will be explained below to clarify what the PIP entails. Detailed action steps to carry out introduction and implementation functions will be provided in the following chapters. (Maintenance functions will be discussed in the last section of the book.)

1. Introduce and gain support for the concept of productivity improvement and the PIP. The central PIP unit introduces the PIP to managers and employees (and the public, if desired). This includes explaining what is involved in productivity improvement and the PIP. More importantly, the PIP office works to gain management and employee support for the program by explaining its benefits. Policies or actions to minimize negative impacts will also be explained at this time.

2. Establish a measurement system. In this step, the central PIP office determines what kind of measurement data are available and what additional measures will be needed to monitor productivity improvement. A system for collecting and evaluating this data should be established during the introduction phase of the PIP. Data collection and evaluation continues throughout the life of the program.

3. Analyze agencies and departments to determine where improvements should be made. The PIP office must decide where productivity improvement is most needed and where implementation of improvement methods is most feasible. This is done in conjunction with the agencies or departments that are involved in the program.

4. Select and implement improvement methods. This step also is a cooperative effort involving the participating agencies or departments. There

Table 3-1. Checklist of PIP Functions

INTRODUCTION AND IMPLEMENTATION PHASES
1. Introduce and gain support for the concept of productivity improvement and the PIP
2. Establish a measurement system
3. Analyze agencies and departments to determine where improvements should be made
4. Select and implement improvement methods
5. Monitor newly implemented methods and take corrective action as necessary
MAINTENANCE PHASE
6. Continue monitoring and evaluating data
7. Encourage maintenance of improvement efforts
8. Update or replace improvement methods as needed

Table 3-2. Methods for Improving Productivity through Staff Efficiency

Work or job redesign (including work standards and redistribution of work)
Incentive systems (monetary and nonmonetary)
Job enrichment
Increased participation (including MBO, flexible working hours, and quality circles)
New technology
Organization restructuring
Resource reallocation

are a variety of methods that focus on increasing staff efficiency to improve productivity (a list is provided in Table 3-2). In this step, the PIP office and the department determine which method (or methods), is best suited for each unit's type of work and work environment. Once selected, the central office helps the agency implement the method(s). This may require training for managers and/or staff.

5. Monitor newly implemented methods and take corrective action as necessary. This step is self-explanatory. The central PIP unit and the implementing department will evaluate the impacts of the improvement method. If it does not appear to be improving productivity, or if problems are evident, corrective measures will be taken.

SUMMARY

The heart of the PIP is clearly the selection and implementation of improvement methods. However, the steps leading up to this are important because they pave the way for making appropriate choices and implementing them successfully. Similarly, follow-up steps are necessary because they facilitate continuation of improvement methods after implementation. The remaining chapters in this section will provide information to help operationalize the PIP and perform the activities included in the introduction and implementation stages.

4
ORGANIZING AND STAFFING THE PRODUCTIVITY IMPROVEMENT PROGRAM

This chapter describes how to create the organization that will carry out the Productivity Improvement Program's (PIP's) functions. This includes gaining authority for the PIP, and organizing and staffing the central office. The functions and organization of the central office's counterparts within city agencies will also be discussed.

GAINING AUTHORITY FOR A PIP

As noted in chapter 3, it is likely that the idea for the PIP was initiated by the mayor or city manager, or with the executive's approval, by a close associate. If this is not the case, executive support for the PIP must be attained before the central PIP office can be created.[1] The reasons for this are that executive approval is needed:

To create a new, high-level office and establish policy guidelines.

To allocate resources for staffing and operating the office.

To provide the office with authority to conduct a citywide program.

The first two reasons are self-explanatory. A new, high-level office in city government cannot be formed without the consent of the executive. Creating a new office requires reallocation of resources to staff and operate it. This reallocation is also likely to require executive approval or support.

The third reason may not be as obvious as the first two. The primary role of the central PIP office is to introduce productivity improvement to all city departments or agencies. While some departments may be eager to cooperate in this effort, others may be reluctant to do so. In order to assure necessary cooperation on the part of all departments, the central unit must be perceived as acting on behalf of the executive. The executive, therefore, should authorize the central office to implement the PIP and direct city agencies and departments to cooperate with it.

When executive support is sought, the suggestion for a PIP should be presented on its merits; that is, emphasis should be placed on its potential for helping alleviate fiscal distress. It should not be oversold, however, since it cannot be expected to fully compensate for fiscal reductions in most cases. A clear presentation of what a PIP entails should be made (this book will be useful in preparing such a presentation). Reference to other public sector PIPs and their accomplishments may also be helpful (numerous references appear in later chapters, or other sources can be used to locate examples).[2] The potential political value of a successful PIP may also be a useful selling point. (However, the risks of failure inherent in introducing any new program should also be noted.) Other tactics for gaining support are dependent on the personalities and situations involved. Therefore, this section will not attempt to describe the art of persuasion.

In summary, executive support is a prerequisite for a citywide PIP. Once this has been secured, the next step is to create a central PIP office.

ORGANIZING THE CENTRAL OFFICE

The primary decision to be made in organizing the central office is whether to create a separate office or whether to locate it in an existing department. This section will present the merits of each position.

Separate PIP Office. One way to create a separate PIP office is as a new unit in the office of the mayor or city manager. It might be headed by a deputy mayor or assistant city manager, for example. While an entire new department could be created, this seems unnecessary except for larger cities (or for counties or states).

The primary advantage of a separate unit is its high visibility. This underscores the importance of the program. Locating it in the mayor or manager's office emphasizes executive commitment to the program. Another advantage of a separate office is that the staff will be able to devote all of its time to productivity improvement.

The disadvantages of a separate office are primarily cost related. An entire new staff must be hired or transferred from other units. A separate unit may be more costly to operate than a unit within another department. Finally, it might take somewhat longer to create a separate unit, and, therefore, for it to become operational.

PIP Office in Another Department. The alternative to a separate office is placing the PIP office in a department that performs related functions. The most logical department is budgeting. Other reasonable choices are personnel or program evaluation. The attitude of the department head, staff capabilities, and availability of resources would have to be considered in selecting a location for the office.

The primary advantage of this alternative is that it is likely to be less expensive than other choices. At least some staff from the existing department might be transferred to the new unit, perhaps on a part-time basis. Other department resources could also be shared. Since an entire new structure does not have to be created, the office may be able to start functioning more quickly.

The major disadvantage of this form of organization is that it is less visible than a separate office. Another disadvantage is that members may have other responsibilities within the department and not be able to work exclusively on the PIP.

There are some aspects of this arrangement that could be either advantageous or disadvantageous, depending on the circumstances.

Working with a particular department head is an advantage if he/she is a good executive and is supportive of the PIP. Otherwise, this arrangement can be problematic. Being associated with the image of a specific department can also either help or hinder the PIP. Some people feel that a budget agency is a poor choice for a PIP office because of its typical adversary role with operating agencies, and/or because it may make the PIP seem like a budget-cutting device.[3] On the positive side, the budget office may be a good location for the PIP because it has the power to reallocate resources to expedite improvement efforts.[4]

Choosing a Location. The advantages and disadvantages of the alternative locations for a central PIP office are summarized in Table 4-1. In general, a separate office is likely to cost a bit more and may be slower to operationalize, but creates higher visibility for the program. Visibility can be

Table 4-1. Organizational Alternatives for a Central PIP Office

ALTERNATIVE 1: A SEPARATE OFFICE
Advantages
• High visibility underscores importance of the PIP
• Allows staff to concentrate on productivity improvement
Disadvantages
• More expensive
• Requires entirely new staff
• May take longer to become functional
ALTERNATIVE 2: LOCATED IN EXISTING DEPARTMENT
Advantages
• Less expensive; use some resources of department
• May be able to organize and become operational more quickly
Disadvantages
• Less visibility
• Staff may not be able to work exclusively on the PIP

an important factor in gaining acceptance for the program among departments and agencies. This option may, therefore, be preferable when city agencies are not interested in, or are resistant to, productivity improvement. High visibility can also be a political "plus" in showing the administration's strong response to such problems as federal cutbacks.

A separate office for the PIP also allows for greater control by, or involvement of, the chief executive. This is not necessarily an advantage, but a mayor or manager who has strong interest in the PIP and wishes to be closely associated with it is likely to prefer this option.

Locating the central office in another department will probably be somewhat less costly and may be faster to operationalize. However, this arrangement will have less visibility than a separate office (unless the agency head promotes it vigorously). Low visibility can be a disadvantage unless it is clear that the program has strong support from the start. Alternatively, it may be useful in opposite circumstances, where a hostile environment exists. Keeping the PIP at a low key may help reduce tension. Of course, in this case the agency selected to house the PIP office must generally have good relations with other city agencies.

Making the PIP part of another department makes it less accessible to the mayor or manager. This would probably be preferred by a chief executive who does not have a strong personal interest in the PIP.

An important criterion in selecting a department to house the PIP is willingness (preferably enthusiasm) on the part of the department head involved. The central office should never be forced on someone who has little interest in, or enthusiasm for, the PIP. This will greatly reduce the potential effectiveness of the program and may, in fact, insure that it dies of neglect.

In practice, it is common to find PIP offices organized as separate units in the mayor or manager's office, or, more typically, as part of the budget agency.[5] It may also be desirable to start the program with a separate PIP office, but move the office into another department after the implementation phase is completed.

The above discussion points out the options for organizing the central PIP unit. There is no "correct" way to organize the unit. The final decision should be based on consideration of individual circumstances.

STAFFING THE CENTRAL OFFICE

The people who staff the central PIP office are the primary resources of the PIP. Therefore, careful selection of the staff is vital to program success. This section will describe the skills needed in the PIP office and discuss different methods for obtaining them.

Unit Leadership. The first position to be filled will be that of the director or head of the unit. The specific background or skills of this person are less important than his/her attitudes toward productivity. The head of the central unit should:[6]

- Be committed to productivity improvement and familiar with improvement methods.
- Be familiar with the public sector environment (preferably with the hiring government and/or its environment).
- Have good communication skills and political savvy to aid in dealing with other agencies and departments.

In addition, it would be helpful if the director possessed some of the skills generally needed in the unit, which are described below.

Staff Skills. Because of the variety of tasks performed by the central office, the staff as a whole should be able to provide a number of skills. Each member, however, does not have to possess the full range of skills. Skills commonly used in a PIP are summarized in Table 4-2.

Table 4-2. Staff Skills for the Central PIP Office

ANALYTIC SKILLS
Data collection and analysis
Statistical methods
Program evaluation
PRODUCTIVITY IMPROVEMENT METHODS
Industrial Engineering Skills
methods analysis
process charting
work redesign
work scheduling
work standards
Employee Motivation Skills
incentive systems
participation methods
job enrichment
GENERAL SKILLS
Research and evaluation
Communication

Source: Based in part on Frederick O'R. Hayes, "Resources for Productivity Programs," in: ed. George J. Washnis, *Productivity Improvement Handbook for State and Local Government* (New York: John Wiley & Sons, 1980), p. 40.

One skill group that should be included in the PIP office is analytic skills. These skills are used to determine where productivity improvement is needed. Analysis is also required to monitor and evaluate productivity improvements after their implementation.

Other skills are associated with selecting and implementing improvement methods. These can be categorized into two different groups. Skills typically associated with industrial engineering are one group. These are used to analyze and redesign work processes, a common approach to productivity improvement. (These skills may also be referred to as systems analysis, operations research, or operations analysis.) The other skill group is associated with improvement methods that are related to employee motivation, such as incentive systems or job enrichment.

The final skill group includes more generalized skills such as research and evaluation. They can be useful in seeking out information about productivity improvements that have been applied elsewhere and to monitor new developments in the field. Good communication skills are also needed in a PIP. They can help maintain smooth relations with the agencies and departments, and will facilitate the transfer of information to departments, especially during the introduction and implementation of improvement methods.

Staff Size. There are no hard and fast rules as to how large the central office staff should be. One rule of thumb suggests a staff of five analysts for every 1000 employees. An alternative formulation is to relate staff size to the number of improvement projects underway. One or two staff members should be assigned to each project for three to six months.[7]

Another reasonable approach is to relate staff size to individual conditions. Factors to consider in doing this include:

- Size of the government involved (number of agencies and departments; number of employees).
- Whether productivity improvements will be phased in slowly or introduced simultaneously in all departments.
- Resource constraints.

The impact the PIP office has, or is expected to have, can also be used to determine staff size. Additional staff members should be hired if the value of their work exceeds the cost of hiring them.[8] Of course, if there is initial uncertainty about how large the staff should be, it is always possible to start small and expand the staff as needed.

Using Consultants. Although a variety of skills are needed for the PIP office, it is not necessary for them to be provided by permanent staff members. Consultants can be hired to supplement skills lacking in central office staff or to increase staff size. Although this may seem expensive, it can help control costs because consultants are only hired, and paid, on an as-needed basis.[9]

Consultants have been used by several PIPs to help initiate the program and build capacity. Phoenix, for example, used a consultant to establish its program in 1970. The consultant suggested creation of a new Operations Analysis Division in the Budget and Research Department. The consultant also developed the work planning and control system to be used by the Division, and trained the city employees selected to staff it in industrial engineering and work measurement techniques.[10]

In addition to augmenting internal staff, consultants can be valuable because they are "outsiders." Since they are not part of the administration or bureaucracy they can bring a variety of qualities to the PIP that may facilitate acceptance of the program. These qualities are:

Expertise/Legitimacy
Fresh Perspective
Objectivity

Consultants are hired because of their specialized knowledge and experience. This expertise imparts legitimacy to their suggestions, and increases the confidence clients have in their recommendations. This can lead to greater willingness on the part of affected departments or agencies to accept and act upon their recommendations.

Another quality consultants have as outsiders is a fresh perspective. Consultants are far less inclined than insiders might be to view existing methods or practices as the only "right" way to do things. They are more willing to question why things are done as they are, and are less likely to be influenced by relationships with others in the organization. As a result, consultants may be more willing to deviate from current or traditional practices and to offer more innovative suggestions for productivity improvement.

Consultants can also be valuable because they are perceived as being objective and neutral. They are not involved in existing organization politics. Therefore, their recommendations will be perceived as being unbiased. An insider's recommendations might be viewed as self-serving in some way. However, a consultant's suggestions should not be perceived in this way, and thus should be more readily accepted. In the Dallas productivity program, for example, consultants provided objective validation that helped gain acceptance for City Hall's recommendation for managerial reform in the Water Utilities Department. Consultants also recommended reducing Police Department civilian positions. This was accepted more readily than if it had been suggested in the budget review process, for example.[11]

While the qualities outsiders can bring to a PIP are generally useful, they become more important when the PIP is resisted, or is likely to be resisted. This may occur if there is suspicion about the motives of City Hall in introducing productivity improvement. It may also occur if departments are generally reluctant to make changes, or when the changes suggested are unpopular. Using consultants, therefore, can be particularly valuable in sensitive and/or politicized situations.

Other Sources of Skills. Consultants are probably the most common source of outside skills used to supplement the internal staff. However, some communities may simply not be able to afford, or be willing to hire consultants for even limited periods of time. Such communities may, nonetheless, need external experts or supplemental staff. There are two possible external sources of assistance that may be willing to serve the same functions as consultants, but at little or no cost.

Local universities may be a source of faculty and/or student assistance. Programs in public administration, policy analysis, business administration, and other related fields teach the relevant skills and are usually interested in providing "real world" experience for students, particularly graduate students. Some universities also encourage faculty members to perform public service activities in their communities.

The business community is another potential source of assistance that seems particularly appropriate to use now. This is because it is in keeping with two themes of the Reagan Administration: a greater role for the private sector, and using volunteerism to supplement the public sector. Obtaining assistance for PIPs from the business community predates the Reagan administration, however. The program established in Detroit in 1974, for example, included a Committee on Management Effectiveness in Government. This was a task force of productivity specialists from Detroit businesses who helped transfer private sector technology to the city.[12]

Tacoma also utilized private sector expertise. The city developed a relationship with the Boeing Company to help develop and transfer technology. Over a four-year period, Boeing made substantial contributions of staff time. In 1972-73, for example, it contributed the equivalent of seven staff years. This level of involvement was not based purely on feelings of civic responsibility, however. Boeing expected to reap future profit from its experience in analysis and technology development for cities.[13] Although this level of support cannot be generally expected, the local private sector may be able to donate some staff to the PIP.

Voluntary assistance from the private sector or universities is cost-advantageous when compared to hiring consultants. It does have a drawback, however. The city has less control over a voluntary relationship than one that is governed by a contract. With volunteers, for example, the city is not in a position to make demands about the speed with which work is performed. This can be an important consideration when there are time schedules to be kept. Of course, the work performed by volunteers can be perfectly satisfactory in its timeliness and quality. The point here is that the benefits of low or no-cost assistance should be weighed against the lack of control inherent in a voluntary relationship before making a final decision on the source of external staff.

Summary. Creating the central PIP office is important because it represents the start of the program. Little can be done in the way of organized, citywide productivity improvement without an office to coordinate and control improvement efforts. Making good choices about how to organize and staff the central office will help it, and the rest of the program, operate smoothly.

This chapter has explained what is involved in creating a central PIP office. Major steps and/or decisions to make in organizing and staffing the office are summarized in a checklist in Table 4-3. The first step is to be sure that the mayor or manager supports the program and authorizes creation of the central office and the extension of improvement efforts to city agencies. The next step is to decide whether to have a separate PIP office (most likely in the mayor's office), or whether to place the unit in another city agency.

The final two steps regarding staff selection actually occur simultaneously. Personnel to direct and staff the unit must be hired. At the same time, a decision must be made whether to use consultants (or similar outside sources) to supplement the staff, or whether to hire a larger staff instead. The latter is affected by both cost considerations and an assessment of the value of the other benefits outsiders can bring to the PIP. In practice, consultants are commonly used to some degree in many PIPs. This decision, therefore, may really be about how much to use consultants.

In all decisions about organization and staffing, factors such as cost, degree of commitment to productivity improvement, personality, interpersonal relationships, and organizational "politics" are important. For best

Table 4-3. Checklist for Establishing the Central PIP Office

I. Be sure the chief executive has approved of the program
II. Select location of office
 A. Independent office reporting to chief executive
 B. Part of related agency (such as budget office)
III. Select Staff
 A. Director
 B. Other staff members
IV. Decide whether or not to use consultants or other outsiders

results, decisions must be based on local conditions. Giving careful consideration to organizing and staffing the central unit will pay dividends in helping get the PIP off to a smooth start.

THE DECENTRALIZED PIP UNITS

The central office plays the major role in the PIP, as explained in chapter 3. It must work *with* and *through* city agencies and departments, however, to achieve the goal of citywide productivity improvement. Each agency and department involved in the PIP should, therefore, have an office or unit responsible for productivity improvement functions and for acting as liaison with the central unit. It is not necessary for these decentralized units to be created simultaneously. If the PIP is being phased in slowly, for example, they can be formed as each agency becomes actively involved in improvement efforts. It is up to the central unit to determine when there is a need for them. This section will describe the functions of the decentralized offices and the options for organizing and staffing them.

Functions. The main purpose of decentralized units is to help the central office select and implement improvement methods. The functions of the decentralized unit are shown in Table 4-4. Note that most of the functions involve *helping* the central office. This is a deliberately ambiguous term, and can represent anything from a fairly subordinate helping relationship to a more independent role involving consultation and cooperation.

It is up to the central office to determine the degree of independence the departmental units will have. This can vary according to each department's ability to handle responsibility based on their size and staff capabilities and willingness to cooperate with, and enthusiasm for, productivity improvement. Delegation of responsibility will also depend on the capabilities of the central unit. A small central unit is almost forced to decentralize responsibility because it cannot do all the work itself. A larger central unit can grant more independence to departments that can handle it, and less to others.

The degree of delegation also can, and probably should, vary by function. For example, department staff cannot be expected to have the skills necessary to devise improvement methods. Data collection, however, is logically a departmental activity. Data analysis may or may not be. Analytic capabilities must be present in order to delegate this responsibility. Enthusiasm for productivity improvement should also be considered. If this is lacking, analysis of productivity data may become a low priority, especially in busy departments. This was the case in Milwaukee's program, which relied on central analytic staff.[14] Alternatively, decentralized analysis may be welcomed by departments enthusiastic about the PIP since it provides rapid feedback.

Table 4-4. Functions of the Decentralized PIP Units

Help the central office introduce the PIP and productivity improvement concepts
Help the central office assess current practices and select where improvement is needed
Help select and implement improvement methods (may involve employee training)
Collect productivity data and help assess progress
Help monitor, evaluate, and maintain the PIP in the maintenance phase of the program

This will boost morale if results are positive, or allow for quick corrective action if not.[15] Retraining employees in new work methods is another function that can usually be delegated, although large departments may need assistance in this because of the volume involved.

Departments should have input into the decision process concerning delegation of PIP responsibilities. This will lead to better decisions based on real departmental capabilities and willingness to perform specific tasks. It will also prevent resentment about too little or too much responsibility being assigned unilaterally.

Organization and Staffing. Because the decentralized PIP office is small, organization and staffing issues are closely related. In essence, an "office" should be created to manage and coordinate improvement activities within each agency or department and to act as a liaison with the central office. These responsibilities will require less than a full-time staff person (except for large departments, where one or more people could be assigned to the task). Therefore, these functions could be added to the responsibilities of an existing staff member.

The most important skill the coordinator should have is the ability to work well with others. This person will be working closely with the staff of the central PIP unit and with the staff of his/her own agency. The ability to work closely with others and to communicate well are important for the success of the program. In addition, he/she should be enthusiastic about productivity improvement.

Specific skills related to productivity improvement are not likely to be found among departmental staff. Training necessary to carry out PIP responsibilities can be provided by consultants or by members of the central unit staff. This was done in Detroit, for example, where staff of the Productivity Center trained departmental coordinators in industrial engineering and management techniques.[16]

In most instances, the coordinator's position should be placed in the department's administrative office. This is desirable because of its visibility and because it underscores the department head's commitment to the program. Therefore, someone from the excecutive's staff is a logical choice for the position of coordinator. An assistant or deputy director would be a good candidate, for example. Of course, it is possible to select a staff member from another part of the agency who will work in the PIP unit on a part-time basis. The ideal candidate is someone with the appropriate skills whose schedule can be arranged to accommodate working on the PIP.

In large departments, other options for the location of the PIP unit become available. A budgetary unit or an evaluation and analysis unit could be used for the coordinator's office, for example. This is particularly appropriate if the person selected as coordinator is on the staff of one of the units.

Other staff functions related to the PIP may be decentralized. Data collection and analysis, for example, can be handled by the unit that normally performs such functions.

Operating managers in the direct service-providing units of the department play a major role in the PIP. They help introduce the program, and they supervise and manage the implementation of improvements. Both the central and departmental unit staffs should work closely with managers in assessing existing work processes and selecting improvement methods for their units. This will help managers build commitment to carrying out improvements.

In summary, departments and agencies play an important role in the citywide PIP. They work cooperatively with the central PIP office in performing some tasks, and carry out other functions independently. Therefore, some kind of decentralized organization and staff must be created in each agency before that agency becomes actively involved in productivity improvement.

The discussion of the role of departments and agencies thus far has been limited to their participation in a citywide program. In some cases, departments or agencies act independently to improve internal productivity where no citywide effort exists. In such cases, the department is essentially playing the role normally played by the city. It should, therefore, create its own PIP office to carry out the functions of the citywide PIP office, but a smaller scale. In such cases, decentralized offices would not be necessary unless the department was very large and/or geographically separated (e.g., a state agency with branches in different locations).

SUMMARY

This chapter has explained the first steps necessary for getting a PIP off the ground. These involve creating and staffing an organization to introduce and implement the program on a citywide basis. Similarly, counterpart organizations need to be created to help the central office carry out its work in departments and agencies. Putting care and thought into this phase of the PIP will contribute to the smooth functioning of the program in its later stages.

NOTES

1. For a discussion of the importance of executive support, see Frederick O'R. Hayes, *Productivity in Local Government* (Lexington, Mass.: Lexington Books, 1971), pp. 243-244.
2. Descriptions may be found in, for example: John M. Greiner, et al., *Productivity and Motivation: A Review of State and Local Government Initiatives* (Washington, D.C.: The Urban Institute Press, 1981); Hayes, *Productivity in Local Government;* George J. Washnis, ed., *Productivity Improvement Handbook for State and Local Government* (New York: John Wiley & Sons, 1980). Recent articles in journals such as *Public Productivity Review* may be used to provide the most current examples.
3. See: Hayes, *Productivity in Local Government,* p. 37; and Edgar G. Crane, Bernard F. Lentz, and Jay M. Shafritz, *State Government Productivity: The Environment for Improvement* (New York: Praeger Publishers, 1976), p. 51.
4. Frederick O'R. Hayes, "Implementation Strategies to Improve Productivity," in: ed. George J. Washnis, *Productivity Improvement Handbook,* p. 28.
5. Ibid.
6. Frederick O'R. Hayes, "Resources for Productivity Programs," in: ed. George J. Washnis, *Productivity Improvement Handbook,* pp. 39-40.
7. National Center on Productivity and the Quality of Working Life, *So, Mr. Mayor, You Want to Improve Productivity* (Washington, D.C.: U.S. Government Printing Office, 1974), p. 13.
8. Hayes, "Resources for Productivity," p. 41.
9. For discussion on selecting and working with consultants, see: Don L. Bowen and Merrill J. Collett, "When and How to Use a Consultant: Guidelines for Public Managers," *Public Administration Review* 38 (September/October 1978): 476-481; Hayes, "Resources for Productivity," pp. 41-44; and John Rehfuss, "Managing the Consultantship Process," *Public Administration Review* 39 (May/June 1979): 211-214.
10. Hayes, *Productivity in Local Government,* pp. 150-151.
11. Ibid., p. 30.
12. Ibid., p. 42.
13. Ibid., p. 182.
14. Ibid., p. 57.
15. Joint Financial Management Improvement Program, *Implementing a Productivity Program: Points to Consider* (Washington, D.C.: Joint Financial Management Improvement Program, 1977), p. 6.
16. Hayes, *Productivity in Local Government,* p. 42.

5
INTRODUCING THE PRODUCTIVITY IMPROVEMENT PROGRAM

This chapter explains how to introduce the Productivity Improvement Program (PIP) in a way that will help build support for it. Introducing the program is the first task of the central unit. It can be managed in a way that will help gain acceptance and create support for the program among managers and employees, which will help insure a successful program. This chapter will explain goals and strategies of the introduction, and provide a model for introducing the program. Timing of the introduction and using a selective approach to help build support will also be discussed.

GOALS OF INTRODUCTION

The two functions of the program's introduction can be summarized as *tell* and *sell.* To this point, only the PIP staff and a small number of people in City Hall have been aware of the program. The introduction should be used to *tell* department managers and employees about the PIP and what their role in it will involve. It should also *sell* the program to them in terms of gaining their support and acceptance. The reasons why these two functions must be covered in the introduction are explained below.

Telling: Filling Information Needs. The need for the *telling* aspect of introduction results from the way the PIP is designed. Since productivity improvement is largely carried out by departmental managers and employees, they must be informed about what they will be doing. In essence, on-the-job training in productivity must be provided. The introduction is the first step in this training process, because it presents an overview of the PIP and everyone's role in it.

Information is also needed to dispel rumors or suspicion. Although the process leading to adoption of the PIP and creation of the central unit involves relatively few people, it probably will not go unobserved. Some managers and employees will be aware that *something* is happening, even if they don't know what it is. As a result, rumors may arise. Information should be provided to prevent or eliminate any inaccuracies and/or dispel suspicion or hostility that could develop if people feel they are being kept in the dark.

Selling: Overcoming Resistance. It is necessary to sell the PIP to managers and employees in order to gain the cooperation and support needed to make the program work. Selling the program involves overcoming resistance to the PIP itself and/or to change in general.

Bureaucratic inertia is often blamed for resistance to change in the public sector. This is an overly simplistic explanation. Resistance is commonly encountered in introducing innovations, including new programs, to any organization.[1] There are a variety of reasons for managers and/or employees to resist change, including:

Fear of job loss if fewer employees are needed because of productivity improvement.

Concern over changes in opportunities for pay increases or promotions.

Fear of failing to achieve improvement and possible sanctions resulting from this.

Concern that implementation efforts will not be evaluated fairly because of difficulties in measuring productivity improvement.

Discomfort over the instability associated with any change (disrupting familiar routines and habits, changing established patterns of interaction, reducing predictability).

Concern that changes will require doing more work, or that work will be harder, or that working conditions will deteriorate.

Resistance to change is rarely expressed as overt refusal to comply with directives. It usually is manifested in less obvious ways, such as low levels of cooperation, halfhearted efforts, delays, or subtle forms of sabotage or noncompliance. It can also be expressed as selective perception, which is the inability to recognize or accept opportunities for improvement. This myopic approach may be used as a way to avoid attempting to make change, as shown in this example:

> Inglewood, California, has used one-man refuse trucks for more than a decade at significantly reduced cost and with fewer injuries and greater satisfaction for personnel.
>
> Informed of the one-man trucks, the sanitation director in an eastern city using four men to a truck said he did not believe it. Having confirmed that they were in use, he opined that Inglewood's streets and contours were different from his city's. Convinced that conditions in both places were generally the same, he lamented that his constituents would never accept the lower level of service. Persuaded that the levels of service were equal,

> he explained that the sanitation men would not accept a faster pace and harder work conditions. Told that the Inglewood sanitation men prefer the system because they set their own pace and suffer fewer injuries caused by careless co-workers, the director prophesied that the city council would never agree to such a large cutback in manpower. Informed of Inglewood's career development plan to move sanitation men into other city departments, the director pointed out he was responsible only for sanitation.[2]

It is likely that some forms of resistance will be encountered during the course of the PIP. Thus, steps should be taken, beginning with the introduction, to lessen employee fears in order to reduce potential resistance. An early step to avoid resistance involves selecting the name used for the PIP. If the word *productivity* seems to generate fear and/or hostility among employees (as it sometimes does, especially with unions), a different name could be chosen. For example, cost containment, efficiency, or work improvement might convey essentially the same meaning in a less threatening way. Although "Productivity Improvement Program" becomes a good acronym, PIP, that is not a sufficient reason to use it if it will create ill will among employees. Any name that makes sense without generating resistance is acceptable. Thus, name selection can be a first step toward gaining program acceptance. Other strategies to help overcome resistance to change will be outlined in the sections that follow.

INTRODUCTION STRATEGIES

There are four strategies that can be used to help overcome resistance to the PIP. These are:

Executive support
Participation
Policies to build support
Persuasive communication

Executive Support. As discussed in chapter 4, support of the chief executive is widely recognized as crucial to the success of any organizational change. It is difficult to resist a program that is personally backed by the mayor or city manager. Executive support also implies that City Hall will help department and agency administrators overcome problems associated with the program.

The introduction of the program provides a good opportunity to exhibit executive support for the PIP. Visible involvement of the mayor or city manager in the program's introduction will help convey the message to administrators and employees that he/she is committed to the continuation and success of the PIP, and that their cooperation is expected.

The importance of the executive's personal commitment has been recognized in the public sector. To cite a few examples, Mayor John V. Lindsay was closely identified with New York City's productivity program in the early 1970s. William Donaldson is known for initiating productivity programs tied to technological change, first as city manager of Scottsdale, Arizona and then in Tacoma, Washington. More recently, a statewide productivity effort was introduced in North Carolina with the strong personal backing of Governor James B. Hunt, Jr. In 1982, New York State's Governor, Mario Cuomo, created a new Cabinet-level position, Assistant to the Governor for Management and Productivity, even before taking office. The new position was created to emphasize the importance of this function, thus underscoring the new governor's intention to do more with less.

Participation. Active participation of administrators and employees in all aspects of the PIP, beginning with the introduction, can help overcome resistance to change.[3] This is because people become more committed to a project they feel is their own than to one imposed on them by others. Taking part in diagnosing problems and selecting improvement methods enables participants to view the decisions as theirs, and to feel committed to successfully carrying them out. Participating in selection of productivity measures reduces fears that evaluation will be unfair. Participation in general provides a mechanism for concerns and objections to be expressed and resolved. It also increases understanding of productivity and the PIP.

Policies to Build Support. Several policies can be adopted to help generate support for the PIP by resolving genuine concerns about the impact of productivity improvement. Policies to share the benefits of the program with administrators and/or employees, or to protect them from negative consequences, serve this purpose.

An example of a policy to share benefits of productivity improvement would be to let agencies or departments retain a portion of the savings generated by their productivity improvement efforts. Without such a policy, administrators would feel they were penalized for improving productivity if, for example, their budgets were decreased to reflect reduced need for personnel. Such a situation would not be likely to encourage cooperation with the PIP. However, allowing a department to keep part of the savings it generates *does* create an incentive to improve productivity. A similar policy would be to share savings with all employees through bonuses or wage increases. (This will be discussed in greater detail in the chapter on incentive systems.)

Fear of job loss is a major cause of employee resistance. One way to overcome this is to adopt a "no layoffs" policy. This assures employees that any reductions in force resulting from productivity improvement will be accomplished through attrition, not layoffs. A policy of retraining displaced employees for other government positions is frequently included in the no layoffs policy. It is often suggested that such policies are essential in order to insure employee cooperation with PIPs. Otherwise, employees would be asked to take actions that might cost them their jobs, a poor incentive for cooperation! Although adopting a no layoffs policy is desirable, it may not be possible to use it in an era of severe fiscal constraints. In such cases, a policy to minimize layoffs as much as possible should be adopted to help gain employee support for the program.

Another policy to help build support is to stress that the PIP will focus primarily on aggregate productivity improvement, not on individual employees. The goal of the PIP is to increase the *overall* productivity associated with providing a particular service. Productivity data will be collected and evaluated primarily at the unit or departmental level.

In some instances, however, it may be desirable to evaluate productivity at the level of work groups or individuals. The reason for this is to bring performance of all employees up to the standards of more efficient workers. In order to achieve this, the productivity of different work groups (e.g., refuse collection crews) would have to be compared. Productivity of individual employees could be the focus of attention for two reasons: to bring group productivity up to expected levels; or if work standards and/or incentive systems are utilized as an improvement method.

Employees should be informed of these potential reasons for focusing on individual rather than group output. It should be made clear, however, that the intent of the PIP is not to single out and punish employees for low productivity, but to achieve higher levels of productivity overall.

Persuasive Communication. The final strategy, persuasive communication, relates to both the "telling" and "selling" goals of the introduction. Transmitting information about productivity and the PIP requires communication. *Good* communication means the information is provided in a way that is clear and easily understandable to its intended audience (administrators and employees).

Communication can go beyond providing information, however. It can be used to help build support for the program. To accomplish this, communication must be treated as a dialogue. It includes seeking feedback about the PIP in order to repond in a way that will overcome objections to the extent possible. In this way, communication is used for *persuasion* as well as information.[4] An outline of the persuasive communication process is provided in Table 5-1.

Persuasive communication requires determining the listener's feelings about the information provided, and reacting to them. For example, a PIP staff member may brief a department administrator on how productivity improvement will help in coping with fiscal problems, how it will operate, and how it will provide specific benefits for that department (e.g., retention of part of savings generated). The administrator's response should then be solicited. If it is favorable, the staff member can briefly restate the benefits, ask if there are questions, then close the conversation with a positive statement about the manager's cooperative attitude and/or by asking for his/her commitment.

If the administrator's initial reaction is unclear, questions should be asked to determine his/her attitude. If it is negative, the staff member should ask questions to be sure objections are understood. When it is clear that an objection is understood, it should be refuted directly, if possible, or minimized to the extent possible. For example, if the administrator is concerned about lack of productivity improvement expertise in his/her department, the staff member can explain that the central PIP office will provide information about, and help implement improvement methods. Wherever possible, benefits should be restated, or additional ones mentioned, to help win over

Table 5-1. Persuasive Communication*

1. State General Benefits of PIP
2. Provide Information about the PIP
3. State Benefits to Listener
4. Listen to Response and Evaluate Attitude. If Attitude is:

POSITIVE	INDIFFERENT	NEGATIVE
5. Agree	Question further to determine attitude	Restate objections as question to clarify
6. Restate benefits	Respond as indicated under the positive or negative columns	Refute directly/minimize to extent possible
7. Ask if there are other questions		Mention other relevant benefits or restate benefits
8. Close with positive statement		Ask if there are other questions
9.		Close with positive statement

*Based on: Logan M. Cheek, *Zero-Base Budgeting Comes of Age* (New York: AMACOM, © 1977), p. 117.

the reluctant administrator. The staff member should then close the conversation as described above.

When utilizing persuasive communication or other techniques to sell the program, one should keep in mind that the program should be "sold" only on its merits. The purpose of "selling" is to win support, not to manipulate people or to brush aside real problems that may be encountered when implementing the program. Introducing any new program is not likely to be trouble-free, and the PIP is no exception.

The best way to handle valid objections is to acknowledge that difficulties may arise in some areas, but that the central office staff will provide assistance to help managers deal with them. This does not negate the concept of persuasive communication, since it can still be pointed out that long-run benefits will outweigh any temporary problems associated with program introduction. Acknowledging the realities managers face will help win their respect. Dishonesty or an overly aggressive approach to selling the program will generate hostility and distrust, not support, for the program.

The four strategies described in this section are not mutually exclusive. They should be used in combination during the introduction of the PIP. They should also be continued throughout the duration of the program.

MODEL FOR INTRODUCING THE PIP

This section will describe a number of action steps that can be taken to introduce the PIP. Each step includes one or more of the strategies discussed above. In combination, the steps encompass all the strategies. The introductory steps described here are intended as a general guide, not as an iron-clad rule. They should be modified to fit the style of operations preferred by the administration launching the PIP.

Orientation Meetings. A series of orientation meetings should be held to *personally* introduce the PIP to as many administrators and employees as possible. The meetings could be designed according to the format shown in Table 5-2. The number of participants in each meeting should be sufficiently small to encourage participation by all persons attending. Therefore, two or three meetings might be necessary to introduce the PIP to all personnel at a given level (e.g., administrators and supervisors).

Orientation meetings are a particularly useful tool for introducing the PIP because they can incorporate the following strategies:

Executive support
Participation

Table 5-2. Suggested Format for Series of Orientation Meetings

1. Mayor (or city manager) and PIP staff meet with top administrators (agency or department heads and their highest level managers) to explain the PIP and generate support.
2. A similar meeting with union officials (if unions exist).
3. Meetings for lower-level administrators, supervisors, etc.
   A. In small communities, the mayor and PIP staff can meet with all personnel at this level as they did with top-level administrators.
   B. In large communities, PIP staff should travel to each agency or department to conduct this meeting. A representative from the mayor's office might also attend. The department head should attend to demonstrate departmental support for the PIP.
4. Meetings for all employees
   A. In small communities, it may be possible to include all personnel in one or two meetings. If so, the mayor and PIP staff should conduct these meetings as described under 3A.
   B. In larger communities, meetings should be held for employees of each agency or department, along the lines described under 3B.
   C. In very large cities or states it may not be possible for the PIP staff to conduct orientation meetings for all personnel. In these cases, supervisors should hold meetings for employees in their own units. Printed material from the PIP office can be used as a supplemental source of information about the program.

Communication for information purposes
Persuasive communication
Explanation of policies to generate support

Since all the strategies to gain support for the PIP can be represented, orientation meetings should be used as the cornerstone of the program's introduction.

The *content* of the orientation meetings should focus on providing information about the PIP, how it will operate, and the role agencies and departments will play in it. The meetings should incorporate persuasive communication concepts by highlighting benefits of the PIP as described above. Care should be taken not to *oversell* the program, however. Productivity improvement is not a panacea for the fiscal problems of state and local government. It cannot be expected to completely counteract the revenue limitations experienced in recent years. Overstating what the PIP can accomplish will only lead to distrust and disillusionment when it fails to live up to its unrealistic billing. Instead, the orientation meetings should emphasize that the PIP will help managers provide as much service as possible with existing resources.

Managers and employees attending these meetings should be encouraged to ask questions, make comments, and raise concerns or objections. This serves three purposes. It provides feedback necessary to accurately judge their response to the program, making it possible to counter objections and thus gain their support (as discussed under persuasive communication). Feedback also can bring to light problems that may require modification of the program. Finally, taking an active part in orientation meetings is a form of participation, which, as noted earlier, helps generate support for a new program.

The *atmosphere* of the orientation meeting is as important as the content. A supportive, nonthreatening atmosphere will help overcome resistance to change and generate support for the program. This atmosphere can be generated in several ways. Points to stress to make managers comfortable with the idea of the PIP include:

Productivity improvement is simply good management, not a completely new concept.

The PIP is viewed as a long-term commitment; results are not expected overnight.

The administration and the central PIP staff are there to help managers achieve improvement goals.

Points to stress to make employees comfortable include:

Adoption of a no-layoffs policy and a retraining program (if applicable).

Productivity means working smarter, not harder.

Employees will have the opportunity to make suggestions/provide feedback about changes in their own jobs.

Informational Materials. Although the orientation meetings will provide information about how the PIP will operate, it is desirable to provide this information in written form as well. This will serve as a reference source employees can turn to at a later date if they forget, or are uncertain about, any features of the program. It is also useful for any employees who were unable to attend the meetings.

The PIP informational material can be packaged in a variety of ways, such as a pamphlet, information sheet, newsletter, memo, and so on. Content can also be displayed in any way that seems appropriate. An example of a "question and answer" format used by the Multi-Municipal Productivity Project in Nassau County, NY, is provided in Appendix A.

Informational material does not have to be restricted to printed form. A slide series or film presentation could also be provided.

Regardless of format, material should define terms and concepts clearly, explain how the PIP will operate and how it will affect employees. It should deal openly with areas of concern to employees (such as job loss) and describe any policies that will benefit them. Informational materials can also be used to stress particular points (e.g., productivity means working smarter, not harder).

Printed materials can be used after the introductory stage to help maintain interest in the PIP and demonstrate the administration's continued commitment to productivity improvement. Periodic newsletters or memos from the central PIP unit or the mayor's office can provide progress reports on improvement efforts. Alternatively, if an employee newsletter already exists, a productivity update column can be added to it.

Participation Mechanisms. Employee participation in the PIP is important for two reasons. As already noted, it helps overcome resistance to change by enabling employees to feel ownership of, and commitment to, the changes adopted. In addition, participation is extremely useful to the central PIP staff when they are analyzing jobs and selecting improvement methods. The employees who regularly perform a job know it better than anyone else. Their insights about better ways to perform the job, or about techniques that would *not* work, are invaluable. Recognition of the importance of employee input underlies the quality circle and Theory Z Management concepts that are currently growing in popularity.[5]

Some formal mechanism to ensure employee participation should be established for each agency or department as it begins to operationalize productivity improvement. One type of mechanism is a productivity task force (or committee, or circle). These require on-going participation during the implementation stage by a relatively small group of employees. The employees selected should be representative of the department's work force. Department management should also be represented, as well as any unions whose employees are affected. Training in group participation and/or productivity improvement concepts is often provided to participants in groups of this nature (a fuller explanation of employee participation methods is provided in chapter 11). Details of how the groups should function can be determined by the central PIP unit and each department. The key point is to create a structure to enable employee representatives to work with the central unit staff when they analyze jobs and select improvement methods.

Task forces and similar mechanisms are not the only way to secure employee input. Alternatives that are somewhat less formal in structure include:

1. Employee surveys using questionnaires or individual interviews (conducted by central unit staff or consultants).
2. Group meetings involving all employees in an agency or department (held by PIP staff and agency management).

3. A "suggestion box" approach, possibly with recognition and/or awards provided to employees whose suggestions are adopted.

These participation mechanisms differ from task forces and related participation approaches in several respects:

Duration of participation is shorter and is generally limited to one event (e.g., a survey interview or group meeting).

As a result, the level of participation will be more superficial than the level that would be expected in formats involving regular meetings of the same group.

However, the above characteristics enable these mechanisms to be applied to a larger number of employees than could be involved in more time-consuming forms of participation.

Of course, it is possible to use both types of participation mechanism. One or more of the broad-scale approaches can be used to give all employees an opportunity to participate, at least to some degree. A more intensive participation method can simultaneously be utilized with a limited number of employees. By combining participation mechanisms in this way, all employees can be involved and, at the same time, some in-depth participation can be generated.

The discussion of participation mechanisms thus far has primarily focused on employees. Generating *management* commitment through participation is equally, if not more, important to the success of the PIP. As discussed in chapter 4, managers at all levels will supervise and control the program in their own units. They will also work with the central and decentralized PIP staffs on all analysis and decision making.

This may not be sufficient to build real commitment to the program, however. Managers may feel it is being imposed on them externally (by the mayor and central PIP office), and/or that it represents interference with their autonomy. Therefore, efforts to generate positive managerial attitudes toward the PIP should be taken.

One way to do this is to create a participation mechanism for managers only (in addition to those that involve employees as well as managers). The central staff can hold regular discussion groups or round tables for all managers in a department or agency. The meetings can cover general aspects of productivity improvement in that agency. Managers can share their own experiences and present problems for open discussion. These meetings can serve the purposes of disseminating information and exchanging ideas as well as providing moral support by demonstrating that others are sharing the same experiences. Some central unit staff members should also attend these meetings. They can offer suggestions, provide encouragement, and praise successful efforts.

It may also be useful to have periodic meetings involving managers from a variety of departments and agencies (or *all* of them in smaller jurisdictions). These can be similar in content to departmental meetings, but will offer a broader perspective to participants.

Another way to involve managers is by having a joint goal-setting process that involves managers and central PIP staff. This is essentially a management by objectives (MBO) approach, but one that is limited to productivity improvement goals rather than all department goals (MBO concepts are discussed in greater detail as a general improvement method in chapter 12). Helping select department goals will increase management commitment to achieving those goals. It will also increase feelings of participation and reduce the feeling that the PIP is being externally imposed.

Union Involvement. If employees are unionized, the concept of employee participation must be expanded to include *union* participation. Union representatives should be invited to take part in participative mechanisms such as task forces, and so on. This should be in addition to their inclusion in informational aspects of the PIP introduction.

The presence of unions means that more than telling and selling may be required to gain cooperation and support. Productivity *bargaining* may also become part of the program's introduction. This is because improvement methods may involve changes in work rules, working conditions, job categories, or a variety of personnel or work practices covered by union contracts. Therefore, changes cannot be made unilaterally, but management can bargain with unions to achieve the desired changes. Bargaining may have to be delayed until the current contract is due to expire, but it may be possible to persuade the unions to bargain over productivity changes early—or to accept them temporarily and bargain later.

Productivity bargaining means management may have to pay (in money or other concessions) to achieve the changes it desires. This is no different than any other bargaining situation. The key is to avoid paying too much. Payments made to obtain specific changes should not exceed the value of the productivity improvements generated by those changes. Although this may seem obvious, it is a goal that is not always reached. For example, in New York City in the early 1970s, the city agreed to wage increases in exchange for changes in work rules. However, once in operation, the work rule changes did not generate productivity gains equal to the wage increases.[6] The way to avoid such problems is this:

Only agree to payments in advance if gains are absolutely certain (e.g., if new equipment will supplement or replace employees).

Otherwise, agree that payments will be made (or other benefits granted) after it has been demonstrated that productivity gains have occurred.

Unions are sometimes characterized as inhibitors of productivity. However, their real intent is to fulfill their functions of securing benefits for their members and preventing job loss. This can lead them to oppose certain kinds of changes, or to seek benefits in exchange for accepting them. But it is often the case that there are alternatives that the union will find more acceptable if one proposal is problematic.

Due to declining economic conditions, however, there appears to be a changed attitude in recent years on the part of unions in general. Some private sector unions, most notably in the automobile industry, have made significant concessions to employers to help financially troubled companies stay afloat. Some public sector unions have responded to fiscal problems encountered in their jurisdictions. New York City unions, for example, agreed to generate their own cost-of-living allowances through productivity gains during the city's fiscal crisis.[7] In a climate of fiscal retrenchment, unions can be expected to be more accepting of productivity improvements than otherwise. However, bargaining and concessions should still be expected as part of the process of dealing with unions while introducing a PIP.

Publicity. Publicizing the PIP to the general public through newspapers, television, and so on, is an optional step that can be taken during the introduction. Administrations that routinely publicize internal improvements will do this as a matter of course. Administrations that are not as comfortable using the media in this way should not feel compelled to do so.

There are some advantages to generating publicity for the PIP:

It reinforces the image of executive commitment to the program.

It builds public support for the program, which may have a positive effect on employee attitudes.

It builds public and legislative support for the mayor/manager for practicing fiscally responsible behavior in an era of taxpayer discontent.

Just as care is taken not to oversell the PIP to employees, its potential accomplishments should not be oversold to the public. Creating unrealistic expectations can lead to embarrassment if the program's performance does not match its publicity. In fact, the major potential disadvantage of publicity is that it can make the problems of a less-than-successful program more obvious and, therefore, more embarrassing.

Another possible disadvantage is that drawing attention to the PIP may increase the hostility of any groups opposed to it. Therefore, careful consideration should be given to potential advantages and disadvantages of publicity if the PIP is likely to encounter a strong negative reaction from employees.

The various action steps included in the model for introducing the PIP should be undertaken more or less simultaneously. Orientation meetings should be the first introductory activity, but informational materials can be used during these meetings. Participation mechanisms should not be initiated until the employees involved have been through the orientation meetings. Unions should be contacted as early as possible to maintain good will. Publicity can be generated at various points during the introduction. However, initial publicity should be delayed until employees have been notified about the program directly.

The introduction of any new program requires that a number of activities take place in a relatively short period of time. One of the questions to be resolved before the introduction begins is *when* it should take place.

TIMING THE INTRODUCTION

The introduction of the PIP requires making two decisions related to timing. The first decision is when the entire program should be introduced on a citywide basis. The second timing decision involves whether it should be implemented in all departments simultaneously, or whether it should be introduced selectively. Appropriate timing can help gain acceptance for the program. Therefore, timing decisions should be viewed as strategies to build support.

When to Introduce the PIP. There are two factors to consider in determining when the PIP should be introduced:

1. Workload
2. Labor Relations

The ideal time to introduce the PIP (or any new program), is when people are not particularly busy with other work, and can give it their full attention. Obviously, this ideal time does not exist! However, one can come as close as possible to it by avoiding obviously busy periods, such as when budgets are due.

The second factor to consider is labor relations. The PIP should not be introduced during periods of strained relations, since it is unlikely that employees would be cooperative at that time. Times to avoid are when there is an actual or threatened strike (or similar job action), or during any period of unusual tension between labor and management.

Admittedly, it is difficult to find the perfect time to introduce change into any organization. However, a quick assessment of work cycles and labor relations can prevent introducing the program at a *bad* time, which could jeopardize its chances for success. The central PIP unit should, therefore, give some consideration to the timing of the introduction and be prepared to delay it until conditions are more appropriate, if necessary.

Selective versus Simultaneous Implementation. Once the PIP is introduced on a citywide basis, the next stage is to implement it in each agency and department. This necessitates another timing choice: should the PIP be implemented simultaneously or on a selective basis? Selective implementation can be done on a one-by-one basis, or can involve a few departments at a time. Simultaneous implementation of course, involves *all* departments at once.

Simultaneous implementation has the advantage of getting all units involved in the PIP at the same time. However, unless the city is very small, it would probably overtax the resources of the central PIP office. Therefore, a selective implementation approach is preferable in most circumstances because of resource limitations. It is also helpful to the central PIP unit because it provides a less hectic environment for its staff to operate in.

An important advantage of selective introduction is that it can be used to help gain support for the program. The successes generated in the initial departments will help sell the PIP to other departments by proving that it works.

Choosing Showcases. The departments that are selected for early implementation of the PIP will, in effect, be showcases for the program. They should be chosen carefully to maximize the likelihood that productivity improvements will occur and that implementation will be as smooth as possible. There are several characteristics that can be used to help the central PIP unit determine which departments are good candidates for the initial round(s) of the selective introduction. A checklist of these characteristics is shown in Table 5-3.

The checklist can be used by the central unit staff to perform a quick analysis of candidates for selective introduction. The analysis should be based primarily on the existing knowledge about the department and the nature of productivity improvement. Formal research is not necessary at this

Table 5-3. Checklist for Selecting Departments for Early PIP Introduction

DEPARTMENTAL CHARACTERISTICS	SCORE
	1-5 (Low-High)
Leadership	
Supportive of productivity improvement?	________
Competent managerial skills?	________
Generally cooperative with City Hall?	________
Good relations between management and employees?	________
Nature of Work Performed	
Repetitive, routine services?	________
Use of equipment or machinery?	________
Extent of routine paperwork?	________
Direct client interaction?	________
Work outputs readily quantifiable?	________
Impacts of Improvement Methods	
Expense?	________
Likelihood of success?	________
Employee satisfaction?	________

stage, although a variety of sources can be utilized to help perform the analysis. These include:

Existing reports, documents, correspondence, or other material in city or departmental files.

Opinions and information from persons knowledgeable about the department, including its own personnel.

Information about productivity improvement methods in general as well as those used in similar situations.

The checklist shown uses a scoring system to determine the relative strength or likelihood of occurrence of each item. A score ranging from 1 (low) to 5 (high) should be assigned for each characteristic. A numerical scoring system is used instead of a verbal one because it facilitates comparison between departments.

The first group of characteristics in the checklist analyzes departmental leadership in terms of its competence; its relations with City Hall and its own personnel; and its attitudes toward productivity improvement. High scores in this group indicate the department will be cooperative and should have relatively few implementation problems.

The second group assesses the nature of the work performed. This may be used to identify suitable improvement methods as well as the likelihood of achieving productivity improvement. For example, repetitive work which makes extensive use of machinery or equipment suggests that improvement methods such as job redesign or new technology could be employed. Since these methods have good track records, it is reasonable to assume improvement will occur if they are utilized. The final item in this group asks if outputs are readily quantifiable (such as refuse collection). This is desirable in a showcase department because it means program success can be easily documented.

The third group on the checklist deals with the expected impacts of improvement methods in each department being analyzed. In order to generate scores here, a "best guess" must be made about which methods are most likely to be used in each department. The "guess" or assumption should be made without extensive research. It can be based on information from the rest of the checklist, knowledge about the department and about methods typically used in similar departments. Note that methods used in this checklist should *not* be automatically operationalized in any department without more extensive analysis of their appropriateness (a step described in chapter 7).

Types of impact included in the checklist are expense, likelihood of success, and employee satisfaction. The PIP's impact in these areas in the showcase departments will be viewed as indicators of what is likely to happen when the PIP is implemented in other departments. For obvious reasons, a method with a strong likelihood of success is desirable. An expensive method is not desirable in the showcase. Other managers may be reluctant to try productivity improvement in their own departments if they believe it will be a major drain on their resources. A method that creates employee dissatisfaction (e.g., because it causes layoffs or makes working conditions less pleasant) is also undesirable because it may lead to employee resistance in other departments.

The final selection of departments to be used as showcases may require exercising judgment in addition to using the cumulative scores on the checklist. Ideally, the analysis will identify some departments with high scores in all of the appropriate categories. This may not be the case in reality, however, where it is possible that no departments are obvious "winners." In such cases, the *distribution* of high and low scores among and within categories should be considered.

Scores in the categories of work performed and improvement impacts are generally more important than in the leadership category. However, uniformly low scores in leadership indicate that it may be difficult to implement productivity improvement. This will jeopardize chances for achieving productivity improvement as well as creating a negative image of the PIP process for other departments. Scores *within* categories should not always be viewed as being of equal importance. For example, the score on "likelihood of success" is usually more important than scores on expense and employee satisfaction. In cities where resource limitations or employee resistance appear to be major obstacles, however, scores on the latter items should be viewed as more important. In short, individual circumstances should be considered when analyzing the checklist scores.

SUMMARY

This chapter has outlined how to introduce a PIP in a way that will gain support for the program. A summary is provided in Table 5-4.

The goals of the introduction outlined here are to provide information and generate support for the program. Strategies to achieve these goals include: executive support; participation of employees and managers; policies to reduce negative impacts; and communication. These strategies are employed in the various steps of the introduction. Orientation meetings are the cornerstone since all strategies can be included in them. Other introductory devices include informational materials, participation mechanisms (including union involvement), and publicity.

Table 5-4. Introducing the PIP

GOALS
Tell: Provide information about the PIP and productivity improvement *Sell:* Overcome resistance to the program and gain support by using strategies
STRATEGIES
Executive support to generate cooperation Participation to build commitment Positive policies to minimize negative side effects (for example, no layoffs, or sharing benefits) Persuasive communication to provide information and explain the benefits of the PIP
COMPONENTS OF THE INTRODUCTION
Orientation meetings Informational materials Participation mechanisms Union involvement Publicity
TIMING STRATEGIES
Introduce PIP when conditions are "normal" Use selective introduction to build support

The final aspect of introducing the program is to time the introduction as strategically as possible. This means introducing the program when conditions are "normal" (i.e., avoiding busy seasons or periods of labor strife). It also requires using a selective introduction process. This process uses the successful introduction of the program in selected "showcase" agencies to build acceptance and support for it in the remaining agencies.

The steps involved in introducing the PIP have been covered in detail here because the introduction is an important phase of any new program. Working to create a smooth introduction will facilitate implementation. Building support for the PIP during the introduction will also increase the likelihood of program acceptance. Thus, time and effort expended in the introductory stage should result in a more successful PIP.

NOTES

1. Discussions of resistance to change can be found in the literature on organizational development and innovations. See, for example: Robert A. Cooke, "Managing Change in Organizations," in: ed. Gerald Zaltman, *Management Principles for Nonprofit Agencies and Organizations* (New York: AMACOM, 1979); Don Hellriegel and John W. Slocun, Jr., *Organizational Behavior: Contingency Views* (St. Paul, Minn.: West Publishing Co., 1976); Ian Mangham, *The Politics of Organizational Change* (Westport, Conn.: Greenwood Press, 1979); Robert H. Schaffer, "The Psychological Barriers to Management Effectiveness," in: ed. Peter H. Burgher, *Changement* (Lexington, Mass.: Lexington Books, 1979); Goodwin Watson, "Resistance to Change," in: ed. Gerald Zaltman, *Processes and Phenomena of Social Change* (New York: John Wiley & Sons, 1973); Gerald Zaltman, *Processes and Phenomena of Social Change* (New York: John Wiley & Sons, 1973); Gerald Zaltman, Robert Duncan, and Jonny Holbek, *Innovations and Organizations* (New York: John Wiley & Sons, 1973).
2. Committee for Economic Development, *Improving Productivity in State and Local Government* (New York: Committee for Economic Development, 1976), p. 46.
3. Watson, "Resistance to Change," pp. 130-131.
4. The discussion of communication for persuasion is based on: Logan M. Check, *Zero-Base Budgeting Comes of Age* (New York: AMACOM, 1977), pp. 116-128.
5. See, for example, Frank M. Gryna, Jr., *Quality Circles: A Team Approach to Problem Solving* (New York: AMACOM, 1981); William Ouchi *Theory Z Corporations: How American Business Can Meet the Japanese Challenge* (Reading, Ma.: Addison-Wesley, 1981); Philip C. Thompson, *Quality Circles: How to Make Them Work in America* (New York: AMACOM, 1982).
6. Raymond D. Horton, "Productivity and Productivity Bargaining in Government: A Critical Analysis," *Public Administration Review* 36 (July/August 1976): 409-410.
7. Victor Gotbaum and Edward Handman, "A Conversation with Victor Gotbaum," *Public Administration Review* 38 (January/February 1978): 19.

6
ESTABLISHING AND USING A PRODUCTIVITY MEASUREMENT SYSTEM

One of the first activities that should take place during the introductory stage of the Productivity Improvement Program (PIP) is establishing a productivity measurement system to be used for evaluating improvement efforts. Chapter 2 described the kind of measures used to monitor productivity. This chapter will explain how to set up a measurement system to perform this function, beginning with an explanation of why measurement is needed, then describing how to select measures to monitor productivity improvement and quality control.

THE NEED FOR A MEASUREMENT SYSTEM

Measurement should never be undertaken for its own sake. A measurement system should help accomplish the goal of productivity improvement. It can help do this in three ways:

- Identify areas needing improvement
- Provide feedback on improvement activities
- Help motivate managers and employees

Identifying Areas Needing Improvement. The measurement system is used for this function before improvement methods are operationalized on a citywide basis or within a particular department. Current levels of productivity (and, possibly, levels in the recent past), are required for this purpose. The PIP staff can analyze this information to locate departments and agencies, or units within them, that seem to have particularly low levels of productivity. These areas can be targeted for early implementation of improvement efforts (assuming other factors are also favorable).

Feedback. A more important use of the measurement system is to provide feedback on the success of improvement efforts that are already underway. Evaluating productivity levels after an improvement method has been fully implemented indicates whether or not it is performing satisfactorily.

Initial declines in productivity, or stable productivity ratios, do *not* necessarily mean the method is not working. They are often associated with the "breaking in" process of a new work method.[1] This occurs for a variety of reasons, most obviously because people work more slowly when they are learning new techniques. Psychological factors, such as stress or dissatisfaction due to changes in work methods and/or the work group, may also play a role. Lack of improvement, or even deterioration in productivity, that occurs when a method is introduced should be regarded as normal. However, if this continues for an extended period (which can vary in length as explained below), the central PIP unit and departmental management should check to see if methods are being used correctly, if more training is needed, or if modifications in methodology should be made. Evaluation should continue after putting such changes into effect.

If productivity still does not improve, another method should be considered, but this should not be done until the PIP staff and others involved feel that the first method has received an adequate trial. This period could vary in length according to the importance of the work performed; the degree of deterioration experienced; the complexity of the new method; the number of people involved; and the intensity of conviction that the chosen method will improve productivity in that setting.

The feedback aspect of the measurement system does not end when it is determined that the improvement method is working satisfactorily. Productivity should continue to be monitored to insure that it remains at a satisfactory level. If it falls at some future time, it is up to the PIP staff and department management to determine the causes and take corrective action.

Motivation. Feedback can help motivate managers and employees involved in the PIP. Productivity analysis helps create expectations, and can be used to set formal goals or standards, if those are used in the PIP. These expectations or goals have motivating power by themselves. In addition, performance feedback is necessary for formal reward systems, such as incentive plans or suggestion awards, and for productivity bargaining.[2] A measurement system also helps provide positive reinforcement by letting people know where they stand through feedback on their performance.[3]

In short, in order for managers and employees to improve productivity, they must know their current performance levels and whether their improvement methods are working. Knowledge of successful efforts reinforces their desire to maintain the accomplishment and motivates them to improve on it. Knowledge of unsuccessful efforts leads to corrective action. Thus the measurement system plays an important role in *achieving* productivity improvement, not just monitoring it.

Making Measurements Systems Useful. The three uses of a productivity measurement system have just been described. There are also three criteria that make a system *useful*. These are:[4]

Timeliness
Accuracy
Relevance

Timelessness and accuracy refer to collecting and processing data. The importance of these two criteria for the usefulness of a measurement system needs no explanation. Ways to achieve these goals will be described later in this chapter. Relevance refers to selecting measures that accurately reflect changes in productivity, and is discussed in the following section.

SELECTING OUTPUT MEASURES

The productivity measurement system must include both output and input measures. Since labor or staff hours are generally used as input measures (as discussed in chapter 2), the choice of appropriate output measures is the major task involved in setting up the measurement system. Output measures should be chosen for all services or jobs that will be involved in the improvement program (a discussion of how to select these services is included in chapter 7).

The same people who take part in other aspects of the PIP introduction should be involved in selection of output measures. Central PIP staff members should guide the process. Employees and managers responsible for the particular job or service (and union representatives, if applicable), should participate for two reasons. First, their familiarity with the service provision process and existing data collection efforts can be extremely useful. They can provide insight about which output measures are most appropriate, and/or whether proposed measures would present data collection problems. This can increase both the accuracy and relevance of the measurement system. Second, their involvement will help build their confidence in the productivity measurement process. Before they can support a PIP, managers and employees must believe their improvement efforts will be evaluated fairly. Involving them in designing the measurement system will assure them of that, and thus will reduce resistance to the program.

Multiple Output Measures. The most important consideration when selecting output measures is that they reflect changes in productivity as accurately as possible. This means they must also accurately reflect the work performed. Measures that meet these objectives will fulfill the relevance criterion discussed above. When measuring public sector outputs, it is usually necessary to use multiple output measures to fulfill these objectives.

As explained in chapter 2, completed service activities, such as number of clients served, miles of streets cleaned, etc., should be used as output measures. These can be viewed as service products.[5] Any internal activities that are the object of improvement efforts, such as clerical, maintenance or repair work, should also have their output measures identified. Since most departments and units perform multiple services, at least one output measure should be used for each service undergoing productivity improvement. However, delivering even one service often involves performing different kinds of work activities, which may be done by different people. Each major type of work that is regularly provided should be represented by its own output indicator.

For example, a social service agency might perform the following kinds of work as part of its service:

- Screen clients for problem identification, eligibility, and referral
- Provide counseling
- Prepare and distribute income-maintenance checks

Each of these activities should be represented by its own output measure:

- Number of clients screened
- Number of clients counseled
- Number of checks prepared

To accurately reflect work performed, output categories should only include work requiring a fairly uniform degree of effort or difficulty. A broad output category, such as counseling, could include dissimilar activities, such as counseling related to family problems, and job counseling. Family counseling might require different skills and techniques, and may be performed by different people, than job counseling. In this case, it would *not* be appropriate to use only one output measure for both. Each form of counseling should have its own measure:

- Number of clients receiving family counseling
- Number of clients receiving job counseling

Even activities that fall within the same work category can require significantly different levels of effort to produce the intended output. This is because the incoming workload (e.g., clients or cases) is not uniform in level of difficulty. For example, it usually takes longer to provide a particular output (e.g., placement in a foster home, job training) for clients with more severe problems. Services of this kind should be grouped by severity and/or nature of client problem to reflect variations in difficulty, even though the same service is provided to all.[6]

This type of variation in work difficulty is not restricted to social services. Multiple output measures may be needed for a wide variety of services. Police activities could be grouped by type of crime and/or amount of information available, for example.[7] Refuse collection could be classified as commercial or residential; street cleaning could be categorized by type of terrain; firefighting, by type of structure; repair or maintenance work, by type of equipment and/or problem, and so on. As these examples indicate, the type and number of multiple output indicators used must be "customized" for each service since work difficulty is affected by different factors for different services. However, this should not be done just as an exercise in categorization. Multiple output categories should only be used when significantly different amounts of effort are required to achieve the same level of output. Thus, if the fact that trash is residential rather than commercial does *not* significantly affect collection productivity, there is no need to use those categories. If it *does* make a difference, then they should be used.

Weighted Output Measures. In some cases, weights can be used to reflect differences in work effort in place of multiple output measures. This can be done when the differences follow a regular pattern. For example, the local health department may be responsible for inspecting both restaurants and fast food shops. However, fast food inspections might *consistently* take only 20 percent as long as restaurant inspections.[8] While inspections could be grouped into two categories, in a case such as this a weighting procedure can be applied so that both kinds of inspections can be reflected in one output measure. In order to use this procedure, the amount of time required for each type of work must be determined. This may be done by having employees keep records of the amount of time spent on each type of work for a period of time. It also might be possible to determine this from information in department files.

An example of how the weighting procedure should be applied is given in Table 6-1. The number of fast food inspections is multiplied by 0.20 in each time period *before* it is added to the number of restaurant inspections to generate the total inspections output figure. Restaurant inspections are not adjusted in any way (their weight is expressed as 1.0). The weighted inspections figure is then used in the final productivity ratio.

This example provides a good illustration of how using *un*weighted outputs in this kind of situation would be misleading. Neither staff hours nor

Table 6-1. Example of Applying a Weighting Procedure to Output Measures (for Health Department Food Inspections)*

BASIC INFORMATION

	Year 1	*Year 2*
Staff Hours (input)	4,200	4,200
Fast food inspections	6,000	5,000
Restaurant inspections	2,400	3,400
Total inspections	8,400	8,400

APPLYING WEIGHTS

	Output	×	*Weight*	=	*Weighted Output*
Year 1					
Fast Food	6,000	×	0.20	=	1,200
Restaurants	2,400	×	1.00	=	2,400
Total					3,600
Year 2					
Fast Food	5,000	×	0.20	=	1,000
Restaurants	3,400	×	1.00	=	3,400
Total					4,400

PRODUCTIVITY RATIO

Year 2 $\frac{4{,}400}{4{,}200} = 1.047$

$$\frac{1.047}{.857} = 1.22$$

Year 1 $\frac{3{,}600}{4{,}200} = .857$

*Source: National Center for Productivity and Quality of Working Life, *Total Performance Management: Some Pointers for Action* (Washington, D.C.: National Center for Productivity and Quality of Working Life, Fall 1978), pp. 14-15.

total *un*weighted inspections changed between the two years. This would be interpreted as representing no change in productivity for this service. However, the *composition* of output did change. There was an increase in the volume of restaurant inspections, which are more time consuming, and a decrease in fast-food inspections. Combining the *weighted* output measure with the stable input measures reflects the situation more accurately. There was, in fact, a 22% increase in food inspection productivity. However, as noted above, the weighting procedure can be applied *only* if the activities have a consistent relationship to each other (e.g., one *always* takes twice as long to perform as the other). If this is not the case, *substantial* variations in difficulty should be reflected by using multiple output categories.

Using Existing Data. Most government agencies or departments collect and maintain information about their activities. Records are kept to show the amount and kinds of service provided to the public or to other government units, to plan for personnel and budget needs, to analyze workload and spending patterns, and so on. Much of this data includes output measures that can be utilized for productivity measurement. Data on inputs in terms of staff hours associated with providing particular services may also be available from time sheets or similar records.

Using measures that are already available will greatly facilitate the measurement process. It means an entirely new data collection system does not have to be put into place (although some additions to the existing system may be needed). It also means productivity comparisons can be made sooner than they would be if a new measurement system had to be installed. In order to determine whether productivity has improved, you need "before" and "after" output and input measures. If no "before" data exists, data must be collected before improvement methods are introduced in order to be able to determine the impact of those methods. Thus lack of available data would delay the implementation of improvements.

It is likely, however, that existing information is not completely satisfactory for some reason. All of the necessary output or input measures might not be available, or outputs may not be categorized into homogenous groups, etc. In such cases it is preferable to delay program introduction in order to collect relevant baseline measures than to use unsatisfactory measures just because they are available. It may be possible to implement improvement methods in one agency while baseline data are being collected in another. This kind of situation only represents a delay for the departments lacking data, not for *all* departments.

The data for baseline indicators should represent fairly typical periods of service delivery. Some services have regular periods of particularly high or low activity. For example, trash collection outputs are probably higher in December because of the holiday season. Police crime-related activities tend to follow seasonal patterns. Extreme weather conditions can affect a variety of services. Using an abnormally high or low base figure in the productivity ratio will distort the resulting information and you will not know the *real* impact of the improvement method used. Using an average output per staff hour figure based on a year or six months of service provision should be sufficient to insure that the base period reflects normal activity. Services that do not usually vary much could use a shorter period, perhaps three or four months.

Another reason to be careful that existing data reflect a normal period of work is because they may be used to set goals or targets for improvement. If the measures chosen are from an atypical period, targets will be set unrealistically high or low, either of which could create a credibility problem for the PIP.

MONITORING QUALITY

In addition to monitoring productivity improvement, the measurement system should be used to help exercise quality control. This means that a set of quality measures will have to be selected, and data on them will have to be collected and analyzed. This system should be handled as a part of the output measurement system, and the same people should be involved. The points made above about using available data and the need for before and after information apply to quality measures as well. This section will only focus on those aspects of quality measurement that differ from output measurement.

The Need for Quality Control. Quality control is needed in a PIP to insure that service quality is not adversely affected by efforts to improve productivity. Monitoring service quality provides feedback for correction purposes. As discussed in chapter 2, service quality is interpreted to include some or all of the following:[9]

- Effectiveness
- Lack of negative side-effects
- Prompt delivery
- Adequacy and equality of provision
- Citizen and/or client satisfaction
- Courtesy to citizens

One of the primary arguments for monitoring service quality is the belief that quality reductions are not acceptable in order to improve efficiency. The standard example is that of changing refuse collection from back door to curbside pick-up. This increases efficiency but decreases quality because residents would have to do some of the hauling formerly done by trash collectors. Therefore, some would argue this productivity improvement is not acceptable because it reduces the quality of service provided.[10]

However, it is maintained here that some trade-offs in quality, such as the example above, may be acceptable, especially in times of fiscal constraint. Indeed, more serious service reductions than that are currently the norm in cities across the country that are operating under "cutback management" or "taxpayer revolt" conditions. This is not to suggest that any and all quality reductions are acceptable. However, some can be, and it is up to city, departmental, and PIP administrators to determine what they are and to set definitions or ranges of acceptable quality for services involved in the PIP.

The other reason for being concerned about quality is that people tend to pay particular attention to aspects of work that are evaluated. If only productivity was evaluated, employees might focus on that exclusively, while allowing quality to deteriorate. If quality is monitored in addition to productivity, employees will pay attention to both aspects of work, thus maintaining acceptable standards of quality while increasing productivity.

A Separate Quality Monitoring System. One way to handle the quality control function is to establish a separate set of quality measures to be monitored just as the output measures are. This requires selecting one or more indicators of quality for each service involved. It would be possible to generate a substantial list of quality indicators for each service. An Urban Institute Study listed 15 to 25 unique quality measures for each basic service.[11] However, a long list of quality indicators means considerably more time and effort must be devoted to the evaluation function. Thus it is preferable to keep the list as short as possible while still reflecting major quality aspects. If the city is already evaluating service effectiveness and/or other quality attributes, PIP evaluation can be reduced by relying on the existing measurment system for some (or all, if possible) of the quality indicators.

If the city does not have such a system, the PIP staff, working with department administrators and employees, should select appropriate indicators for each service. Concepts of effectiveness and undesirable side-effects can vary substantially by service. A sample list of these indicators for major services is shown in Table 6-2. Other aspects of service quality, such as promptness, courtesy, extent of service provision, and citizen satisfaction, do not vary in meaning. However, they do vary in relative importance. Prompt service delivery is a critical quality indicator for police, fire, and emergency health services, for example. Similarly, adequate coverage of all neighborhoods by police, fire, and sanitation service is more important than coverage by recreation or library service.

The list of quality indicators for a specific service should include only those that are most important for that service. This is preferable to compiling a general list of quality indicators to use for all services, whether or not all items on it are relevant to all of them. Such a list would result in excessive evaluation for some services, and inadequate evaluation of others if items relevant to them are missing from the general list.

Another approach to service quality is to monitor the number and percent of outputs that do not pass specific tests or standards of quality. In effect, they represent "defective" outputs.[12] These might include measures such as

Table 6-2. Examples of Service Quality Indicators: Effectiveness/Undesirable Side Effects

Indicator	Measured by
SANITATION-SOLID WASTE COLLECTION	
Cleanliness of streets, alleys, etc.	Percent rated satisfactory in appearance
Health and fire hazards	Number and percent of blocks with hazards
Lack of offensive odors or noise	Complaints received
Lack of spillage or damage during collection	Complaints received
POLICE PROTECTION	
Indicator	*Measured by*
Reported crime rates	Reported crime per 1000 population
Physical injuries and property loss	Number/dollar value reported
Crimes solved	Percent of cases cleared
Stolen property recovered	Percent recovered
FIRE PROTECTION	
Indicator	*Measured by*
Property loss	Average dollar loss per fire
Time for fire suppression	Time to control fire
Casulaties	Injuries and deaths reported
Rescue effectiveness	Number of people saved
RECREATION SERVICES	
Indicator	*Measured by*
Usage	Attendance records (or estimates)
Crowding	Peak attendance divided by capacity
Cleanliness and equipment condition	User survey or observation
LIBRARY SERVICE	
Indicator	*Measured by*
Use—visits	Number of visits
Use—circulation	Circulation data
Quality of reference service	User survey

Source: Harry P. Hatry et al., *How Effective are Your Community Services? Procedures for Monitoring the Effectiveness of Municipal Services* (Washington, D.C.: The Urban Institute, 1977), pp. 9-124 passim.

these: clients who do not reach specific "improvement" targets; paperwork that must be reprocessed because of errors; clients who are inappropriately classified or "placed"; arrests that do not survive preliminary hearings, and so on. Measures of defective outputs could be compiled and monitored in place of, or in addition to, positive indicators of quality. If these are used in addition to positive quality indicators, only those "defective outputs" that provide significant additional information should be included to keep the monitoring process from becoming overly burdensome.

Composite Measures. Instead of analyzing quality indicators separately, it is sometimes suggested that they be joined with output measures in the productivity ratio, thus creating a composite measure. There are two ways to accomplish this. One is to define the output measure in specific quality terms, such as:[13]

- Repairs made within "x" working days
- Forms processed with fewer than "x" errors
- Clients counseled who reach specific levels of functioning
- Arrests that survive preliminary hearings

While this approach has its merits, it does present some measurement problems. Many of the quality indicators cannot be determined at the time the output is produced, for example. The approach recommended here (i.e., include only nondefective outputs in the ratio, and monitor quality separately) seems to serve the same purposes in a simpler way.

A second way to bring quality into the ratio is to adjust outputs to reflect changes in quality. In practice, this means one or more quality attributes are measured and combined with the output measure in the productivity ratio. This approach is generally favored by those who prefer to define productivity broadly. It is also similar to total performance measurement (TPM), which attempts to monitor all major service attributes. Unfortunately, there are some difficulties associated with the interpretation of composite indicators, so their use is not recommended in the PIP. However, since they are frequently mentioned in the context of productivity measurement, it is worthwhile to understand how they work. Therefore, a more detailed explanation of composite indicators is presented in Appendix B.

From the perspective of the measurement system, composite measures do not reduce the amount of information needed, since both output and quality measures will have to be collected. From the perspective of evaluating progress and taking corrective action based on feedback, individual measures for productivity and quality are still required. Therefore, for the sake of clarity and simplicity, it seems preferable to report productivity and quality measures separately.

Availability of Data. Most departments or agencies collect information relating to the quality and/or effectiveness of their services. Records of the extent to which problem conditions are alleviated are often maintained. Agencies that provide direct services to clients may keep records of client progress and/or achievement (sometimes reflected in test scores). Some departments keep information on the promptness of service delivery, its accuracy, completeness, or similar attributes. Records of citizen complaints, which may be about any of the quality indicators, are commonly retained by departments or by a city office.

Other ways of gathering data about quality have been proposed and put into effect in some places. One of these methods is trained observer ratings. In this approach, people are trained to rate specified conditions, such as the cleanliness of streets. Photographic scales have been devised that depict street scenes reflecting varying degrees of cleanliness. Trained observers compare *actual* street conditions to those in the photographs to give the street an objective cleanliness rating. These scales have been used in a number of cities. Scales have also been devised to rate pavement condition and traffic sign visibility, and could be developed for other service quality variables that can be similarly observed or monitored.[14]

Another way to measure service quality is through surveys of all citizens, or of specific groups (such as users of a particular service), or of the business community. Such surveys provide information on perceptions of service quality. This is especially useful for aspects of quality that are otherwise difficult to assess, such as employee courtesy. They can also provide information about participation patterns. A single survey can gather information on a variety of services. Such multiservice surveys of a sample of the population can be repeated at regular intervals (usually annually) to allow for comparisons. Surveys can be conducted as personal interviews or as mail-in questionnaires. A number of communities have used these surveys.[15]

While such methods increase the information about service quality, they require additional resources, notably staff time. Communities with limited in-house resources would probably have to use survey firms. The additional costs involved (staff time or dollars), may be worthwhile if other quality information is lacking, or if a particular method is the best way to assess some conditions (e.g., street cleanliness). The data generated from such surveys can also be used to plan for improvements in quality/effectiveness. However, if sufficient quality indicators already exist or can easily be generated, surveys or observer ratings are not necessary for quality control monitoring for most services.

Assuring that service quality does not deteriorate is an important aspect of the PIP. However, it adds to the complexity of the measurement system and evaluation process. While it is possible to monitor many aspects of quality, it should be kept in mind that *productivity* is the primary focus of the PIP. Therefore, quality should be monitored only to the extent necessary to insure that major aspects of quality are maintained at satisfactory levels.

SETTING UP A COLLECTION SYSTEM

This chapter has focused thus far on identifying output and quality indicators to be used in the measurement system. The remaining sections will explain how to collect data on them.

Who Collects Data? As discussed in chapter 4, data collection is one of the decentralized aspects of the PIP. Thus each agency or department, or unit within them, should collect its own data.[16] Data collection can best be viewed as a "bottom-up" process. Most data originates at or near the point where work is performed, with records kept by individual employees. These are eventually added to similar data from other work units in that department. Someone in each department or agency should be responsible for supervising data collection. This person should also be responsible for compiling and processing the data, if that function is a decentralized PIP unit responsibility. If not, he/she is responsible for submitting the data to the central unit. Initial data collection can be performed by:

- Individual employees
- Work groups
- First line supervisors

Collecting the Data. There are two basic types of information needed to monitor productivity: the outputs produced, and the inputs used to produce them. Providing these kinds of data is complicated by the nature of work in the public sector. Most employees divide their time among a variety of services, each with its own output. A time-monitoring system is probably the simplest way to keep track of both the kinds of outputs produced and the time spent producing them.

Time monitoring can be operationalized through daily time logs for each employee. The "lines" on the log sheet can represent time intervals of 15 or 30 minutes. Column headings can reflect each major work output. These can be subdivided into whatever subcategories and/or levels of workload difficulty are necessary to accurately reflect the work performed. (These should have been identified when output measures were solicited).

To use the time logs, employees simply fill in the number of outputs of a particular type produced in a given block of time. This does not mean they have to stop working every 15 or 30 minutes to record output data. If they are working steadily on one type of work for an extended period, they can record the output produced when they are finished, and indicate how many time blocks were spent on it. In allocating time to a particular output, all tasks necessary to production of that output should also be included. Thus, time spent gathering and preparing (or putting away) materials, getting/giving instructions or information, or waiting should be allocated to the major service output. Minor interruptions (e.g., taking a phone call, etc.) do not have to be subtracted. A "miscellaneous" column can be provided for breaks and activities that are infrequently performed, or are not included in the productivity program.

Alternatively, this kind of intensive time keeping could be performed for a limited period, perhaps a few weeks, to establish standards to be applied when calculating future input measures. If such time monitoring indicates that 50% of caseworker time is typically devoted to intake interviews, for example, then 20 hours a week (for 40-hour weeks) per caseworker will be used as the input figure when interview productivity is calculated in the future. This kind of norm can only be used for services where approximately the same amount of time is regularly spent on a given activity. Such regularity may be due to job descriptions or regulations. Because such standards can become outdated, time recording should be repeated periodically to be sure they continue to reflect current work patterns. Another alternative would be to use sampling techniques to gather information on time allocation of employees selected for the sample. This would be used to estimate the proportion of time spent by all similar employees on each type of work.[17]

In some cases, time logs are not necessary because an employee (or groups of employees) produce only one kind of output which does not vary significantly in workload difficulty (e.g., clerks in a vehicle registration office).[18] Although each person performs a variety of different tasks, there is only one kind of output, completed vehicle registrations. The daily total of registrations can be tabulated by a supervisor and divided by the number of hours worked by the group to derive the average number of registrations per staff hour. This approach to monitoring group output is applicable to standardized paper-processing functions of government where there are few variations in difficulty.

As noted previously, defective or incomplete outputs should not be included in the productivity ratio. Thus pages that have to be retyped, forms that have to be reprocessed, repairs that must be redone, etc., should not be included in the work logs. Unfortunately, it is often difficult to identify "rejects" at the time they are produced. This is particularly true of services involving interaction with the public or clients (e.g., arrests, training sessions, etc.). Completeness or adequacy of such services is difficult, if not impossible, to determine in the short run. In such cases, all service outputs should be counted.

The measurement system should record quality control information as well as output data. If quality indicators are available when work is performed, they should be collected then along with the output data. The types of quality information that fit this description can include speed of response, completeness, and accuracy. Other quality indicators, such as effectiveness, presence or absence of negative side-effects, and citizen satisfaction, usually are not immediately observable. Thus these must be monitored separately, especially those requiring techniques such as observer ratings or citizen surveys. Such monitoring is generally best performed by central PIP staff members or department personnel.

Determining who collects data should be based on doing whatever makes sense and is simple to operationalize. Many employees, particularly those who have direct contact with the public, typically report some or all of their activities (e.g., arrests, investigations, clients served, etc.). Thus the notion of recording one's work should not be particularly unusual to them, or to other public employees. If it seems difficult or overly burdensome for some types of employee, the responsibility can be given to their first line supervisors. The PIP staff should hold brief orientation sessions to familiarize all personnel involved in data collection with the chosen format and how they should record information. Care should also be taken to stress the importance of accuracy in record keeping.

Frequency of Collection. There are really two aspects to frequency of data collection: how often should original output data be collected, and how often should it be compiled as a report for feedback purposes? As is true of other aspects of the PIP, individual circumstances must be considered when making these decisions. Staff capacity to collect, aggregate, and record data is the key factor affecting frequency of collection. Computer availability is helpful, but is not absolutely necessary except for large and/or scattered government units. It would, however, facilitate and speed up the data collection process for smaller jurisdictions.

In general, data kept by employees on their own output, or by groups or supervisors on group output, should be *recorded* daily and may be collected by supervisors on a daily or weekly basis. Data should be compiled on a weekly basis, if possible, to be sure original records are not misplaced. This level of compilation will probably be the responsibility of the decentralized PIP staff.

For the most part, average productivity figures should be reported on a monthly basis (e.g., tons of trash collected per labor hour for the month of January). These reports could be compiled by the central or decentralized staff, depending on how responsibilities were allocated initially. However, when the improvement method has been newly implemented, it is preferable to report output ratios on a weekly or bi-weekly basis. This provides faster feedback on whether or not the method is working satisfactorily. After the breaking-in period, monthly reports will be sufficient. Reports should show productivity figures for the prior months of the year and for the base period. Percentage increases or decreases over the prior month should be included. Percentage change from the prior year average and the base period might also be included.

Quality measures that require special collection efforts should be monitored somewhat less frequently, perhaps quarterly. Those that are readily available can be reported on a monthly basis along with the productivity measures.

It should be kept in mind that the primary purpose of data collection is to provide feedback. When a method is newly implemented, members of the central staff should promptly review the reports with managers of the department or unit to determine whether the data indicates that the method is working properly. After a method has been functioning properly for a while, the reports can be treated in a more routine fashion. It should become primarily the responsibility of the decentralized PIP staff to check them for problems. However, the central staff should also review them.

Monitoring for Accuracy. As noted earlier, it is important for a measurement system to be accurate. The way to insure this is to build in an accuracy-monitoring component. This involves regularly checking different aspects of the system for accuracy. For example, compiled data could be checked against individual time logs. Time logs could be checked against tangible work products (such as forms completed). If the nature of the work does not allow this, a sample of employees could be interviewed to check the correctness of the log system.

Accuracy monitoring should be an on-going part of the measurement system. Some, or all, of the monitoring should be done on a random basis to promote greater accuracy in all records, not just in those subject to monitoring. The knowledge that there is a *possibility* that data will be checked encourages people to be more careful, which is a major goal of the monitoring system. Sanctions for deliberate misreporting should also be part of the monitoring system to discourage "cheating."[19]

Personnel to perform the monitoring can come from the central PIP staff, the decentralized staff, or a combination of both. Decentralized staff should be responsible for regular random checks within their department, while central staff members can make less frequent checks. Employees should be informed that these checks are a part of the system, so they are not completely surprised by them. It should be made clear that the checks are not intended to harass or intimidate anyone, but that this is a normal procedure to determine whether information is being accurately recorded.

SUMMARY

The purpose of a measurement system in the PIP is to provide information that will help achieve the goal of productivity improvement. The key function of measurement is providing feedback on whether improvement methods are working, so corrective action can be taken if they are not. Quality control monitoring serves a similar feedback function so decreases in quality can be corrected.

Paying attention to the details of setting up a measurement system will assure that the system provides relevant information in a timely, accurate manner. Important aspects of setting up the system include:

- Involving people affected by the system
- Selecting output measures that reflect major work activities
- Grouping outputs into homogeneous categories, or weighting them when appropriate
- Selecting quality control measures for all services involved
- Using available data whenever possible
- Teaching the decentralized staff how to collect data
- Monitoring for accuracy
- Using data for feedback and correction

Establishing the measurement system is one of the final aspects of the introductory phase of the PIP. The next step is to begin selecting and implementing improvement methods.

NOTES

1. Walter L. Balk, "Toward a Government Productivity Ethic," *Public Administration Review* 38 (January/February 1978): 48.
2. Walter L. Balk, "Improving Government Productivity: Some Policy Perspectives," Sage Professional Papers in Administrative and Policy Studies, vol. 1, series 03-025 (Beverly Hills, Ca.: Sage Publications, 1975, p. 13.
3. Ibid., p. 25.
4. Samuel A. Finz, "Productivity Measurement Systems and Their Implementation," in: ed. George J. Washnis, *Productivity Improvement Handbook for State and Local Government* (New York: John Wiley & Sons, 1980), p. 143.
5. James F. Budde, *Measuring Performance in Human Service Systems* (New York: AMACOM, 1979), p. 47.
6. Harry P. Hatry, et al., *Efficiency Measurement for Local Government Services* (Washington, D.C.: The Urban Insitute, 1979), p. 143.

7. Ibid., p. 77.
8. The example used here is taken from: National Center for Productivity and Quality of Working Life, *Total Performance Management: Some Pointers for Action* (Washington, D.C.: National Center for Productivity and Quality of Working Life, Fall 1978), pp. 12-15.
9. Harry P. Hatry, "Measuring the Quality of Public Services," in eds. Willis D. Hawley and David Rogers, *Improving Urban Management* (Beverly Hills, Ca.: Sage Publications, 1976), p. 7.
10. Ibid., p. 13.
11. Harry P. Hatry, et al., *How Effective are Your Community Services? Procedures for Monitoring the Effectiveness of Municipal Services* (Washington, D.C.: The Urban Institute, 1977), p. 5.
12. Hatry, *Efficiency Measurement,* pp. 37-38.
13. Ibid., p. 36.
14. For more information on using and developing observer ratings, see Hatry, *How Effective are Services?* pp. 207-213.
15. Ibid., pp. 215-225.
16. For a discussion of data collection, see National Center for Productivity and Quality of Working Life, *Improving Productivity: A Self-Audit and Guide for Federal Executives and Managers* (Washington, D.C.: National Center for Productivity and Quality of Working Life, 1978), pp. 23-24.
17. See Hatry, et al., *Efficiency Measurement,* pp. 164 and 179, for a discussion of sampling.
18. Balk, "Improving Government Productivity," p. 29.
19. For a discussion of this subject, see: James E. Swiss, "Unbalanced Incentives in Government Productivity Systems: Misreporting as a Case in Point," *Public Productivity Review* (March 1983): 26-37.

7
SELECTING PRODUCTIVITY IMPROVEMENT APPROACHES

This chapter focuses on selecting the methods that will be used to improve productivity, based on the concept of a tailor-made approach to productivity improvement. It explains how to analyze conditions in the work environment and the way the job is performed, and how to use this analysis to select appropriate improvement methods for different jobs.

THE TAILOR-MADE APPROACH

The key to a successful PIP is to tailor improvement approaches to fit individual circumstances. The method that "worked" in a city 100 miles away, or that received a favorable write-up in a professional journal, is not necessarily the right one for your city. Bringing this concept to a lower level, an improvement method that works in one *department* is not necessarily appropriate for another deparment in the same city. A method that improves productivity in jobs requiring physical labor may not be as effective in white-collar positions.

A standardized approach will not yield optimal results because every service is different. Each has its own method of production, and is performed by a different type of employee. Each exists in its own organizational framework that influences the way work is performed. Therefore, each service should have a productivity improvement method (or methods) selected to fit its unique characteristics.

Of course, some types of work included in the PIP will not display much variation. Office work and support services (such as cleaning and maintenance), are examples of activities that involve very similar production methods regardless of where they are performed. Organizational factors can still affect the potential usefulness of different improvement methods for such jobs. Therefore, methods should be individually determined for *all* work targeted for productivity improvement.

There are two major implications that follow from the tailor-made approach. First, it implies that some combination of improvement methods is being selected, rather than one approach. It is possible that a different improvement method may be employed for each job in a given department.

Or two or more methods may be applied to one job (simultaneously or sequentially). The second implication is that a careful analysis of each service or job must be done in order to select the method(s) to apply to it. This analysis should take place after the PIP has been introduced to the department.

OVERVIEW OF IMPROVEMENT METHODS

Before discussing how to analyze services to determine selection of improvement methods, a brief overview of different approaches to improvement will be given in this section.

Motivation and Productivity. Since several improvement approaches are related to motivation, basic motivation concepts will be briefly reviewed first.[1] Applied motivation theories focus on those factors organizations can use to motivate employees to produce more. Offering appropriate amounts or mixtures of these factors should motivate employees to improve their work performance.

The best known and accepted motivation theory is Abraham Maslow's hierarchy of needs.[2] According to this theory, there are five categories of need common to everyone. Attempts to fulfill these needs initiate action. The needs are viewed as a hierarchy:

1. Physiological needs—for basic life support (food, water, etc.)
2. Safety needs—for security, stability, and the absence of danger.
3. Social needs—for love, affection, a sense of belonging, and so on.
4. Esteem needs—for self-respect and respect, recognition, and so on, from others.
5. Self-actualization needs—for self-fulfillment or realization of one's potential.

According to the theory, only unfulfilled needs can motivate people. As one need is satisfied to a sufficient degree, the next level need takes over as a motivating force. The lower-level needs, physiological and safety needs, must be met before the higher-level needs, with their more psychological orientation, begin to motivate. At the highest level, self-actualization, the need is never fully satisfied. People continue to want more growth and self-fulfillment even after they have achieved some satisfaction in this area.

A variation on Maslow's needs hierarchy is Frederick Herzberg's two-factor, or motivation-hygiene theory.[3] Hygiene factors are identified as characteristics of the work environment, such as pay, personnel policies, relations with other employees and supervisors, and so on. Insufficient quantities of these factors lead to dissatisfaction. However, sufficient quantities of them will not motivate employees to produce more. Only factors associated with job content are considered to be motivators. These include achievement, recognition, responsibility, and advancement. In effect, Herzberg's theory is that only the two highest level needs of Maslow's hierarchy actually motivate people.

Different needs have been emphasized as motivators at various points of time. Money was initially viewed as the only motivator because it was linked to survival needs. Security and social needs were emphasized in turn. As general societal and/or working conditions have improved over time, these basic needs have been largely satisfied for the majority of the population. The primary focus of motivation theories is currently on the upper levels of the needs hierarchy.

Improvement Methods Based on Motivation. *Incentive systems* are a longstanding productivity improvement method. These use money or other benefits, such as time off, as incentives for increasing production. Some systems use work standards to determine "normal" levels of production, and offer bonuses for exceeding these levels.

A currently popular technique that focuses on higher-level needs is *job enrichment.* This involves increasing the content, variety, and significance of jobs. This gives employees greater responsibility and enables them to derive more satisfaction from their work. Job rotation and team approaches to work are variants of job enrichment.

Increasing *employee participation* is also related to higher-level needs. Several improvement methods focus on participation. Participation can involve groups of employees, as in labor-management committees and quality circles. It can be based on individual participation, as in management by objectives (MBO). Flextime systems are also viewed as a participation related method because employees exercise more choice in regard to work schedules.

Work or Organizational Redesign. One of the earliest approaches to productivity improvement was work redesign. Commonly associated with industrial engineering, it involves changing the way work is performed (i.e., the production process). Redesign typically improves productivity by reducing the amount of labor needed and/or increasing output by using more efficient production methods. Redesign frequently accompanies other improvement methods, such as new technology.

Just as work redesign focuses on the production process, *organizational redesign* focuses on organizational structure. It generally involves rearranging components of the organization to reduce duplication of effort, unnecessary steps, and so on. Parts of the organization may be restructured to promote a more efficient flow of work. Other methods that can be viewed as kinds of organizational redesign include contracting out for service delivery and intergovernmental agreements.

Another method of productivity improvement focuses on *resource allocation.* This includes better deployment and/or rescheduling of services. It can also involve relocation of facilities, such as fire stations. Although reallocation is usually associated with improving effectiveness of service delivery, it can also contribute to more efficient use of personnel.

New Technology. This may be the oldest and most familiar approach to productivity improvement. New technology involves introducing or expanding the use of labor- and/or cost-saving equipment. New equipment is often associated with services noted for "hardware" usage, such as sanitation, fire protection, and so on. The most widely used type of new technology in recent years is computers, which can be utilized for a broad range of services or activities.

ANALYZING CURRENT CONDITIONS

In order to successfully apply the tailor-made approach it is important to be familiar with:

- The characteristics of the service or job undergoing improvement
- Constraining factors in the work environment
- Improvement methods and how they work

The remaining sections of this chapter explain how to analyze work characteristics and environmental factors. Section III provides detailed descriptions of improvement methods.

Which Jobs Should Be Analyzed? If the approach taken by the PIP is that *all* jobs within a department are to be involved in improvement, then no choice is necessary. However, it is not always feasible to work on improving all jobs simultaneously because of resource constraints. In this case, the first stage of analysis is to select jobs that will be initially targeted for improvement (other jobs can always be included at a future time).

If a limited number of jobs are to be selected for improvement, those selected should be jobs where improvements will have the greatest impact. In general, these are jobs that account for major portions of the department's work, or jobs that are done by large numbers of people (these categories often overlap). Services that are provided irregularly (e.g., fall leaf collections, removal of bulk refuse such as furniture or appliances), should not be included. Their sporadic nature reduces the impact of any improvements that might be achieved. (This type of job might be considered after all regularly performed jobs have been "improved.") The PIP staff and department management should be involved in identifying jobs where improvement will have a substantial impact. Once these jobs have been selected, the next step is to determine the characteristics of the work involved in them.

Identifying Job Characteristics. The analysis to be performed at this stage should not be a detailed, industrial engineering style of analysis. The intent at this point is to identify major aspects of the way work is performed. These will be used to help narrow the range of improvement methods to be considered for each service or job.

Information about job characteristics can be collected in a variety of ways, including:[4]

- Observation of work performed.
- Interviews with employees who do the jobs. (Employees can be interviewed individually, or those who perform the same job can be interviewed in groups.)
- Interviews with supervisory and/or managerial personnel.
- Questionnaires distributed to any of the above personnel.
- Have employees keep a record or diary of their work activities.
- Utilize information in departmental files.

It is not necessary to use *all* of these sources to identify job characteristics. Interviews with people familiar with the job and/or observation should be sufficient in most cases, and are generally convenient to use. If these do not provide sufficient information, or if there are difficulties in using them, the other sources listed can be used instead.

Developing a Job Characteristics Profile. One of the easiest ways to collect and display information about a job is to develop a job characteristics profile. This form lists major job characteristics that should be identified for each job. The person conducting the analysis simply has to fill in the blanks for each job studied.

A job profile provides a broad overview of how the job is performed, who does it, and what equipment is used in the process. A sample profile form is shown in Table 7-1. Answers are provided for refuse collection as an example of the kind of information that should be included in this analysis.

Table 7-1. Job Characteristics Profile

1. *Prepared* for (Instructions: enter name of service, job title, etc.)
   Example: Refuse Collection
2. *Employee Characteristics* (Instructions: describe the characteristics of employees performing the job, e.g., skills used, attributes required. Where applicable, note the number of employees and any variation in their duties)
   Example: Three employees are assigned to each crew. One acts as the driver, two are loaders. Work is of an unskilled nature, involving physical labor (picking up full trash cans and emptying them into truck). Work force is all male. Department is unionized; labor relations have traditionally been good.
3. *Equipment* (Instructions: list all equipment, machinery, tools, etc., used in normal performance of this job. Note age and condition where relevant).
   Example: Rear-loading trucks with a capacity of 20 cubic yards are used. Average age of fleet is 9 years. Breakdowns are frequent.
4. *Production Process* (Instructions: briefly describe how the work is performed, extent of variation, etc.)
   Example: Driver stops truck where refuse cans are placed at curb. Loaders carry cans to truck, empty them, and replace at curb. Loaders may walk or ride between stops, depending on distance, weather, etc. When truck is full, or route completed, truck is driven to disposal site and contents are dumped. Work is of a routine, repetitive nature.
5. *Other Characteristics* (Instructions: note any other relevant aspects about how this job is performed. These could include: location; when or how frequently it is performed; if it is part of a sequence of activities, etc.)
   Example: Only household refuse is collected. Pickup is at curbside. Average time spent driving to disposal site is 1½ hours per day.

The first entry is the name of the service, activity, or job that is being profiled. The second describes who performs the job. This should include the number of employees involved, if it is a group effort, and the specific functions each performs. Characteristics of the employees, such as skills utilized, should be included here. In the refuse collection example, there is one driver and two loaders per truck. The work involves physical labor and does not require special skills.

The example includes two characteristics that are not requirements of the job. First, the work force is exclusively male. Second, it is unionized, but labor relations have not been a problem. This type of detail could be helpful in selecting improvement methods. Therefore, any information that describes significant attributes of the work force should be included in the profile, even if they are not directly job related.

The third entry requires a listing of any equipment, tools, and so on, needed to perform this job. Age and condition of equipment should be included for machinery or similar equipment. This helps indicate where new technology should be considered. In this example, the type of truck used (rear loader) is not one of the newer styles. The fleet is getting old and breakdowns are a problem.

The fourth entry provides a description of how the work is performed (the production process). This should be kept as brief as possible. The extent of variation in the job should also be noted. This entry is useful in determining whether jobs are good candidates for improvement methods that focus on the work process, such as redesign or job enrichment.

The final category is reserved for noting any characteristics that do not fit in the previous four categories and that might be useful. These can include items such as frequency or location of performance, average amount of time spent on a task, and so on. The types of information included in this category can be expected to vary considerably with the job performed.

Understanding the characteristics of a job is necessary in order to select an improvement method that is responsive to those characteristics. However, this information is not sufficient for selecting a method. The environment in which the job is performed must also be understood. This is discussed in the next section. Information about the job and its environment can then be utilized *together* to help determine which improvement methods are appropriate for the job.

Developing a Job Environment Profile. Systems theory emphasizes that work is not performed in a vacuum. It is performed in an organizational environment, which is part of a broader social environment. Factors in these environments, particularly the organizational environment, may act to constrain the types of changes that can be made to any given job. This is because changes associated with particular improvement methods may have negative impacts on certain parts of the environment. Or it may occur because the changes are not compatible with the environment as it exists, or they may violate some of its rules and regulations. In effect, environmental factors may rule out the use of *certain* improvement methods but not *all* methods. Therefore, it is important to identify potential constraints as part of the analysis of current conditions.

A profile of factors in the job environment can be developed and used in the same manner as the job characteristics profile. An example is shown in Table 7-2. As in the previous profile, the first entry is job title. Refuse collection will be used again as an example. The second step is to identify jobs or activities *directly* related to the one under study. These include jobs that precede or follow it in sequence. Jobs that provide inputs to the job being profiled, or that use its output, should also be noted here. Jobs included in this category do not have to be in the same department or agency as the profiled job. Interdependencies frequently cross department lines. Looking at the refuse collection example, this job does not follow in sequence from any other. However, it necessarily precedes, and provides input to, refuse disposal.

Table 7-2. Job Environment Profile

1. *Prepared for* (Instructions: enter name of service, job title, etc.)
   Example: Refuse collection
2. *Directly related jobs or services* (Instructions: (a) List jobs or services that must precede the subject job in sequence and/or that provide materials necessary for its performance. (b) List jobs that depend on it for input and/or must follow it in sequence).
   Example: (a) None. (b) Refuse disposal (incineration and landfill)
3. *Indirectly related jobs or services* (Instructions: (a) List indirectly related jobs or services that precede and/or provide materials to the subject job. (b) List indirectly related jobs that follow it and/or depend on it for input).
   Example: (a) Vehicle maintenance and repair (b) None
4. *Relations with citizens* (Instructions: Describe the nature of contact with citizens; e.g., provide direct services, respond to demands for service, provide information and referral, collect information, fees, etc.)
   Example: Provides a direct service in terms of refuse collection, but involves little direct contact with citizens themselves.
5. *Rules Affecting Change* (Instructions: Describe rules, regulations, etc., that may limit changes in this job. Include items such as civil service rules, union agreements, or other regulations affecting personnel change; city, state, or federal regulations affecting service delivery, etc.)
   Example: Union agreement stipulates one driver and two loaders per truck.
6. *Organization Structure/Managerial Style* (Instructions: Describe factors in the structure of the organization and/or its style of management that affect the job.)
   Example: Hierarchical style of management with little employee participation.

There are two reasons for looking at jobs that are sequentially related to the job being improved:

1. Changes in the profiled job may have adverse effects on related jobs. For example, they may hamper ability to synchronize with related jobs. This may disrupt work patterns in the related job.
2. Changes in related jobs may be beneficial to the profiled job. For example, changes in a preceding job may improve outputs to, or coordination with, the profiled job. This may help improve productivity in the latter as well as the former.

The first example shows how related jobs can act as constraining factors. If an improvement method will have a major adverse effect on other jobs, it should generally not be used. The second example shows how related jobs can provide opportunities for improving two jobs with one improvement method.

The rationale for analyzing directly related jobs is applied to indirectly related jobs in the third step. Indirectly related jobs, as used here, are jobs that are not as closely linked as those in step 2, but still may have a significant impact on the profiled job, or may be affected by it. General administrative and supportive activities should *not* be automatically included here, even though they can be viewed as indirectly related to almost any job. Refuse collection provides a good example of a supportive service that is sufficiently important to the functioning of the job to be listed: vehicle maintenance and repair. Improvements in this job could have significant positive effects on refuse collection as well.

The fourth step looks at the nature of the realtionship between employees performing the job and citizens. The latter can also act as a constraining factor if particular job changes have a negative impact on them. For example, job changes might cause reductions in the amount or convenience of services provided. This kind of problem is most likely to occur in jobs characterized by direct contact with citizens. Of course, it may be decided that some kinds or degrees of inconvenience are acceptable trade-offs for a given level of productivity improvement.

The fifth factor is any rules, regulations, or laws that restrict the kind of changes that can be made. Many of these may be related to personnel changes. Civil service regulations and/or union agreements are likely to pose some constraints. Local laws may include stipulations about service delivery that may prevent certain kinds of change. Some services may also be affected by regulations of higher-level governments. If it is sufficiently important, it may be possible to get changes made in constraining rules. However, this is likely to be time-consuming and/or difficult to achieve. Therefore, it may be preferable to accept some constraints and seek another improvement method that is not restricted by them.

The final factor to consider is whether the way the organization is structured and/or the style of management used may limit the ability to use certain improvement methods. For example, a department with a hierarchical structure and an authoritarian style of management is not a likely candidate for methods using increased participation and/or flexibility. Such methods *could* be successful, but it would require more effort than a method that is more compatible with the organization's style.

The purpose of identifying environmental factors that may constrain changes is *not* to discourage attempts at change. The intent is to make constraints obvious *before* initiating change. This allows avoidance of improvement methods that are doomed to fail because of multiple and/or major constraints. In other words, it helps select methods that are more likely to succeed. By identifying constraints in advance, it may be possible to either:

- Revise the improvement method to reduce its negative impacts.
- Make changes in the constraining environmental factor(s) to allow the change to take place, and/or to reduce its negative impacts.

USING JOB PROFILES TO SELECT IMPROVEMENT METHODS

The prior sections explained how to develop profiles of the job and its environment. This section will explain how the information in these profiles can be used to help identify ways to improve staff efficiency that are most suitable for a given job.

Turning first to the refuse collection job characteristics profile, the information can be interpreted fairly easily. The service is clearly labor intensive, with three men assigned to each truck. Work is of a routine nature, involving physical labor but no special skills. Capital equipment (trucks) plays a critical role in performing this job. However, existing equipment is growing old and is not functioning well. A fair amount of time is wasted driving to and from the disposal site each day.

This information alone indicates some methods to consider for this job. First, new technology would help solve the problem of the aging truck fleet. Some of the newer model trucks are designed to reduce the number of loaders necessary, which would also alleviate the labor-intensiveness of this job. However, the fact that the department is unionized may make it difficult to adopt technology that would reduce the labor force. This would probably become a matter for negotiation.

The job does not provide opportunities to use a variety of skills, and is repetitive in nature. This implies employee motivation may be low. Efforts to enrich the job might help. Other motivation techniques, such as incentive systems, might also be considered.

Efforts to reduce wasted time traveling to the disposal site should be considered. New technology in the form of trucks with larger capacity could help. Establishing transfer stations might also be considered. This would be viewed as a modest form of job redesign, since trucks would no longer be driven to the final disposal site, they would be driven to transfer stations. Transfer stations can be sites where the refuse is directly transferred to larger collection vehicles. Or they can be sites where loads can be dumped into a large container or pit before being reloaded for trips to the final disposal site. This system allows the collection trucks to return to their routes more quickly than if they had to drive to the final dump site.

The same type of interpretation should be applied to information in the job environment profile. Refuse collection is not directly related to many other jobs. It provides input to refuse disposal operations, and relies on the support service of vehicle maintenance and repair. Although it involves a direct service, there is little contact with citizens. Few constraining rules exist, but crew size is stipulated in the union agreement. Managerial style is of typical hierarchical nature and does not encourage employee participation.

Environmental factors should be analyzed in terms of constraints posed.

In this example, directly or indirectly related jobs do not constrain choice of methods. The indirectly related job, vehicle maintenance and repair, does provide an opportunity for improvement, however. If productivity of this operation was improved, trucks would break down less often. This alone would probably increase refuse collection productivity to some degree.

Citizens could be a constraining factor because the service directly involves them, even though they have little contact with the employees. Changes that reduce frequency of pickup would probably be resisted, for example. However, the types of change mentioned here are unlikely to do this. Changing to some of the newer, self-loading trucks might require citizens to use special kinds of refuse containers. If they have to purchase new containers, they might resist this change. If the city supplies new containers, they should not have problems accepting it.

Union rules are an important constraint. The contract agreement calling for a crew of three underlies the labor intensive nature of the service. Any change affecting crew size, such as a self-loading truck, would have to be bargained for. However, trucks with larger capacity (to reduce driving time to the disposal site), will probably not be resisted. The prospect of transfer stations should not be particularly problematic to unions.

Management style is somewhat constraining. It is not particularly conducive to applying job enrichment, which works better in a less rigid setting. However, incentive systems would fit this environment without difficulty.

To summarize the analysis, four general approaches to improvement were identified as likely candidates: new technology, job enrichment, job redesign, and incentive systems. Improving productivity of the related job, vehicle maintenance, should also be considered, but this must be done in a separate analysis of that job. New technology is strongly constrained by union regulations. The union may agree to it, but they would probably demand higher pay in exchange, and/or provisions to assure none of their employees is laid off. However, if past relations with the union have been good, they may be willing to adjust their demands to reach an acceptable compromise. Job redesign (transfer stations) seems feasible. Job enrichment is a possibility as a motivation-related technique, but incentive systems look stronger because they seem to fit the managerial environment better.

The job profile analysis can be used to fairly quickly identify improvement methods that are likely to work for a given job. Methods that did not immediately come to mind might also be considered for inclusion in a final list of candidates. In this case, a closer look should be given to other motivation-related techniques, since this method in general does not seem to be constrained. Flextime may be a good candidate to consider, for example. However, each improvement method suggested by this analysis should be examined more thoroughly before a final choice is made. This requires greater familiarity with the workings of each method, which is provided in section III.

COSTS OF IMPROVEMENT METHODS

The preceding sections explain how job characteristics and environmental factors can be used to help identify improvement methods appropriate for a particular job or department. Costs of improvement methods are an additional criterion to be considered when making final selections. In the face of revenue constraints, there may be some temptation to reject more expensive improvement methods, or even to avoid productivity improvement completely, because of costs involved. This kind of attitude is counterproductive and should be discouraged. Productivity improvement should be viewed as an investment that will generate savings (even though they may not be realized in the short run). Thus efforts should be made to identify ways of financing the different improvement methods, rather than simply estimating their cost and possibly rejecting otherwise appropriate methods because of costs.

For example, new technology is generally the most expensive kind of improvement method. However, if the expense budget is constrained, new technology can be financed through bonds, since it is a capital expense. This will make it affordable in many circumstances. Unfortunately, this mechanism is not applicable to other improvement methods. However, it may be possible to secure grants for productivity improvement purposes, or to apply portions of intergovernmental revenues to them.

Another way to deal with fiscal constraints is to select one of the lower-cost methods within a general category. For example, the analysis may indicate that a motivation-related method is appropriate for a particular job. Within that category, monetary incentives probably have the highest cost (although other types of incentives could be used instead). Methods such as job enlargement or quality circles are relatively low cost, since the only costs normally associated with them are related to designing and/or establishing the method in its new location. Thus they might be a better choice in situations where fiscal constraints are severe. Efforts can also be made to get volunteers from universities or the business community (as discussed in chapter 4) to help reduce the "start up" costs associated with launching the improvement methods (unless this can be handled by the central PIP staff). In short, efforts should be made to work around cost constraints to the extent possible, rather than let them become the dominant criterion when selecting improvement methods.

SUMMARY

This chapter has explained how to apply a tailor-made approach to productivity improvement. The philosophy underlying this approach is that methods must be individually selected for each job. They should be chosen for compatibility with the way the work is performed and the environment it is performed in.

In order to help apply this approach, two analytic tools should be used. The job characteristics profile helps identify major aspects of the way a given job is performed. These include:

- How the work is done
- Who performs it, and what skills they use
- What equipment is employed

Once job characteristics are isolated in this manner, problem areas are fairly easy to identify. The next step is to select improvement methods that can help alleviate those problems and that are compatible with the characteristics of the job. Using the job characteristics profile should be helpful in generating a list of improvement methods that are candidates for further appraisal.

The next step of the analysis is to profile factors in the job environment in the same way that job characteristics were profiled. The purpose of this is to identify possible constraints that may make it difficult, or even impossible, to utilize particular methods on the list of candidates. Factors that frequently act as constraints include:

- Related jobs that are negatively affected by changes in the profiled jobs
- Rules and regulations concerning personnel and/or service delivery
- Citizens who may be adversely affected by change
- Managerial style

The constraints identified in this profile should be compared with the methods identified as candidates in the previous step. It is generally not possible to utilize methods that are strongly affected by environmental constraints. However, it may be possible to remove or diminish the constraint, or modify the method in some way to reduce its impact on the constraining factor.

A final factor to consider when selecting a method is the cost associated with it. Although cost is an important concern in a time of revenue constraints, efforts should be made to find ways to finance improvement methods or to identify "affordable" methods rather than allow costs to overly restrict the selection process.

NOTES

1. Material in this section relies heavily on summaries of motivation concepts from: John M. Greiner et al., *Productivity and Motivation: A Review of State and Local Government Initiatives* (Washington, D.C.: The Urban Institute Press, 1981), pp. 1-9; Herbert G. Hicks and C. Ray Gullett, *Organizations: Theory and Behavior* (New York: McGraw-Hill Company, 1975), pp. 275-299; and Katherine Janka, *People, Performance . . . Results! A Guide to Increasing the Effectiveness of Local Government Employees* (Washington, D.C.: National Training and Development Service Press, 1977), pp. 11-22. For more complete discussions of motivation concepts see, for example: Ramon J. Aldag and Arthur P. Brief, *Task Design and Employee Motivation* (Glenview, Ill.: Scott, Foresman, 1979); Robert C. Beck, *Motivation: Theories and Principles* (Englewood Cliffs, N.J.: Prentice-Hall, 1978); Kae H. Chung, *Motivational Theories and Practices* (Columbus, Ohio: Grid, 1977); Edward E. Lawler, III, *Motivation in Work Organizations* (Monterey, Calif.: Brooks/Cole Publishing Company, 1973): V. Vroom, *Work and Motivation* (New York: John Wiley & Sons, 1964).
2. Abraham Maslow, *Motivation and Personality* (New York: Harper & Row, 1970).
3. F. Herzberg, B. Mansner, and B. Snyderman, *The Motivation to Work* (New York: John Wiley & Sons, 1959).
4. Ernest J. McCormick, *Job Analysis: Methods and Applications* (New York: AMACOM, 1979), pp. 23-24.

Section III

Productivity Improvement Methods

The next step in the Productivity Improvement Program (PIP) is to select and implement improvement methods in the various departments, agencies, and work units involved in the PIP. In keeping with the tailor-made approach discussed in chapter 7, different methods should be chosen for different situations. This section will provide information that can be used to help make the appropriate choices.

In keeping with the theme of this book, the chapters in this section describe those methods (outlined in chapter 7), that focus on improving productivity by increasing staff efficiency. Therefore, those methods that fall outside the scope of this book, such as cost cutting, are not discussed. This section brings together descriptions of a number of improvement methods, with sufficient information about each to provide guidance for selecting improvement methods for use in the PIP.

The discussion of each method includes an explanation of:

- How the method improves productivity
- Where it is applicable
- How to use it
- Factors affecting implementation

Since a substantial number of improvement methods are included here, it is not possible to provide detailed discussions of all of them. Therefore, the notes to each chapter provide references to sources of additional information for those who are less familiar with particular methods.

8
IMPROVING PRODUCTIVITY THROUGH WORK REDESIGN

This chapter will explain how various types of work redesign can be used in a PIP. It will provide information that can be used to help:

- Decide whether to use job redesign
- Select the appropriate type of redesign for different work situations
- Implement redesign

Work redesign is one of the earliest and most basic improvement methods. This chapter begins by explaining how redesign works and where it is applicable. It will then explain differences among major kinds of redesign techniques, and how to apply them. The techniques include: methods analysis and improvement; work flow and distribution; work-place design; and work measurement. The final section will discuss factors affecting implementation of work redesign techniques.

HOW REDESIGN IMPROVES PRODUCTIVITY

This section will explain how work redesign can improve productivity by changing the way work is performed. The primary concern of work redesign is the way work is organized and how inputs, such as people and equipment, are utilized. The goal of redesign is to increase the efficiency with which work is produced by changing one or more of the following:

- Work processes
- Sequence of tasks
- Staff responsibilities
- Physical layout

Work redesign is needed because it is often the case that work methods were never originally designed or planned; they simply evolved. Alternatively, the original work process may have gotten lost under a variety of incremental modifications made over the years. This means that inefficient methods, unnecessary procedures, steps that no longer serve a purpose, duplication of effort, and similar barriers to productivity may be built into existing work practices. Redesign is used to identify these problems and remove them. It can be viewed as applied common sense, or as "working smarter not harder."

Redesign Methods. Several different types of techniques for redesigning work exist. This section will provide a basic description of these methods and how they work. They will be explained in greater detail later in this chapter.

Work redesign is associated with the following management disciplines: method study; organization and methods (O & M); and work measurement, each of which takes a slightly different perspective.[1] They are explained here to illustrate the diverse activities included in work redesign:

Method study looks in detail at the sequence in which specific tasks are, or should be, performed. Physical layout of the workplace may also be a subject of study. Job content may be reviewed to better match job specifications and employee skills.

Organization and methods originally evolved to bring method study techniques from the factory to the office. In addition to the usual method study subjects, it also concentrates on the organization of people, both as work groups and in terms of responsibility and supervisory functions. Forms design also fits under this discipline.

Work measurement is primarily concerned with the amount of time involved in performing a task or job. Its main purpose is to determine standard times in order to establish production levels and evaluate performance.

Although each method uses some different techniques they all employ a similar approach to work redesign. Each begins by analyzing in detail the way a job is currently performed, and then looks for ways to improve the work method. This typically means simplification of the process and/or reduction of waste. The key goals in improving work methods are:

Eliminate any unnecessary actions, waste, duplication, delay, and so on.

Simplify those processes and/or physical activities that remain.

Combine tasks or activities.

Organize space, equipment, people, and the sequence of activities to improve the flow of work.

Making changes to achieve one of these goals will often help achieve others. For example, eliminating duplication of effort should also simplify the work process; or reorganizing space may help reduce delay. The ability to accomplish some of these goals may be affected by factors in the organizational environment such as civil service rules, legislation affecting staff requirements, and so on.

The basic redesign process is not overly complex. Most methods can be applied by persons who have not had extensive training in it. Some techniques, such as work measurement, do require more expertise. If it seems desirable to use this method, consultants could be used. However, the core of work redesign can be performed by existing PIP staff who have had moderate amounts of training or self-study in the fundamental methodology.

The extent of improvement gained from redesign will vary from job to job, depending on the nature of the work performed, how well it was originally designed, and how many procedural problems exist to be eliminated. Most improvements will be related to a reduction in time needed to perform a particular job, which ultimately translates into a reduction in staff hours needed for that job. It is assumed that other meaningful work exists to occupy the hours freed by work redesign, and/or that it reduces the need to hire additional personnel. These are realistic assumptions for the public sector in general, especially in times of fiscal constraint.

APPLICABILITY OF WORK REDESIGN

Although work redesign was developed to improve manufacturing productivity, it is applicable to many jobs in the public sector. The basic requirement for using redesign is a repetitive work process. While many public sector jobs do not meet this criterion, a large portion of them *can* benefit from redesign.

Jobs that can benefit from redesign include those that require physical labor of a fairly repetitive, routine nature. Public sector jobs that meet these criteria include street patching, park maintenance, refuse collection, street cleaning, meter reading, and vehicle maintenance and repair. Much office work is of a repetitive nature as well, particularly the processing of forms or other kinds of information. All aspects of a job do not have to be repetitive for redesign to be applied. It can be used for those parts that are repetitive and still enhance productivity of the whole job. Nor does work have to be completely repetitive in the style of assembly line jobs. As long as procedures or activities are *basically* the same, redesign methods can be utilized.

Of course, there are some public sector jobs that are not good candidates for redesign. These include jobs requiring individualized responses to specific cases or situations, or those where thinking or creative work dominates, such as research. Some nonrepetitive jobs, however, might benefit from redesign techniques that *don't* focus on how work is performed. Reorganization of space or redistribution of responsibilities, for example, could increase productivity in these jobs, although gains are not likely to be as significant as those associated with redesigning work processes.

All repetitive jobs are good candidates for redesign. However, it is likely that some jobs are being performed about as well as possible, while others could benefit more from redesign. Therefore, one should try to identify jobs that are in greatest need of improvement by looking for problems such as backlogs, delays, waste, or other acknowledged trouble spots. Departmental management can help identify both repetitive jobs and problem areas.

METHODS ANALYSIS AND IMPROVEMENT

This section will describe the most basic redesign technique, methods analysis and improvement, and explain how to use it. This technique is easy to understand and can be readily applied to any job eligible for redesign. It uses an analytic tool that facilitates looking at a job in terms of its component parts. This tool, called process charting, is helpful in analyzing and redesigning the job. The basic redesign principles—eliminate, simplify, combine, and organize—are used to redesign the job for improved productivity. Methods analysis and work redesign for any given job is typically not an overly time-consuming or costly technique. It also has the advantage of being reversible or modifiable if the new method does not increase productivity, or if other problems develop.

Parts of the Job. The process chart technique facilitates studying work in terms of its basic components. Work can be viewed as a three-part cycle whose parts are:

Get ready
Work
Clean up

The get-ready phase includes gathering materials or information, setting up equipment, and so on. The work phase involves activities that directly contribute to the output or finished product associated with each job. Clean-up includes distributing or putting away the work produced, as well as removing materials not needed for the next task. An example of a clerk preparing a supply requisition will help clarify what each stage includes:

Get ready—Activities include: reading memo from supervisor requesting that certain supplies be ordered; getting a supply requisition form from file; getting supply catalog and looking up order numbers for items requested.

Work—The requisition is typed and proofread; it is brought to the director for approval.

Clean up—The order form is separated into copies for distribution; several are sent to the supply department; one is sent to the supervisor; one is filed with the supervisor's memo; the catalog is returned to its shelf.

Since only the work phase is truly output oriented, isolating it in this way is helpful in understanding the purpose of the job and is useful in the critical analysis stage of the process chart method.

Process charts. The method currently used to perform a job must be thoroughly understood before it can be redesigned. This section will explain a technique to use to help understand how a job is currently done. This technique, called a flow process chart, is an industrial engineering tool that describes a job in terms of a sequence of basic activities. There are five basic activities, each with a corresponding symbol, that are commonly used in preparing process charts:

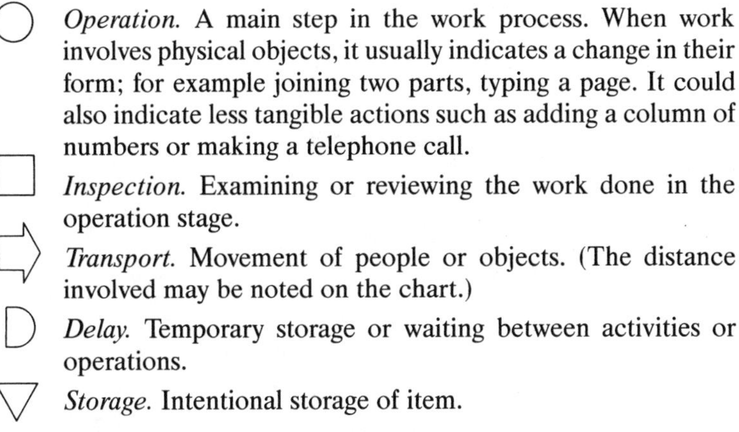

Operation. A main step in the work process. When work involves physical objects, it usually indicates a change in their form; for example joining two parts, typing a page. It could also indicate less tangible actions such as adding a column of numbers or making a telephone call.

Inspection. Examining or reviewing the work done in the operation stage.

Transport. Movement of people or objects. (The distance involved may be noted on the chart.)

Delay. Temporary storage or waiting between activities or operations.

Storage. Intentional storage of item.

Chart entries can be grouped by stages of work, to highlight those that are most important. Only activities that are actually part of the job should be recorded on the process charts. Interruptions such as telephone calls or coffee breaks, should not be noted. The purpose of the chart is to study the steps that are normally taken to perform a particular job, not to study behavior patterns of a particular employee. To be sure that the chart for a given job is accurate, those preparing the chart should make several observations of how the job is done, observe different people doing it, and consult the job supervisor to check if the chart reflects current practice. Random samples are not required for this technique, however.

For an example of a process chart, return to the clerk typing a supply requisition, which is shown in chart form in Figure 8-1. (Charts can be individually prepared, as in this figure, or a preprinted form can be used, as in Figure 8-2.) The chart focuses on explaining the activities performed by the clerk. Since the object of this particular analysis is a narrowly defined job, the chart presents a fair amount of detail about what is done. However, it does not go to extremes in showing detail; for example, it does not indicate that the typewriter is turned on or off, or that margins are set, and so on. Process charts can take broader or narrower perspectives than used in this example, which will affect the level of detail shown in the chart (other types of process charts will be described later).

In deciding the level of detail to include in a chart, it is helpful to

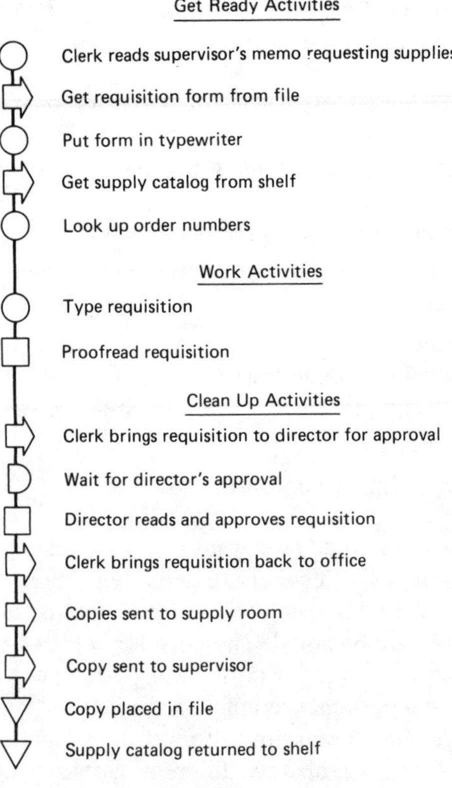

Requisitioning Supplies
Get Ready Activities
Clerk reads supervisor's memo requesting supplies
Get requisition form from file
Put form in typewriter
Get supply catalog from shelf
Look up order numbers
Work Activities
Type requisition
Proofread requisition
Clean Up Activities
Clerk brings requisition to director for approval
Wait for director's approval
Director reads and approves requisition
Clerk brings requisition back to office
Copies sent to supply room
Copy sent to supervisor
Copy placed in file
Supply catalog returned to shelf

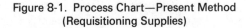

Figure 8-1. Process Chart—Present Method (Requisitioning Supplies)

FLOW PROCESS CHART	NO.	PAGE NO.	NUMBER OF PAGES
PROCESS			
☐ MAN OR ☐ MATERIAL			
CHART BEGINS	CHART ENDS		
CHARTED BY	DATE		
ORGANIZATION			

SUMMARY						
ACTIONS	PRESENT		PROPOSED		DIFFERENCE	
	NO.	TIME	NO.	TIME	NO	TIME
○ OPERATIONS						
⇨ TRANSPORTATIONS						
□ INSPECTIONS						
D DELAYS						
▽ STORAGES						
DISTANCE TRAVELED (feet)						

STEP NO.	DETAILS OF METHOD ☐ PRESENT ☐ PROPOSED	OPERATION	TRANSPORTATION	INSPECTION	DELAY	STORAGE	DISTANCE (in feet)	QUANTITY	TIME	ANALYSIS (why?) WHAT?	WHERE?	WHEN?	WHO?	HOW?	NOTES	ANALYSIS ELIMINATE	CHANGE COMBINE	SEQUENCE	PLACE	PERSON	IMPROVE
		○	⇨	□	D	▽															
		○	⇨	□	D	▽															
		○	⇨	□	D	▽															
		○	⇨	□	D	▽															
		○	⇨	□	D	▽															
		○	⇨	□	D	▽															
		○	⇨	□	D	▽															
		○	⇨	□	D	▽															
		○	⇨	□	D	▽															
		○	⇨	□	D	▽															
		○	⇨	□	D	▽															
		○	⇨	□	D	▽															
		○	⇨	□	D	▽															
		○	⇨	□	D	▽															
		○	⇨	□	D	▽															
		○	⇨	□	D	▽															
		○	⇨	□	D	▽															
		○	⇨	□	D	▽															
		○	⇨	□	D	▽															
		○	⇨	□	D	▽															
		○	⇨	□	D	▽															
		○	⇨	□	D	▽															

Figure 8-2. Sample Process Chart

remember that the intent is to improve the way a job is done. Things that obviously are not targets for change (at least in the context of the PIP), such as turning the typewriter on, may be omitted. Care should be taken not to omit too much, however, because this would defeat the purpose of the chart. The discussion of critical analysis in the next section will clarify how the chart is used, thus providing more guidance about what to include in it.

The process chart used here displays a fairly simple task. Chart format can be varied to reflect more complex activities. One common way to do this is to use branches from the main chart to show activities that are performed simultaneously or to show alternative courses of action. Examples of this type of chart are provided in Figures 8-3a and 8-3b. Figure 8-3a shows simultaneous activities performed during a motor vehicle license examination. In this example, one inspector grades written responses to the test while another simultaneously administers a vision test to the applicant.

Figure 8-3b uses branching to show that different courses of action are taken when specific criteria or conditions exist. In this case, permits are issued automatically to residents, while nonresidents must fill out an additional form. These alternative forms of action are readily displayed in separate branches.

Critical Analysis. After preparing a process chart showing how a job is currently performed, the next step is to analyze the work methods used. In effect, this analysis involves asking and answering "who, what, when, where, why, and how" questions for each activity shown on the chart. After answering these questions, it should be possible to identify one or more alternative ways of performing the activity. The alternatives, of course, will be geared

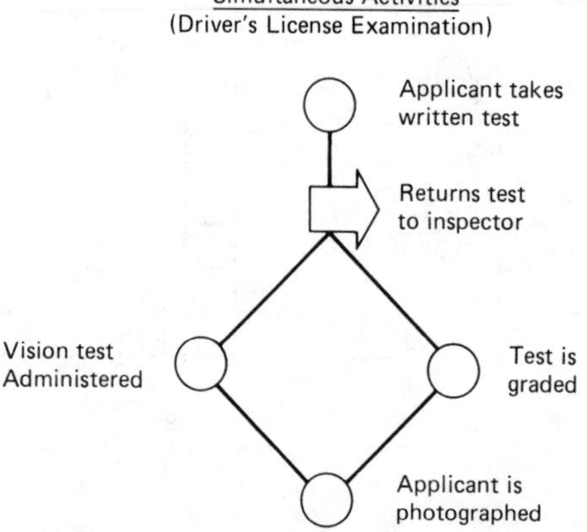

Figure 8-3a. Example of Process Chart With Branches

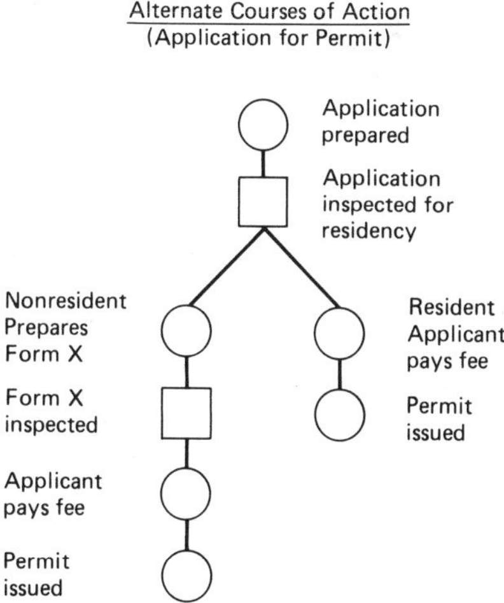

Figure 8-3b. Example of Process Chart With Branches

toward improving productivity, mainly through elimination, simplification, combination, and reorganization. They may also help work flow more smoothly, thus reducing backlogs and delays. A form such as the one shown in Table 8-1 could be used to help organize the critical analysis.

Critical analysis should begin with the major work activity in the job under study. Although it may seem odd not to start with the first activity in the sequence, the reason for this is simple. If the *major* activity is eliminated, then all related activities will automatically be eliminated, without need for analysis. If one starts in sequence, time spent analyzing preliminary activities is wasted if elimination of the major task removes them as well.

The first thing to ascertain about any job activity is whether it can be eliminated completely. This is addressed by the "why" and "what" questions, which look at the purpose of the activity. Returning to the supply requisition example, the major activity is typing the requisition. This is done in order to have supplies sent from central storage to the office originating the request. The ultimate goal is to have necessary materials on hand to carry out basic office activities. There appears to be no problem with the purpose or goal in this case, although either *could* be unnecessary or misdirected in other instances.

The next area of consideration is possible alternatives to typing the requisition. At this point it is advisable to write down *all* alternatives that come to mind, even though some appear to be unworkable or less efficient than current methods. This "brainstorming" is useful because it may lead to

Table 8-1. Analysis of Activity Form

STAGE 1 EXAMINATION	STAGE 2 ALTERNATIVES POSSIBLE ALTERNATIVES	BEST ALTERNATIVES
1. *Why?*		
Why is this operation performed?	______	______
What goal is involved?	______	______
2. *What?*		
What is the purpose of the operation?	______	______
Is it necessary?	______	______
3. *Where?*		
Where is the operation performed?	______	______
Why this place?	______	______
4. *When?*		
When is it performed in sequence?	______	______
Why then?	______	______
5. *Who?*		
Which person performs the operation?	______	______
Why this person?	______	______
6. *How?*		
How is it done?	______	______
Why that way?	______	______

Based on Alan Fields, *Method Study* (London: Cassell & Company, Ltd., 1969), p. 24./P. E. Randall, *Introduction To Work Study and Organization Methods* (London: Butterworths, 1969), p. 36 and Victor Smith, *Modern Practice in Work Study* (Brighton, The Machinery Publishing Co. Ltd., 1970), p. 19.

other, more appropriate, alternatives. Some alternatives to the "what" and "why" questions are as follows:

Eliminate the central supply unit; let each office keep its own stock of supplies, purchasing from outside vendors as needed.

Eliminate typing the requisition; it could be handwritten.

Eliminate typing the requisition; the order could be telephoned to the supply unit.

The first alternative does not appear realistic since central purchasing and storage is generally more efficient. The next two alternatives are plausible, however, and might be developed further as other questions on the form are answered.

The "where" and "when" questions in this case are not particularly useful, although they can be in other circumstances. The activity takes place in an office, at the clerk's desk. It is the sixth step in sequence, and could not logically be moved unless earlier steps are eliminated.

The "who" and "how" questions are more useful in generating alternatives.

A clerk currently types the requisition. Telephoning and handwriting have already been noted as alternatives to typing. Alternatives to the clerk include the supervisor who originally requested the supplies, or the supervisor's secretary (if there is one). One could also consider using a different clerk or other office worker if there was some reason to believe this would improve overall office efficiency.

Critical analysis of the main work activity alone has identified some major potential changes. If the supervisor filled out a requisition form by hand, or telephoned the request directly to the supply room, for example, the number of activities would be reduced considerably. Although the "get ready" and "clean up" activities should be subjected to the same degree of analysis as the work portion, only some key points will be noted here since the process should now be clear.

One issue to be resolved is use of a requisition form. The "why" and "what" questions will probably indicate that it is used as a record-keeping and control device. Therefore, it is unlikely to be abandoned completely. It would be possible to adopt the process of telephoning for supplies and still fill the need for a written record by having a clerk in the supply unit fill out the form from the telephone order. A copy of this form could be sent with the supplies. The recipient's signature on the form would acknowledge both approval and receipt.

Another key point is whether it is really necessary for the person requesting supplies to use order numbers for them. Omitting numbers reduces preparation time by removing the need to look through the supply catalog and by simplifying the typing task. The resolution of this point probably depends on the variety of supplies kept in the central unit; a large volume might necessitate this step.

Turning to "clean up" activities, the most obvious candidate for elimination is sending the requisition to the director for approval. This is clearly another control device, yet it adds steps and delay time to the job. It should be decided whether the added control is really needed. In this case, it might also be possible to eliminate sending a copy of the requisition to the supervisor. This is probably done for informational purposes, but results in duplication of effort because several people keep the same material on file.

The most valuable aspect of critical analysis is that it forces one to question the way things are done and whether all the steps involved are necessary. This may be the first time anyone has seriously looked at and challenged work procedures, so it is possible that many alternatives will be found. As the example indicates, even the most basic actions can be candidates for elimination or change. Therefore, an open mind is an important prerequisite for performing this analysis.

The final step is to devise a new work process from the alternatives generated. If there is more than one good candidate, a process chart should be prepared for all of them so that comparison of the number and kinds of activities can be made to facilitate the decision. If such comparison is unnecessary, a chart should still be made to examine the new method to insure that it is both workable and an improvement over the old method. The chart can then be used to help explain the new process to the employees involved and to check that it is being performed properly.

The proposed method for requisitioning supplies is shown in Figure 8-4. The decision was made to have a clerk or secretary call in the order to the supply room, rather than have a supervisor fill in a form or make a call, since it is more efficient for supervisory personnel to spend their time on more important tasks. A supply clerk will fill in an order form from the telephone conversation. A copy of the form will be sent with the supplies for the supervisor to sign, indicating both approval of the original order and receipt of supplies. The number of activities performed by the office requesting supplies has declined considerably from the original process (see Figure 8-1). The main work activity, typing the requisition, is no longer performed, thus eliminating the associated get-ready and clean-up activities as well. It has also been decided that the director's approval is not necessary, eliminating another activity and the transportation and delay associated with it.

It is not suggested that this represents a model procedure for supply requisition nor an indicator of the amount of productivity improvement that can be expected whenever this process is applied. The extent of change possible will vary according to the job under study and the unit in which it is located. It would be unlikely for elimination of control mechanisms such as a written requisition form and approval by the director to occur in a large department with a strong emphasis on control. Nor could one expect to move the responsibility for preparing the requisition to a supply room clerk if that unit was very busy. These are all aspects that must be investigated in the analysis and redesign process. Alternatives should not be rejected on the assumption that such changes cannot be made; those assumptions must be

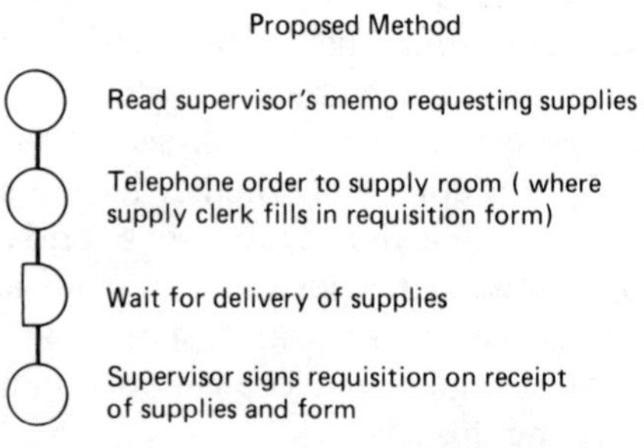

Proposed Method
Read supervisor's memo requesting supplies
Telephone order to supply room (where supply clerk fills in requisition form)
Wait for delivery of supplies
Supervisor signs requisition on receipt of supplies and form

Figure 8-4. Process Chart—Requisitioning Supplies

verified. The structure provided by the process charts and critical analysis encourages careful consideration of alternatives, which is a major benefit of the methodology.

Examples. Some examples of public sector applications of redesign concepts will help illustrate their relevance to a variety of jobs and show how they have been used in practice. One possible result of critical analysis is elimination of jobs. The Department of Building Services in Dallas, for example, eliminated the job of floor waxing, which is intended to prolong the life of vinyl tile flooring in public buildings. A study determined that the cost of waxing was six times greater than replacing the flooring more frequently.[2]

Jobs may also be eliminated by having them performed by another government entity. In effect, this springs from the "who should do the job" portion of the critical analysis. Milwaukee eliminated city meat inspections and arson inspections on the grounds that these are state responsibilities in Wisconsin.[3] Asking who should perform a service might also lead to contracting it out to the private sector, a step which has been taken by many local governments for a wide variety of services. Of course, this does not eliminate the service, but presumably allows for its provision at a lower cost.

Analysis of current work methods more typically leads to elimination of portions of jobs or to redesign than to elimination of entire jobs. In the Dallas Department of Building Services, it was discovered that cleaning practices were outdated and inefficient. New methods were established, and a training academy created to provide instruction in methods and equipment use.[4] Although this redesign did not involve new equipment, many redesigned jobs involve new technology, which will be discussed under that heading in a later chapter.

The Pennsylvania Department of Transportation has recently made efforts to eliminate unnecessary work. They reduced equipment maintenance work by identifying and disposing of obsolete equipment, thus decreasing the number of pieces to be maintained. They also began a program to eliminate at least 10 forms per month, which resulted in removal of 330 forms. This not only eliminated work involved in preparing and processing the forms, but saved about $100,000 in annual printing costs as well.[5]

Work redesign analysis was applied to a variety of office procedures in the California Department of Motor Vehicles (DMV). For example, the original procedure for suspense documents involved date stamping on arrival, but reading and routing at a different time. The documents were counted by one unit before passing them to the next unit, which also counted them for its records. This job was revised so that stamping, reading, and routing became one operation, and the count made by the first unit was passed on to, and used by, the second. While this is a minor example, the DMV made a total of

125 improvements in an 18-month productivity improvement program which was believed to bring about $1 million in savings annually, largely from staff reductions and avoidance of staff increases.[6]

PROCESS CHART VARIATIONS

The basic flow process chart was explained in depth because it has the greatest potential for use in a wide variety of public sector situations. There are variations in the basic process chart that are used for more complicated work situations, or when a different perspective on work flow is needed. These variations and their use will be explained in this section.

Variations in Chart Perspective. The process chart described in the previous section has traditionally been referred to as a man type chart because it shows activities of the person performing the job. This distinguishes it from two charts that take slightly different perspectives.

One of these is a material type chart, which follows what happens to materials during the work process. In the public sector, material could include anything from a form being prepared in an office, to a client going through an application process. Material type charts are used when the focus of redesign is on the *flow* of work, rather than the *method* of work. Material charts follow work as it crosses unit or department lines. Redesign based on this chart will primarily focus on reducing the number of people/steps involved in processing the material.

The other chart variation is an equipment-type chart, which follows what is done with a certain piece of machinery or equipment. Equipment-type charts are used when machinery or equipment dominates the work process. Redesign based on this chart will focus on improving utilization of the equipment, reducing backlogs, conserving energy, and so on. While either of these charts could be used to analyze some public sector jobs, the person-centered chart will be applicable to more situations.

Multiple Activity Chart. Another process chart variation is used for more complex work processes where more than one person and/or machine work together to perform a job. This is called a multiple activity chart. It uses a bar chart format to represent all people and equipment involved. An example of this kind of chart is given in Figure 8-5, which shows some of the activities of a two-person custodial crew cleaning the rug of a small office. Note that the amount of time expended is typically indicated on such charts. The chart thus shows how much of a person's or machine's time is idle, usually due to waiting for other members of the team. In this example, the rug cleaner is

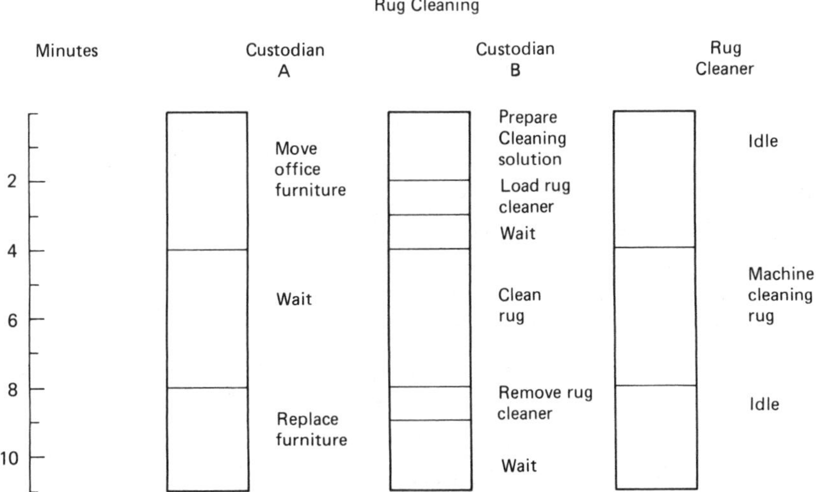

Figure 8-5. Multiple Activity Chart (Rug Cleaning)

idle for the first four minutes while one custodian removes office furniture and the other prepares the cleaning solution and loads the cleaner. Then one custodian is idle while the second uses the machine to clean the rug, and so on. The goal of a study using this kind of chart would be to reduce the amount of idle time, or possibly to reduce crew size.

An example of an analysis of multiple activities comes from the Water Distribution Division of the Milwaukee Department of Public Works. In studying water main repair, it was discovered that the work crew arrived at the site of the break, then waited while their truck returned for a compressor to operate the pneumatic hammer, which was then operated by one person while the rest of the crew waited. Other equipment tended to arrive late, and the trucks used to haul debris from the site were too small, causing delays when they left to be emptied. Finally, the original work crew would have to wait for a specialized caulking crew to arrive to make the repair. In short, the entire process kept either people or equipment idle for considerable portions of the work time. Analysis led to revisions in repair procedures and a new management system in the division.[7]

Two-handed Charts. Another variation on the basic flow process chart is the two handed process chart. This type of chart is used when fairly detailed repetitive work is done with both hands, such as assembling or repairing an object, or performing some types of office functions. It shows the activities performed with each hand in a separate column. Figure 8-6 shows a two-handed chart of the present method used by a clerk stamping some forms. The goal of analysis using this kind of chart would be to increase the use of principles of motion economy to improve productivity. The basic principles are:

Minimal movements. This includes reducing the number of movements and the level of effort involved. For example, finger or wrist motions are less tiring than arm or body motions. This also includes reducing transportation distance, preferable keeping all items and movements within a space that can be reached without stretching.

Simultaneous movements. Both hands should start and stop at the same time.

Symmetrical movements. Each hand performs the same activities.

Habitual movements. Positioning materials and tools in a fixed pattern helps build habits and reduce searching.

Rhythmical movements. Repeating a regular pattern leads to establishing rhythm.

Continuous movements. Curved, continuous motions are preferable to straight motions which lead to short changes in direction and abruptness.

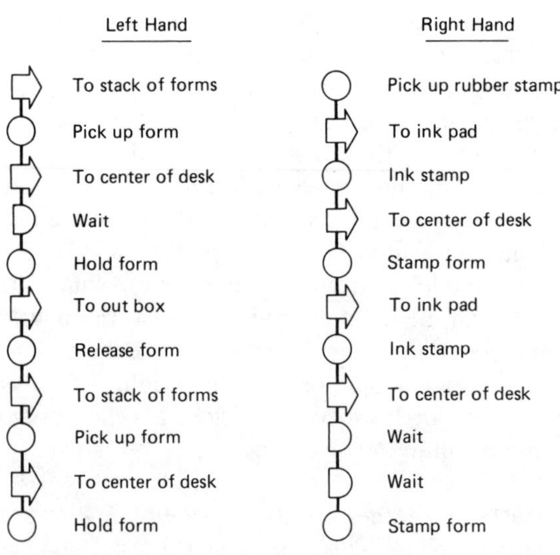

Figure 8-6. Two-Handed Process Chart (Stamping Forms)

Natural movements. Movements should take advantage of the natural shape and path of the hands, feet, or body; for example, the normal reach of the arm. Momentum generated by a motion should be completed to form a natural rhythm.

There are undoubtedly fewer opportunities to use this kind of chart in the public sector than in manufacturing. However, there are many tasks, including office work, to which it can be successfully applied. For example, a fairly obvious improvement can be made in the form-stamping job described in Figure 8-6 by simply moving the forms waiting to be stamped to the center of the desk. This reduces transportation distance and most of the movement of the left hand, and eliminates some of the delay that occurs because the left hand is performing more activities than the right.

WORK DISTRIBUTION

This section will explain another redesign method, which improves productivity by changing the way work is distributed. Work distribution analysis can be applied to jobs that involve less routine work processes than needed for process charts and redesign. However, the distribution of work must be fairly consistent over time for this method to be employed. Work distribution can also be used *with* redesign to improve both aspects of work.

Work distribution analysis begins with an initial examination of current distribution of work and/or responsibility to identify problem areas such as:

- Overburdened employees
- Underutilized employees
- Duplication of effort
- Mismatches of job requirements and employee capabilities

Work distribution should primarily be analyzed within units or departments. However, some comparisons should be made *among* units to check for duplication of effort in cases where similar jobs are performed in different departments or agencies.

Job Content Charts. One of the primary tools to help analyze work distribution is a job content chart (see Table 8-2). This is used to identify the kinds of activities or tasks done by an individual employee and how much time is spent on each. This information can be gathered by having employees monitor and record their own activities over a period of time.

Time should be recorded in terms of the activities that make up the specific task or job. For example, if preparing a report is the task, time

Table 8-2. Job Content Chart

EMPLOYEE: J. Smith

JOB TITLE: Research Associate

ACTIVITY	AVERAGE HOURS/WEEK
Data gathering	10
Data processing	5
Analysis	10
Writing	5
Accuracy Checks	2
Delays, transportation	2
Staff Meetings	1
Handling Inquiries	2
Preparatory/Clean-up Functions	3
Total	40

should be recorded for activities such as gathering information, manipulating data, writing the report, and so on. If cleaning a building is the job, record time in terms of activities such as washing floors, dusting, vacuuming, and so on. Recording time in terms of activities instead of whole jobs gives a clearer picture of what is really being done by each employee and what skills are being used. This can help pinpoint duplication of effort. In addition, it will help in reassigning responsibilities in a way that is compatible with employee skills and other work duties. Miscellaneous and nonproductive activities, such as time spent waiting, in transit, attending meetings, or performing get-ready and clean-up functions should also be recorded.

Work Distribution Charts. Once individual job content charts are prepared for all employees in a unit, an aggregate chart can be prepared from them to show work distribution within that unit. This chart is essentially the same as the job content chart, but it indicates the typical or average number of hours per week each employee in the unit spends on each task (see Table 8-3).

Critical Analysis. After preparing the work distribution and job content charts, the next step is to combine information from them to analyze and improve the distribution of work. Information contained in one chart frequently sheds additional light on that contained in another. Referring back to process charts may also help clarify situations and/or design solutions. This section will provide examples of how these tools can be used together to analyze the existing situation and make changes in work distribution.

Using the work distribution chart, one can determine what proportion of

Table 8-3. Work Distribution Chart (Sample Format)

	TITLE: Research Analyst NAME: J. Smith	TITLE: Programmer NAME: A. Jones	TITLE: Research Director NAME: R. Armstrong	
TASK DESCRIPTION	AVERAGE HOURS/WEEK	AVERAGE HOURS/WEEK	AVERAGE HOURS/WEEK	TOTAL HOURS/WEEK
Data Gathering	10	2	4	16
Data Processing	5	20	2	27
Analysis	10	2	12	24
Writing	5	1	10	16
Accuracy Checks	2	2	3	7
Delays, Transportation, etc.	2	4	2	8
Staff Meetings	1	1	5	7
Handling Inquiries	2	4	2	8
Preparatory/Clean-up Functions	3	4	2	9
Total	40	40	42	122

Based on: Monroe S. Kuttner, *Managing the Paperwork Pipeline* (New York: John Wiley & Sons, 1978), p. 142.

unit time is spent on each task. Are the tasks using the most time most important in terms of unit/organizational goals? Is excessive time spent on unproductive activities? Problems in these areas can be viewed as priority-setting problems. They might be related to insufficient supervision. This may be because the immediate supervisor is overburdened, which can be ascertained from his/her job content chart. Or the problem may be due to work flow, which can be ascertained by checking the process chart. Delays might be reduced by changing the sequence in which tasks are performed, or the people responsible for them.

Again looking at work distribution, it can be determined whether many employees perform the same task. If so, is this necessary? Does it result in a poor match between skills and job content? Work might flow more smoothly and/or be of better quality if a smaller number of employees specialized in an activity. Turning to the job content charts, are any employees performing numerous unrelated tasks? This can reduce productivity because of interruptions due to frequent changes in activity. As in the previous case, increased specialization may be helpful.

Looking at both the work distribution chart and the individual job content charts, it is possible to determine whether jobs are assigned to people with appropriate skills for performing them. Are highly skilled employees spending too much time on work requiring lesser skills (e.g., filling out forms)? Are some tasks being performed by people who lack sufficient skills to perform them well? Is work distributed fairly evenly, or are some employees doing too much or too little? Such problems may be organizational in nature, stemming from the way departments are defined and responsibilities are assigned. They may also occur because staffing patterns have not changed to meet current needs or priorities, leaving too many employees in units or positions where workload has declined. Other units that have experienced increased workloads may be performing tasks in a haphazard way that does not closely relate job content to skills.

Examples. Most examples of work redistribution in the public sector are intended to reduce duplication of effort or better utilize the time of highly skilled employees. For example, duplication of effort among departments was found to exist for building inspections in both Phoenix and Milwaukee. Both cities had inspectors in different departments to perform specific kinds of building inspections. Both redesigned the inspection job and trained generalist inspectors to perform all types of inspection. In Milwaukee, functions formerly conducted by five departments were merged into a new Department of Building Inspection, eliminating 22 positions (by attrition), for an annual savings of $270,000.[8]

A similar reassignment of inspection responsibilities occurred within the

Building Safety Department in Phoenix, Arizona. Prior to work redistribution, separate inspectors performed electrical, plumbing, building, and mechanical inspections. Inspectors were retrained to perform all these tasks for single-family homes. This reduced the number of inspectors needed for this type of building, as well as the number of trips to construction sites. Annual savings were estimated at $750,000 from this redistribution of work.[9]

The solution to the problem of highly skilled employees doing jobs requiring lower skill levels may lead to reclassification of jobs or creation of new job categories. It has not been uncommon to find uniformed police or fire personnel performing desk jobs. Many cities have moved to put less costly civilian employees in these positions instead. Some cities (including Scottsdale, Arizona, Fort Lauderdale, Florida, and Jackson, Michigan), have moved beyond this to train and use civilians for a variety of routine police tasks, such as preliminary crime investigations and reporting, accident investigation, traffic control, and noncriminal service calls.[10]

The development of paraprofessional positions is also a response to the need to more fully utilize specialized skills. So is the development of employees trained to perform more than one job, usually in emergency services. In some areas, mainly smaller residential communities, the job category of public safety officer has been created, in which employees provide both police and fire services. Fire and paramedic services are also provided jointly in some localities.[11]

WORKPLACE DESIGN

Thus far charting techniques have been used to examine and revise the work process and responsibility for job performance. Similar methods can also be applied to physical layout. This can mean the layout of an entire office or workplace, or of a work station such as an individual desk and its immediate surroundings. The study and design of physical layout is an industrial engineering technique. A thorough application of the appropriate methodology would probably require use of consultants, unless industrial engineers are part of the PIP staff. However, physical layout generally does not represent a major factor in public sector productivity, as it often does in manufacturing, so it is unlikely that the PIP staff will find it necessary to use consultants. An understanding of major concepts and readily applicable methods will be presented here as an aid to analysts facing relatively minor layout problems.

Layout Analysis. Physical layout is closely related to work flow. Indeed, the reason for changing layout is to improve work flow, mainly by reducing transportation of people and/or work. This can typically be achieved by arranging the workplace so work can move in a logical sequence, eliminating backtracking and shortening distances to be traveled. Physical layout should be studied after job redesign has taken place.

It should be pointed out that layout analysis deals with a whole office or department, not with only one job or work process. Since many different jobs are usually performed in the same space, layout is not tied to the work-flow pattern of a single job.

Two simple methods useful in studying layout can be applied without use of consultants or special training. The first approach uses a diagram of the office or department under analysis. The purpose of the diagram is to facilitate analysis of traffic patterns, which will be used to rearrange the layout if necessary. Blocks are used to represent each work area. A work area could be an individual desk or office, or a group such as a typing pool or a duplicating department. Work areas are drawn to indicate relative size and proximity, but a scale drawing is not necessary. The next step is to draw lines between blocks to represent trips made between work areas. A line should be drawn for each trip made, which means there will be many lines on the chart. One way to calculate trips is to refer to the work flow charts and draw lines to indicate transportation linkages between work areas. Trip frequency information can also be supplied by supervisors or employees. Alternatively, observation can be used to chart trips made, or employees can be asked to record them for a period of time.

Figure 8-7 represents a fairly simple work-flow diagram. It can be readily seen that two sets of work areas have far more interaction than the others,

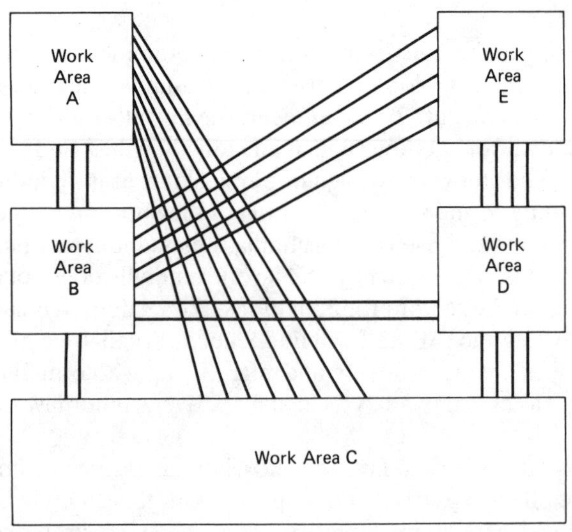

Figure 8-7. Work Flow Diagram.

namely A and C, which have the heaviest pattern, and B and E. However, area A is located at the furthest distance from C, and B and E are also not adjacent. In this example, a fairly obvious change will improve matters considerable. Switching the positions of work areas A and B will put A next to C and greatly reduce the time spent in transit. It will also reduce distance traversed between B and E.

Similar information could be presented in matrix form by showing the number of trips between work areas. The trips diagrammed in Figure 8-7 are placed in a trip frequency matrix in Table 8-4. Although the matrix does not show the physical layout under analysis, it does identify the work areas that interact most in the work process. These areas should logically be placed near each other in space. The matrix can be used to check against the actual layout to see if these areas are near each other. If not, space can be rearranged to place them closer together.

Although it is desirable to manage space to reduce transportation and facilitate work flow, it is not always easy to accomplish this. Work areas may include fixtures or equipment that would be expensive and/or difficult to move. It is also possible that the productivity improvement that would result from rearrangement would be relatively small. In such cases it does not make sense to pursue a layout change since there may be a variety of other ways to improve productivity that would have greater potential for success in these circumstances.

WORK MEASUREMENT

The final topic under the general heading of work redesign is work measurement, which is a fairly technical aspect of industrial engineering. Specific training is required to conduct the most accurate kinds of work measurement analysis. Therefore, consultants will probably be needed by most PIPs undertaking such studies, although training in specific measurement skills can be provided for staff members. Because of their technical nature, only the basic concepts of these methods will be outlined here to help in determining whether they are of potential use. If so, further exploration should be con-

Table 8-4. Trip Frequency Matrix

			TO WORK AREA		
FROM WORK AREA	A	B	C	D	E
A	—	3	8	0	0
B	3	—	2	2	5
C	8	2	—	4	0
D	0	2	4	—	4
E	0	5	0	4	—

ducted. Texts on work measurement, methods study, and industrial engineering will provide greater detail about what is involved in these methods.[12]

The primary focus of work measurement is on how long it takes, or should take, to perform a task. Its major application has been in manufacturing processes, but it can be applied to any repetitive physical activity, including many jobs in the public sector. Work measurement is usually undertaken with the intent of having employees perform in accordance with the established time. This may or may not involve an incentive system, a subject that will be discussed in chapter 9. Standard times can also be used to determine staffing needs, for work scheduling, and for employee evaluations.

Although its concern is with timing, work measurement is related to work redesign because timing only takes place after the job has been designed. Thus the first step of work measurement is really job redesign.

Standard Time. Once the job is designed so it is being performed in the best possible way, actual work measurement can begin. The goal of the measurement phase is to establish the amount of time needed for a qualified worker, working at a normal rate of speed, to perform the task at a satisfactory level of quality. In establishing the standard time, it is recognized that, for a variety of reasons, employees do not maintain a continuous pace throughout the day. Thus the standard time has adjustments built into it for personal time (coffee breaks, restroom trips, etc.); delay (waiting for instructions or supplies, equipment preparation, etc.); and normal slowing of pace due to fatigue. Time standards are generally established in one of two ways: time study or use of predetermined time standards.

Using the time study approach, employees are timed as they perform the task, using a stopwatch to time the elements that make up the job. These are summed to determine the time for the whole job. This method requires determining the appropriate number of observations to be made and using random sample methods to select employees and times for observation, in addition to the timing process. Use of predetermined time standards does not require timing employees at their jobs, but it does require observing the job and identifying each work element in it. Predetermined times exist for all fundamental motions (e.g., grasp, reach, move, or assemble). These are modified by characteristics of the particular task, including weights and distances involved, complexity of motion, and so on. The predetermined times for each element are then summed to find the standard time for the whole job.

These brief descriptions of what is entailed in time studies and predetermined time systems do not do justice to the complexity of the tasks. However, it should be clear that the level of intricacy involved requires using trained practitioners to employ these methods. At times, it is possible to utilize engineered work standards without going through the measurement stages described here. Published time standards may be available for jobs that are common in the private sector. It is also possible to utilize standards established by another department or jurisdiction, *if* the jobs concerned are performed the same way.

While the most accurate methods of establishing work standards are complex procedures, there are simpler, and therefore less accurate, techniques that can be applied by analysts without industrial engineering backgrounds. One method is to utilize historical records that indicate volume of output and hours worked over time. Such data can be used to determine average output per hour, such as the average number of paychecks prepared, applications processed, clients interviewed, and so on. A major problem with this method is that it is not necessarily based on the best work methods. In fact, past inefficiencies are included in the standard.

That problem can be avoided by analyzing work that has been redesigned, but by using simpler, less precise approaches to timing. The amount of work accomplished in a period of time, such as an hour, can be quantified. Several hour-long periods can be used to establish an average. Quantification can be done by observers or by employees keeping logs of their activities and output. Neither of these methods needs to be adjusted for personal needs, fatigue, and so on, since those are already reflected in the data gathered. Since these methods are less precise than time study or predetermined standards, it is not advisable to use them in incentive systems or for individual evaluations, although they can be helpful in scheduling work and planning for staff needs. It should also be emphasized that the times established by these methods reflect how long it *did* take to perform the task, not how long it *should* take. The more accurate methodologies should be used to determine the latter.

Examples. Time standards have been applied in a variety of public sector jobs. Perhaps the most traditional use is for motor vehicle maintenance and repair, following the common use of "flat rates" in the private sector. But a wider range of application can be found. In Seattle, both the Water and Engineering Departments have utilized time standards, for jobs ranging from water meter repair to drafting. Staff reductions resulted (through attrition or transfer) in both departments, and the standards are also used for planning and scheduling work.[13] The U.S. Bureau of Census has applied time standards to a variety of office operations, including key punching, coding, typing, filing, printing, mail opening, sorting, collating, operating equipment, and so on.[14]

Although work measurement and standards generally deal with the amount of time needed to perform a job, one sometimes finds standards expressed differently, most likely in terms of output or costs. This was the case in a public works performance standards program jointly undertaken by three New Jersey townships. Performance standards established included: road maintenance program—3 tons of asphalt per staff-day; leaf collection—15 cubic yards per staff-day; street sweeping—75 swept miles per unit per week; sanitation—$30.42 total cost per collection point (in 1979 dollars). In a three-year period, use of standards resulted in annual net savings/avoidances of approximately $280,000 for the three townships.[15]

IMPLEMENTING WORK REDESIGN

The foregoing descriptions of redesign methods have already covered the major implementation topics, when and how to apply particular tools. This section will discuss the other major implementation concern, which is potential trouble spots that may act as barriers to employing the methodology. Ways to deal with these problem areas will be suggested.

One possible problem area affecting redesign is regulations or laws that make it impossible to reassign responsibilities or redesign work. Civil service regulations, union contracts and legislation affecting service delivery falls into this category. The existence of such barriers does not completely preclude use of redesign. It generally will affect a limited number of jobs, not all jobs; or may restrict some kinds of redesign, not all kinds. Thus redesign can be freely used in nonaffected areas, and may be used to a limited extent in others. It may be possible to remove some of the barriers to change, especially labor contracts, but this will involve delaying implementation.

Any efforts to improve productivity might generate adverse reactions from employees, largely due to concern about losing jobs, changing working conditions, and so on. Most work redesign methods have particulary negative connotations, which makes the potential for creating dissatisfaction among employees the major drawback of this approach. Industrial engineering techniques, particularly work measurement and time standards, have had a negative image with employees, particularly union members, for a long time. Even without a bad reputation, it is easy to see that these methods have some characteristics that could cause employees concern.

Employees will be observed, and possibly timed, at their jobs, which may be intimidating to many people. This may be viewed as an indication that unit or individual performance is not satisfactory.

Work redesign, particularly time standards, may be interpreted as meaning that employees will have to work faster or "harder," that their work will be more closely monitored, and that they will be subject to penalties for failure to meet standards.

Changes in work method may seem unsettling to employees comfortable with their habitual work methods. There may also be concern that jobs will be so routinized or simplified that they will become boring, or that working conditions in general will become less pleasant.

There may be concern that the motive behind work redesign is to dismiss some employees.

The best ways to deal with these problems have already been discussed in chapter 5, so they only need to be noted briefly in this context. Good communication and employee involvement are the key factors. Employees should receive clear explanations of what will happen in the job redesign and/or work standards analysis. Explaining time standards clearly will also reduce apprehension because employees will see that personal allowances, fatigue, and so on are built in. Care should be taken to emphasize that time standards will be attainable and to avoid taking a punitive attitude when discussing failure to meet standards. It should also be made clear that redesigning jobs should make them easier for employees, since the goal is to work smarter, not harder. A fair and appropriate distribution of work is also one of the concerns of work redesign. Adoption of a "no layoffs" policy will alleviate fear of job loss; staff reductions can be achieved through attrition.

Although employee involvement and input is stressed for all productivity improvement methods, it is particularly important in redesigning work. No one should be more familiar with problem areas, bottlenecks, and poor work procedures than the people performing the job. Not only can they point out what should be changed, they are a very good source of ideas for improvements. Making it clear that employee input in redesigning work is desired and valued will also help decrease concern about being observed. Perhaps more importantly, it will also reduce worry about the nature of the revised work process, since employees will understand they will have input into its design.

The possibility of generating employee opposition or apprehension can be greatly reduced by communication and involvement measures similar to those outlined earlier. However, these additional employee relations efforts should be viewed as a cost, rather than a negative feature, of this method. Use of work measurement and time standards usually involves additional costs for consultants or staff training. It also implies future commitment to monitoring employees to see that standards are met to a satisfactory degree. Work redesign may also have a hidden cost aspect to it. Job simplification has traditionally occurred through the addition of technology. Thus the costs of some types of equipment may be associated with this method. Even without this cost, all but the simplest kinds of redesign implies a need for retraining and a breaking-in period during which productivity may be lower as employees adjust to new methods. These should also be anticipated as costs of this method.

SUMMARY

This chapter has described a group of productivity improvement techniques that are related to work redesign. The main characteristics of the methods discussed and the type of results that can be expected may be summarized as follows:

Methods analysis uses process charts and critical analysis to study how tasks are performed in repetitive jobs. It leads to changes in work method through simplification, elimination, and so on. The result is a reduction in the amount of staff time needed for the job. It may also lead to changes in the people/units involved. Results may include a smoother flow and a reduction in the number of steps, delays, and duplication of effort.

Work distribution/job content analysis looks at how each employee spends his/her time and how work is distributed within each unit. It leads to changes in distribution of work. Results include a better allocation of work time in accordance with priorities, a better match between employee abilities and work assignments; and a more equitable division of workload.

Workplace design studies traffic patterns in the workplace to improve the flow of work. It leads to changes in physical location of offices, units, and so on, resulting in reduced time spent in transit.

Work measurement/time standards is applied to repetitive jobs after methods analysis establishes a standard time for each task which employees will be expected to meet. Results include less wasted time plus information useful for work scheduling, evaluation, etc.

The key to using redesign methods in a PIP is to select the method that is the best fit for the job to be improved. In general, methods analysis and work standards should be applied only to repetitive type jobs. They have the strongest impact on increasing the quantity of output produced, and thus the greatest likelihood of increasing productivity. Work distribution and workplace design can be applied in conjunction with them. The latter can also be applied to jobs that are not repetitive enough for methods analysis.

Work redesign methods have a history of considerable success in improving private sector productivity. The examples in this chapter have illustrated that these methods can be successfully employed in the public sector as well. Thus one should carefully consider using them for the kinds of public sector work where they are appropriate.

Redesign methods also have a number of positive features that facilitate their use in a PIP. In general, this approach is fairly easy to use. Most redesign methods can be applied by in-house staff without extensive training. Redesign methods can be applied to a variety of jobs. These features are highly desirable. This approach also establishes the habit of questioning the way work is done; an attitude that supervisors and administrators are likely to apply to jobs other than the ones identified for study under the PIP. Thus the practice of looking for the most productive way of performing tasks can reap benefits in the future as well as the present.

It should be kept in mind that redesign methods are not necessarily used alone. They may be applied in combinations of two or more, or one may prove useful if another has been tried without much success. Of course, they could also be used in conjunction with other improvement methods that will be explored in later chapters.

NOTES

1. Refer to basic texts in these fields for more detailed discussions of analytic methods discussed here. See, for example: Ralph M. Barnes, *Motion and Time Study: Design and Measurement of Work* (7th ed. New York: John Wiley & Sons, 1980); Harry P. Cemash, *Work Study in the Office* (2nd ed. London: Current Affairs Ltd., 1961); Owen Gilbert, *A Manager's Guide to Work Study* (New York: John Wiley & Sons, 1968); Patricia Haynes, "Industrial Engineering Techniques" in: ed. George J. Washnis, *Productivity Improvement Handbook for State and Local Government.* (New York: John Wiley & Sons, 1980); Ernest J. McCormick, *Job Analysis: Methods and Applications* (New York: AMACOM, 1979).
2. Frederick O'R. Hayes, *Productivity in Local Government* (Lexington, Mass.: Lexington Books, 1977), p. 21.
3. Ibid., p. 63.
4. Ibid., p. 21.
5. James I. Scheiner, "Productivity Improvement in the Pennsylvania Department of Transportation," *Public Productivity Review,* 5 (March 1981): 17-19.
6. National Center for Productivity and Quality of Working Life, *Improving Governmental Productivity: Selected Case Studies* (Washington, D.C., U.S. Government Printing Office, 1977), pp. 75-77.
7. Hayes, *Productivity in Local Government,* p. 60.
8. Ibid., pp. 60-61.
9. Ibid., pp. 160-161.
10. George P. Barbour, Jr., "Law Enforcement" in: ed. George J. Washnis, *Productivity Improvement Handbook for State & Local Government* (New York: John Wiley & Sons, 1980), p. 938.
11. Ibid., p. 1053.
12. See, for example: Donald L. Caruth, *Planning for Clerical Work Measurement* (New York: American Management Association, Inc., 1970); Edward V. Krick, *Methods Engineering: Design and Measurement of Work Methods* (New York: John Wiley & Sons, 1962); Dennis A. Whitman, *Measurement and Control of Indirect Work* (New York: American Elsevier Publishing Company, 1971).
13. National Center for Productivity, *Improving Governmental Productivity,* pp. 34-44.
14. Frederick W. Hornbruck, Jr., *Raising Productivity: Ten Case Histories and Their Lessons* (New York: McGraw-Hill Book Company, 1977), p. 53.
15. U.S. Office of Personnel Management, Office of Intergovernmental Personnel Programs, *The New Jersey Public Works Performance Standards Study,* by Laurel M. Burcham (Washington, D.C.: U.S. Government Printing Office, 1981), p.v., pp. 20-23.

9
IMPROVING PRODUCTIVITY THROUGH INCENTIVE SYSTEMS

HOW INCENTIVE SYSTEMS IMPROVE PRODUCTIVITY

Incentive systems are based on motivation theories (discussed in chapter 7). They are one of the earliest and most common productivity improvement methods used in the private sector. Incentive systems offer rewards to employees in exchange for achievement of specified goals that will lead to increased productivity. The reward is intended to motivate employees to work toward reaching the goals. The following sections will briefly explain the components of incentive systems. Descriptions and examples of incentive systems using different kinds of goals and rewards will be presented later in this chapter.

Goals. The most common goals in incentive systems are:

- Increased output (quantity produced)
- Improved performance (effectiveness and/or quality)
- Improved behavior (e.g., reduced absenteeism or lateness, better safety habits)

Goals may be directly related to productivity improvement, for example, increased output. Or they may be indirectly related, for example, changing behavior patterns (such as excessive absenteeism) that are detrimental to productivity. Sometimes goals are performance related rather than productivity related; for example, providing higher quality, or prompter delivery of service.

Rewards. The most common reward is money, but nonmonetary rewards, such as time off, are sometimes used as incentives. The distribution of rewards can vary in two major respects: the longevity of the reward and the number of people receiving it.

Longevity refers to whether the reward is continuous or whether it must be re-earned. Rewards most commonly fall in the latter category. They are provided on a one-time basis, like a bonus. In order to get another reward, the employee must again accomplish a specified goal. However, incentive systems sometimes provide rewards on an on-going basis, as a pay increase. In this case the reward continues to be paid in the future without being linked to additional accomplishments.

The number of people receiving incentives can also vary. Rewards are typically distributed on an individual basis. When work is performed by groups or teams, incentives can be awarded to the group and then allocated among its members. Sometimes a whole class of employees can be rewarded. For example, a pay raise might be offered to all sanitation workers if certain street cleanliness goals are met during a given year.

The System. Goals and rewards are linked by a *system* that specifies explicitly what employees must accomplish to earn a particular reward. In effect, incentive systems are similar to contracts in setting out conditions to be met and payments to be made upon their fulfillment.

Incentive *systems* should not be confused with *incentives.* Incentives are rewards or penalties common to any organization. These include, for example, raises or promotions related to good job performance, or demotions or job loss related to inadequate performance. The merit system common to the public sector falls into the category of incentives, although there is some feeling that it no longer functions well in this capacity.[1] In general, organizational incentives are vaguely defined rewards offered for vaguely defined accomplishments. Incentive *systems* provide specific definitions of both rewards and accomplishments.

APPLICABILITY OF INCENTIVE SYSTEMS

Incentive systems can be used for a wide variety of jobs. There are four basic criteria that must exist before they can be applied. It must be possible to:

- Identify behavior that will improve productivity
- Specify behavioral goals and rewards for achieving them
- Verify whether the goals have been reached
- Identify persons or groups to be rewarded

These criteria can be met by many jobs in the public sector.

Applying an incentive system requires making a number of choices. The initial choices are related to the first two criteria on the list: deciding *what* to reward and *how* to reward it (e.g., size and distribution of monetary incentives). Some systems are more technical than others. Piecework systems are the most complex, for example. Designing this kind of system requires some expertise. Therefore, consultants should be used if no PIP or personnel department staff are knowledgeable about designing incentive systems. PIP staff members should be able to design the simpler types of system after self-instruction or training.

A variety of types of incentive systems have been applied in the public sector in recent years. The sections that follow will describe different types of systems and provide examples of their use. The first two sections look at systems that are oriented toward achieving changes in output or behavior. The third looks at a recent variation in incentive systems, shared savings plans.

OUTPUT FOCUSED SYSTEMS

Incentive systems have traditionally focused on output, usually with the goal of increasing the quantity produced. This type of system is most directly related to productivity improvement. Another form of output focused incentive system seeks to improve performance. One or more aspects of service quality or effectiveness can be the target of such a system. Performance can also be more broadly defined to include some combination of quantity, quality, and effectiveness. Performance focused systems are responsive to the belief that service quality and effectiveness are as important as quantity produced. Since these systems do not necessarily reward increased *quantity,* they do not always lead to productivity improvement. The various types of systems will be described here to illustrate how they can be used in a PIP.

Piecework Systems. These are probably the oldest type of incentive system and were traditionally associated with manufacturing. However, they can also be applied in the public sector. Under a piecework incentive plan, pay is directly related to production. They can only be used in cases where work can be defined and measured in unit terms. Rewards are incorporated in the normal paycheck and are thus distributed fairly soon after goals are attained.

The simplest kind of piecework plan provides a specified amount of money for each unit of output produced. A more commonly used variation pays a specified wage for a base level of output, plus a per unit payment for each unit produced above the base. The base wage and base output level should be set at levels near the current wage and output levels. Thus employees will have to improve productivity to earn more than their current wages. Work measurement should be used to determine how many units of output can normally be produced in a specified time period (a day or week). This amount is used to calculate the base production level, base wage, and the per unit bonus.

Piecework systems are designed to allow employees to regularly produce above the basic level and earn bonuses. If this was not the case (i.e., if the base was too high), there would be no incentive for increasing productivity. Thus setting the base production levels, salaries, and bonus amounts is important to the success of the system, and should be done by persons with thorough understanding of the concepts involved. There are also a variety of methods that could be used to calculate bonuses. Therefore, consultants may be required to help design a piecework system if this method is chosen. A detailed explanation of how to make the necessary calculations is too complex to include here, however.[2]

The Philadelphia Water Department was an early user of this approach. It introduced piecework incentives for both field and repair shop personnel in its Meter Division in 1952. Time standards were used to establish basic daily production levels. Employees producing this amount or less only receive their base wage. Earnings for those producing more than the basic amount are calculated by multiplying the number of acceptable pieces produced, or service calls made, by standard times for repairs or calls. Employees are paid for this "excess time" at their regular hourly rate (see Table 9-1 for a more detailed explanation of how bonuses are calculated). The incentive plan resulted in considerable productivity gains in the repair shop (a 113% increase

Table 9-1. Illustration of Calculating Piecework Bonuses

STEP 1: SETTING THE BASE

1. *Determine hourly base.* Use time standards (see chapter 8 on work measurement) to determine how many output units can be produced in an hour. Example: Four water meters can be repaired in an hour.
2. *Determine daily base.* Multiply the hourly base production rate by the number of hours worked each day. Example: In an eight-hour day, 32 meters can be repaired.

STEP 2: CALCULATING THE BONUS

1. *Calculate bonus units.* Determine how many units over the basic output level were produced. Example: If an employee repaired 40 meters in one day, this represents 8 units over the base (40 − 32 = 8).

2a. *Use hourly wage method to calculate bonus.* Determine how many hours of work the bonus units represent. At four meters/hour, the eight extra units are equivalent to two hours of additional work (regardless of how long it actually took to make the repairs). Multiply the employee's hourly wage by two to determine bonus earnings. Example: If the employee earns $4/hour, the bonus for the two hours is $8.

— or

2b. *Use piece rate method to calculate bonus.* Multiply the number of units produced above the base rate by the predetermined piece rate to calculate the bonus. Example: If the piece rate is $1.25/unit, the bonus for eight units is $10.

in meters processed per employee per year), and in the field (a 162% increase in meters in service per field employee per year), between 1952 and 1975.[3]

Another example from Pennsylvania is a piecework plan for data-processing personnel in the state Bureau of Employment Security. Bonuses were paid for each wage record correctly entered into the computer system above a specified minimum. At the end of two years, average output per worker increased from 280 to 450 wage records per hour, and unit costs decreased from 86 cents to 54 cents per 100 records.[4] Examples of other types of jobs to which piecework plans have been applied include maintenance personnel in public housing authorities, meter readers, and animal census takers.[5]

Although piecework systems are commonly used to encourage increases in the quantity of service produced, bonuses can be used instead. For example, a plan to increase output of auto mechanics was implemented in Fort Worth, Texas in 1973. Mechanics could earn a 5% monthly bonus if their monthly output exceeded the flat-rate standards (engineered standards for automotive repair), by at least 10%. Output increased 23% within seven months of the program's introduction.[6]

Although traditionally there has been concern about the feasibility of measuring service output, the examples noted here indicate that there are a variety of jobs in the public sector where output can be measured and piecework or bonus systems successfully applied.

Performance Based Systems. The performance based systems are generally used to improve aspects of service quality or effectiveness. Performance systems sometimes include increased output among their goals, but do not always do so. Employees must meet specific performance goals in order to earn rewards. Rewards are usually viewed as bonuses and are thus distributed less frequently than piecework system rewards. This enables these plans to be used for objectives that need a longer time frame for accomplishment. Performance awards are sometimes given in the form of a pay increase.

There are a variety of examples of use of performance-based incentives in the public sector. One widely publicized example is from the police department in Orange, California. The goal was to increase effectiveness by reducing repressible crimes (rapes, robberies, burglaries, and auto theft). If the crime rate per 1000 population fell by stipulated percentages during the time period covered by the plan (July 1973-March1975), a specified percentage increase in wages would be received by employees participating in the plan (which included all but the highest levels of the department).[7] Thus the reward was earned by a whole class of employees, rather than on an individual basis. This is also an example of a plan where the reward was a wage increase, rather than a bonus, making it an on-going reward.

An example of a performance plan related to work quality comes from

Helena, Montana. The plan covered waste collection employees, who were awarded an extra $5 per day for completing their regular routes and not receiving more than two legitimate complaints from citizens. An interesting point about the origins of this plan is that it was apparently not initiated in response to poor quality of service or unfinished routes. It was offered to gain employee cooperation for a work redesign plan that involved changing to plastic bags and curbside pickup, which led to reduction in the number of collection crews.[8] It would seem that the department did not want to offer raises to gain acceptance of the new system, but found a performance plan more palatable, even though it seems to be designed so all employees should be able to earn a daily bonus. This example illustrates that incentive systems may be utilized to serve more than one purpose. It should be noted, however, that the number of days in which routes were completed with no more than two complaints increased 9% in two years, indicating the plan did have a real performance impact.[9]

Another example of a performance incentive system comes from Montana's Division of Employment Security. This was a group incentive plan, in which local offices could earn both quarterly bonuses and an annual bonus. Quarterly bonuses were awarded according to performance rankings of offices of similar size. Performance criteria for the rankings included both output measures (e.g., individuals or veterans counseled), and effectiveness measures (e.g., individuals or veterans placed). Annual bonuses focused more on quality of placements, such as average hourly wage of persons placed, or percentage of placements in professional or managerial jobs. Overall agency performance increased during the year the plan was used (1976) compared to the previous year. For example, there was a 14% increase in placements and a 23% increase in individuals counseled.[10]

Performance incentive plans can also be related to employee promotions and thus, indirectly, to wage increases. For example, the states of Michigan and Mississippi both have stipulated performance standards (in terms of speed and accuracy) for promotion of keypunch or EDP employees.[11] Such skill related standards for promotion in the public sector are fairly common.

Using Output Focused Systems. Incentive systems that focus on increasing the amount of output produced are most consistent with the productivity focus suggested here. However, there are some limitations on use of incentive systems. For example, piecework systems or bonuses for increased production can only be applied where individual units of output can be identified. Although this may restrict their use, there are still many potential public sector applications for such systems.

Performance focused systems should only be used when improving service quality or effectiveness is one of the goals of the PIP. These systems are generally not related to improving productivity, except in cases where increased output is one of the performance indicators included in the system. In general, output focused systems are preferable for use in the PIP.

BEHAVIOR FOCUSED INCENTIVE SYSTEMS

Piecework and performance plans focus on improving output. This section will describe incentive systems that focus on improving behavior. These systems usually concentrate on behavior that is related to the amount of time employees spend on the job. Some plans focus on increasing the amount of time employees spend on the job by reducing absenteeism, lateness, and accidents. Others try to decrease overtime by rewarding timely completion of work. Some of these plans have mixed motives. For example, reducing accidents also reduces cost, and prompt completion of work improves service quality.

Attendance Plans. Employee attendance is clearly related to productivity. Therefore, discouraging absenteeism and lateness is a good target for an incentive system. Rewards can be offered in the form of bonuses related to lack of lateness or absence over a specified time period. Rewards might also be in the form of extra vacation days.

Attendance plans are fairly common in the public sector. A plan introduced in Sacramento, California in 1969 allows employees who accumulate 60 or more days of unused sick leave in a year to choose between receiving a cash payment of 25% of the value of the unused leave or to accumulate the leave. One-third of the value of unused leave is payable upon retirement, resignation, or death. Average annual sick leave taken dropped nearly 10% the year after the plan was introduced. Kansas City, Missouri allows employees to convert unused sick leave into additional terminal leave on retirement at the rate of one additional leave day for every four unused sick days. As a result of this program, average sick leave per employee fell from about nine hours per month to about six hours per month. A variety of plans in other local and state governments also provide cash bonuses or other benefits for unused sick days upon retirement.[12]

A "well pay incentive program" recently introduced in Tennessee combined both group and individual incentives to reduce absenteeism in the executive branch. The plan stipulated that *overall* sick leave use in this branch had to decline by 15% during a six-month trial period. If this goal was reached, individual bonuses could be earned by employees who used little or no sick leave. For example, the highest bonus, $360, would go to employees using *no* sick leave during a specified 18-month period; employees using no more than 3 days would receive $180. Results for the early portion of the trial period showed monthly reductions ranging from 25 to 35%.[13] In essence, by requiring overall reductions before operationalizing individual bonuses, the plan relied on peer pressure to reduce absenteeism even among those who would not normally try to earn the individual bonuses.

Task Systems. The objective of task systems is to encourage prompt completion of work (which improves service quality), and/or to reduce overtime. One way of encouraging employees to complete their jobs in a timely manner is to let them go home after their work is completed. This kind of system was used in Flint, Michigan, for waste collectors, who were allowed to go home after six hours on the job if their routes were completed. The intention of the Flint plan was to decrease overtime. The plan also shared the savings from reduced overtime payments with employees. The plan resulted in significant reductions in controllable overtime within the first two years of operation, from 6700 hours in 1973 to 2200 hours in 1974 and 45 hours in 1975.[14]

Task systems are fairly commonly used in the public sector for work like waste collection. Such a system was implemented for waste collectors in Xenia, Ohio after work measurement was used to redesign collection routes so they could be completed in five to seven hours. Crews are paid for an eight-hour day even if they use less time to complete their routes. Although many similar plans are used satisfactorily, problems can arise with work quality. This happened in Lake Charles, Louisiana, after a waste collection task system had been in effect for 2½ years. The system deteriorated as employees began accelerating their pace to the point where routes sometimes were completed in only four hours (the work normally took about eight hours, but employees were paid for ten hours on a ten-hour, four-day system). Quality declined significantly, with trash spilled, cans not returned to the appropriate place, stops missed, and so on. The city ultimately returned to its former system.[15] Thus care should be taken to include a quality monitoring system (as discussed in chapter 6) when task systems are utilized.

Safety Awards. Safety awards are used to reduce the amount of productive time lost because of accidents and to reduce the costs associated with them. Safety award systems are generally used only in departments where accidents are common, such as in public works departments where employees operate a variety of vehicles or other equipment. Such plans frequently are designed in the form of competitions. For example, snowplow operators in Bloomington, Minnestoa were divided into teams. The team with fewest accidents during the winter season would win $10 per person; individuals with no accidents also won a $10 bonus. As a result of this program, accidents decreased from 12-15 per winter to 3-5. Kansas City, Missouri, had a similar team approach for public works employees. The team with fewest accidents in a given year won $25 per person; individuals with no accidents were awarded an extra vacation day. Accidents declined 49% after the first year of program operation.[16]

Suggestion Awards. Suggestion award systems offer incentives to employees to make suggestions that lead to productivity or performance improvement, cost reductions, and so on. Rewards are only given for suggestions that are actually adopted. Rewards can be monetary, either as a sum specified in advance, or as some stipulated percentage of the initial savings generated by the suggestion. Alternatively, or in conjunction with the monetary prize, there can be honorary rewards; for example, mention in the local newspaper, a certificate of appreciation or plaque, a luncheon to honor employees who made winning suggestion, and so on. Suggestion awards can be used to encourage employee participation in, and commitment to, the PIP (employee participation in general will be discussed in chapter 11).

Using Behavior-focused Systems. In general, behavior-focused incentive systems should be used primarily if the particular type of behavior targeted is a problem. Thus if time lost and/or costs of absenteeism or accidents are excessive, attendance plans or safety awards should be used. If overtime is too high, task systems should be employed. If there is no behavior problem, techniques that are more directly related to increasing output (e.g., job redesign) are likely to be more effective at improving productivity. However, behavior incentives can still be useful additions in cases where other methods are the dominant improvement approach.

Suggestion awards are not intended to alleviate a problem. They are meant to encourage participation and generate ideas for productivity improvement. Therefore, they could be fruitfully used in any PIP. However, their inclusion should depend on how many *other* participation mechanisms are being employed. Using too many of these techniques may make the PIP appear "gimmicky" and thus could alienate employees.

SHARED SAVINGS PLANS

This section will explain a relatively new type of incentive system, the shared savings plan. These plans focus on generating savings, by, for example, reducing staff or using cost-cutting techniques. The major features of this plan are:

- They frequently rely on employee participation/suggestions to generate ideas for savings.

- Instead of using specified amounts as rewards, the savings accrued from the plan's efforts are pooled. A share of these savings is then allocated among employees.

Because employees know they are generating the savings pool that funds their bonuses, they may be more committed to the system than to a regular incentive system. Instead of receiving specified amounts of money as incentives, employees receive a share of the savings accrued as a result of the improved productivity. Savings generally come from reducing the amount of labor needed to perform a service, or using various cost reduction methods. These include many areas described above, as will be illustrated by the following examples.

As noted earlier, the Flint, Michigan plan to reduce overtime payments for waste collection used two incentives: allowing workers to go home early, and sharing the savings that resulted from lower overtime payments. In Lake Charles, Louisiana, shared savings was used to reduce accidents in the sanitation department. Employees received a share of refunds of workmen's compensation insurance payments resulting from lower accident rates. A $107,000 refund was received by the city in the first year of the program.[17]

Suggestion awards frequently use a portion of the savings generated by the suggestion as the reward. Of course there is typically a ceiling on the amount to be paid, and/or a limit to the length of time over which the savings will be calculated.

A variation on the individual suggestion award involves sharing savings with groups of employees participating in joint labor-management committees to identify ways to improve performance, save money, and so on. This approach relies on participation and worker-management cooperation. It is essentially a variation of Scanlon plans used in the private sector. This approach was used for parks and public works employees in Rockville, Maryland. Two of the cost-savings suggestions resulted in a savings of $6200. They involved doing some work in-house instead of using outside contractors, and having drivers clean and inspect their own vehicles.[18]

A number of shared savings plans in recent years have resulted from union negotiations. Because of New York City's fiscal crisis in the 1970s, union employees agreed to "earn" their cost-of-living salary increases by helping generate cost savings. Forty labor-management committees were formed and helped bring about $7.8 million in savings in the first six months of plan operation.[19]

Shared savings plans may also evolve in response to union demands for wage increases. For example, the City of Detroit agreed to share savings with its sanitation employees. Savings would result from productivity gains expected from use of larger trucks, longer routes, less overtime, and staff reductions. First-year savings were estimated to be $595,000.[20] As fiscal problems affect more government units, it can be expected that union negotiations will result in an increased use of shared savings plans so that employees will "earn" some of their monetary gains, thus easing financial strain somewhat.

Using Shared Savings Plans. Shared savings plans can be used only when the incentive system will lead to actual dollar savings. Thus it cannot be used in plans that focus on increasing output *unless* they result in savings from staff reductions. They can be used in cases where funding for incentive awards is not available, because this system generates its own resources. This is a major benefit in times of fiscal constraint. Shared savings plans can be used to encourage employee suggestions and participation. Although there is some belief that sharing savings is a stronger incentive than other forms of reward, and will thus lead to better results, there is no real proof of this.

APPLYING INCENTIVE PLANS

The previous sections provided information to help you determine what kind of incentive system to use in the PIP. Once a decision has been made about what kind of plan(s) to use, the next step is to implement them. Applying incentive systems in the public sector requires an understanding of the elements that make such plans successful, and of the special problems that may be encountered in the public sector. This section will explain the factors necessary to successfully design and apply incentive systems. It will also describe problem areas that can affect implementation and explain how to deal with them.

Criteria for a Successful Incentive System. The main criteria for a successful system are:[21]

1. Rewards must be clearly linked to performance/behavioral goals.
2. Goals and the overall incentive system must be clearly understood.
3. Goals must be measurable or otherwise subject to objective evaluation.
4. Goals must be challenging but attainable.
5. Goals must be worth working for.
6. The system should be updated over time.

1. Establishing a clear linkage between achievement of performance or behavioral goals and receipt of rewards is important for two reasons. First, it prevents the system from deteriorating into an automatic, unearned reward system, a problem that has plagued the merit system. This would remove the

motivating effect of the system, and it would fail to produce the desired performance goals. Second, the incentive impact is stronger if rewards are received fairly soon after performance is achieved. This leads to greater belief in, and commitment to, the system on the part of employees. Therefore, monthly bonuses are better than annual ones, for example. Rewards received in the more distant future, perhaps as additions to retirement benefits, will probably have less motivating power than rewards received in the present.

2. The second item on the list is essentially self-explanatory. Employees must fully understand how the system works and how it affects them in order to be committed to it. They must also clearly understand what the goals are in order to perform as expected. Thus efforts should be made to explain the system thoroughly when it is introduced.

3. Goals need to be measurable or objectively verifiable to insure fair distribution of rewards. If this is not the case, charges of bias may arise that would destroy confidence in the plan. This factor reinforces the first criterion, that rewards should be linked to performance.

4. Goals should be challenging both to motivate employees toward better performance and to insure benefits to the department or agency involved. They must also be attainable, or else they will not serve to motivate employees for very long. No one will put forth extra effort if they believe the promised reward can never be earned.

5. Rewards must be significant enough to justify the extra effort required. Since many public sector employees do not feel that their compensation is adequate, monetary rewards can be expected to serve as good motivators if they are of reasonable size (which, of course, varies with the general pay levels of employees involved). It is doubtful that purely honorary rewards would have a strong motivating effect on most people.

Although the rewards must be large enough to motivate, care must be taken so that they are not so large that the costs of the program match, or even exceed, the benefits derived. This aspect of the plan requires careful consideration, and preferably should have the involvement of persons knowledgeable about incentive systems. Thus, consultants may be necessary to help design the reward aspects of the system.

6. The system should be monitored over time and updated if necessary. Revisions may be needed because of changes in the way work is done, the equipment used, and/or changes in the nature of work performed or clientele served. If revisions are not made, the goals may become unattainable, or too easily attained, either of which would create problems that have already been discussed. Revisions may also be needed because the novelty of the plan may have been part of the reason it had an initial impact. After the plan has been in effect for some time, performance may decrease. Changing the

plan may revive some of the earlier enthusiasm. Monitoring should also be done to determine whether changes are needed and to check on the system used to record performance to insure that data are not manipulated and that rewards are truly earned.

Legal Barriers to Incentive Systems. There may be some legal barriers present that make it difficult, or even impossible, to use incentive systems. Some state or local governments have laws prohibiting use of monetary rewards, or laws that stipulate pay rates in detail. Uncertainty about possible illegality of such plans may restrain some officials from considering such plans even if they are not really prohibited in the jurisdiction. The necessity of changing the law in areas where incentives are barred might be a sufficiently formidable obstacle to prevent a plan from going forward.

Civil service regulations are another kind of barrier. For example, they may strictly limit the levels at which employees are compensated and the timing and/or nature of wage increases. They may also require uniform pay for employees in similar positions, which precludes using incentives in selected agencies or departments.[22] Overcoming civil service restrictions requires revisions in civil service statutes. Any form of change in rules or laws should not be viewed lightly, since it may be time-consuming and difficult to achieve. Unfortunately, there is no way to sidestep the issue; the only course of action is to try to change the restricting laws or rules, or look for a different productivity improvement method.

Attitudinal Barriers to Incentive Systems. Attitudinal problems can also make it difficult to use incentive systems. This includes potential opposition from the following sources, each of which will be discussed in turn.[23]

1. Employees (and/or unions) in the plan
2. Employees excluded from the plan
3. Managers
4. The media and the public
5. Legislators

(Another area of concern is maintaining relative pay differentials. These may be mandated by law, civil service regulations, union agreements, or merely custom.)

1. Employees themselves and/or their unions are one source of opposition. They may mistrust its impartiality or fairness or not find the rewards sufficient. This problem can be remedied to some extent by careful design

and explanation of the system. Involving some employees or their union representatives in designing the plan will also help.

2. Employees who are not covered may feel they are not being treated equitably, particularly if the work they do is similar to those coverd by the plan. There may be concern that relative pay differentials will be narrowed or even eliminated if lower pay/status jobs are included in the system, while higher status ones are not. These problems are not easily solved unless the disgruntled employees can be offered an incentive system of their own, or if some other mutually satisfactory arrangement can be made to provide some other kind of benefit to those excluded from the system.

The problem of maintaining wage differentials is more difficult, especially if there is a customary or legal ratio between pay rates of certain employee groups. Maintaining the distinction by giving employees excluded from the system a raise is an obviously expensive and probably undesirable solution. It would be preferable to try to design the system so that incentives do not narrow the gap too much. The solutions offered above (provide another incentive plan or other benefit) may also work in this case. In extreme situations, the plan may have to be abandoned.

3. Managerial level personnel may also oppose an incentive plan. Some may oppose it because they feel employees will focus on whatever job aspects will earn them larger rewards instead of on overall service objectives. Some managers may feel uncomfortable about giving employees extra money to be more productive, or to arrive on time, and so on, feeling that this is what their basic compensation is for. The way to deal with managerial opposition is to explain how the plan will benefit their department and the jurisdiction. With respect to concern about deemphasis of service goals, the plan should be designed to reward behavior associated with those goals; for example, by rewarding greater productivity or improved performance in jobs related to the primary service. This should be made clear to managers who are fearful about goal displacement. Providing examples of success stories from other government jurisdictions may also help win over the opposition.

4. The media and citizens might also take one or both of the perspectives described above. How successfully either group can be won over depends on public relations skills and how good the relationship is between each group and the administration. The tactic of explaining benefits to be derived and the overall concept of incentives and motivation should be used. In addition, the long experience of private sector use of incentive programs, as well as public sector success stories, should be emphasized.

5. Other elected officials, such as city council members or state legislators, may oppose the plan because it represents increased expenditure. In some instances, it may also represent real or apparent loss of legislative control

over wage increases. The latter problem is difficult to deal with since power is at stake. In either case the expected benefits from the plan should be stressed, and it should be made clear that they are expected to exceed costs involved. Again, examples of successful plans should be provided to help make the case.

Maintaining the Incentive System. Deciding to use an incentive system requires establishment and maintenance of a measurement system. Records must be kept of whatever behavior is to be rewarded (outputs, performance, attendance, etc.), so that rewards will be distributed correctly and fairly. Of course, some of this data may already be routinely collected. If not, it can be made part of the PIP's measurement system. As noted previously, the effectiveness of the system in terms of continuing to increase desired behaviors should also be monitored so changes can be made, if necessary. These maintenance requirements are relatively minor and should not act as a barrier to adopting an incentive system.

SUMMARY

This chapter has described different types of incentive systems that can be used in the PIP. Incentive systems are designed to motivate employees to reach explicitly specified goals by offering explicitly specified rewards. The major choice to make in selecting a system is what goal should be rewarded. Table 9-2 presents a summary description of occasions when systems focused on different goals can be used.

Table 9-2. Summary of Incentive Systems

FOCUS OF SYSTEM:
Output Quantity Can be used whenever output can be measured in unit terms. Piecework systems link output to regular paychecks. Bonus systems offer less frequent rewards and can be used when goal accomplishment requires longer time periods.
Performance Can be used to improve quality or effectiveness of service instead of, or in addition to, productivity.
Behavior Can be used to reduce nonproductive behavior (such as excessive absenteeism); to encourage prompt completion of work (task systems); to increase safety; or to generate suggestions for improved productivity.
Shared savings Can be used to encourage ideas for savings and/or to generate higher levels of motivation since employees effectively create their own bonuses by the amount of savings they achieve.

In general, systems that reward increased output are most directly related to productivity improvement and are, therefore, most desirable for use in a PIP. Other systems, for example, to reduce nonproductive behavior, can be useful additions to a program where other improvement methods dominate. By themselves, however, they are unlikely to lead to major productivity improvements unless the behavior problems are of substantial magnitude.

Money is the most common reward used in incentive systems, although time off (as vacation days or the shorter workdays) is used fairly frequently. Rewards can be distributed on an individual or group basis. They are most commonly provided as bonuses, although pay increases are sometimes used as incentives.

Although originally designed for the private sector, incentive systems have been successfully employed by state and local governments for a variety of jobs in recent years. They can be applied in conjunction with other improvement methods.

The concept of incentives and how they work is intuitively easy to understand, and the systems themselves are also fairly easy to implement. These features make them good candidates for inclusion in a PIP.

NOTES

1. For discussion of the merit system and its problems, see John M. Greiner, et al., *Productivity and Motivation: a Review of State and Local Government Initiatives* (Washington, D.C.: The Urban Institute Press, 1981), pp. 67-88, and Jacob B. Ukeles, *Doing More with Less: Turning Public Management Around* (New York: AMACOM, 1982), pp. 17-42.
2. The basic calculations would be explained in industrial engineering or other books that deal with incentive systems. See, for example, H. K. von Kaas, *Making Wage Incentives Work* (New York: American Management Association, Inc., 1971).
3. John M. Greiner, et al., *Monetary Incentives and Work Standards in Five Cities: Impacts and Implications for Management and Labor* (Washington, D.C.: The Urban Institute, 1977), pp. 37-41.
4. Greiner, et al., *Productivity and Motivation,* pp. 49-50.
5. Ibid., p. 47.
6. National Commission on Productivity and Work Quality, *Employee Incentives to Improve State and Local Government Productivity* (Washington, D.C.: U.S. Government Printing Office, 1975), pp. 53-54.
7. Greiner, et al., *Monetary Incentives and Standards,* pp. 62-63.
8. Greiner, et al., *Productivity and Motivation,* pp. 37-38.
9. Ibid., p. 44.
10. Ibid., pp. 39-41.
11. Greiner, et al., *Productivity and Motivation,* pp. 78-79.
12. National Commission on Productivity, *Employee Incentives,* pp. 21-23.
13. Catherine A. Turner, "A Well Pay Incentive Program," *Public Productivity Review* 6 (March/June 1982): 127-130.
14. Greiner, et al., *Monetary Incentives and Standards,* pp. 47-53.
15. National Commission on Productivity, *Employee Incentives,* pp. 99-100.

16. Ibid., pp. 24 and 83.
17. Greiner, et al., *Productivity and Motivation,* pp. 57-58.
18. Ibid., p. 53.
19. Ibid., pp. 53-54.
20. Ibid., pp. 54-55.
21. Based on Greiner et al., *Productivity and Motivation,* pp. 33-46, 122, and 154; and von Kaas, *Making Incentives Work,* pp. 4-8.
22. Greiner, et al., *Productivity and Motivation,* pp. 96-99.
23. Material on attitudinal problems relies heavily on Greiner et al., *Productivity and Motivation,* pp. 100-104.

10
IMPROVING PRODUCTIVITY THROUGH JOB ENRICHMENT

HOW ENRICHMENT IMPROVES PRODUCTIVITY

This section will explain the basics of job enrichment: how it works, why it is needed, and what it means. This will provide a foundation for the rest of the chapter, which presents details on different enrichment methods and how to apply them.

Job enrichment is another motivation-based improvement method. It increases motivation through characteristics present *in* the job, rather than with rewards *external* to the job. It changes the job in ways that let the job itself help fulfill employee needs for esteem and self-actualization, the so-called higher-level needs. It does this by adding factors to jobs that will increase opportunities for employees to gain more responsibility, recognition, and growth from the job itself. This leads to greater employee satisfaction and motivation, which results in improved productivity.

Why Enrichment is Needed. Job enrichment has been a major productivity improvement theme in the private sector since the 1960s. This is probably due in part to growing awareness of changes in employee attitudes. Worker discontent with overly simplified, monotonous work was becoming obvious, exemplified in high absenteeism and turnover, poor quality work, and strikes.

In addition, it was recognized that work-force demographics and attitudes had changed. Growth in the number of younger, better-educated workers resulted in different attitudes and expectations about work than could be met by many jobs of a "routine" nature, whether on assembly lines or in offices.[1] These changes in employee attitudes are present in the public sector as well.

Regardless of the reason, job enrichment has received considerable acclaim as a solution to productivity problems. Although lower-skilled jobs are often described when discussing the need for enrichment, it is a broadly applicable technique. The fact that it is not limited to a particular type of work means it is as applicable to the public sector as it is to the private.

What Enrichment Means. Job enrichment involves increasing a group of job characteristics that are described as "core dimensions."[2] These are:

Diversity—performing a variety of different tasks that use a number of skills or talents.

Autonomy—exercising freedom and discretion in performing tasks and making decisions.

Wholeness—performing an identifiable or complete piece of work rather than portions of tasks.

Feedback—providing information about job performance in a clear and direct manner.

A fifth dimension that is sometimes included is task significance, which is the impact of the task on the work or lives of others.

The core dimensions are related to fulfilling higher level needs of employees. Diversity, wholeness, and task significance increase the meaningfulness of the work. Autonomy increases feelings of responsibility, which feedback reinforces by providing understanding of how effectively the job is being done. In combination, these lead to greater satisfaction; more involvement with, and attachment to the job; higher motivation; and better performance.

Performance does not necessarily mean production of a greater quantity of output, although it can mean that. It could include things like higher quality work, less absenteeism, lower turnover, and so on, which are indirectly related to productivity. Enrichment does not provide explicit rewards for specified achievements. The "reward," enrichment, is provided in advance of improvements in performance. Although this differs from the incentive system approach, it is common to motivation-related techniques. However, it should be made clear to the employee that continuation of the enrichment program is dependent on satisfactory levels of performance.

The degree of enrichment that can be achieved will vary with the type of job and the organization it is in. Ideally, an enriched job should contain all core components, but it may not be possible to expand all of them in a given job. For example, a specific change might result in a large amount of autonomy but not very much task variety; or a lot of variety but not much feedback, and so on.

Care should be taken to see that enrichment factors added to the job are significant, not merely token gestures. Enrichment programs often fail to have impact because the jobs were not *really* enriched. Adding one or two unimportant tasks, or responsibility for making decisions of little consequence, will not truly enrich a job.

Enrichment should be viewed from the perspective of the original job. The kind of dimensions that can be added to a clerical job, for example, will not be of the same magnitude as those that can be added to a lower level supervisory position. Therefore, enrichment should not be viewed solely in terms of an idealized enriched job. Efforts should be directed toward adding as much real enrichment as possible given the nature of the job itself.

Jobs are enriched by changing the way work is performed. In effect, enrichment entails job redesign, but instead of simplifying the job, it makes it more complex. Since some core dimensions are interrelated, a specific change in the way work is done may contribute to increasing more than one core dimension. Some of the most common ways to enrich jobs are these:

Combining tasks/forming natural work units. This involves expanding the work content to add variety and use more skills. The added tasks should lead to greater task identity or wholeness. A "natural work unit" is an identifiable, meaningful work product.

Vertical loading. This means expanding employee autonomy by adding factors that may previously have been reserved for management. This could include responsibility for deciding on work methods; work scheduling; priority setting, and so on.

Feedback. Expansion of feedback opportunities can include more direct contact with people in a position to give meaningful feedback on work performance; for example, clients, other employees, and/or supervisors. It can also mean giving the employee quality control responsibilities, which, in effect, provides feedback from the work itself.

If all of these were applied at once, the resulting job could be characterized as a model enriched job. In practice, it is not always possible to accomplish this. Several different methods have been developed to accomplish various enrichment objectives. These will be described in the following section.

ENRICHMENT METHODS AND THEIR APPLICATION

The term "*job enrichment*" refers to the basic method of redesigning a job to increase the amount and/or degree of core dimensions it contains. Job enrichment is also used more broadly to encompass other enrichment techniques including job enlargement, rotation, and team efforts. These involve some or all of the core dimensions. These methods may be appropriate for jobs or work situations where full-scale enrichment cannot be easily applied. This section will explain each of these enrichment methods and provide examples of public sector applications.

Job Enrichment. Since job enrichment itself has already been described, only examples of its use will be provided here.

Clerical or other lower level office jobs are good targets for job enrichment because they are often routine and are designed so that work is fragmented (meaning each employee specializes in one particular function). One example of a clerical enrichment program is from Arapahoe County, Colorado. The program involved clerks who process and record legal documents such as licenses, wills, and so on. Before redesign, the clerks worked in assembly-line fashion, each performing a specific task such as checking applications, certifying documents, or handling money. Restructuring the jobs gave each clerk responsibility for complete processing of a specific document and for correction of his/her own errors. County officals felt productivity and employee satisfaction improved under this system.[3]

Although this appears to be a very simple change, partly because it is a very logical course of action, its significance in terms of enrichment should not be overlooked. All core dimensions were increased by this redesign. Combining tasks added both variety and wholeness. Responsibility and feedback were both increased by having clerks check their own work and correct errors. Since only one clerk now serves each client, feedback is more direct and perception of task significance is probably greater. Thus a seemingly small change can have multiple impacts in terms of enrichment.

Another enrichment effort involving office workers was designed for secretaries in Montgomery County, Maryland. The jobs of about 250 secretaries were changed to administrative aide positions, with added duties of research, preparation of staff papers, letter composition, and other administrative responsibilities.[4] In Tacoma, Washington, personnel analyst jobs were subject to enrichment. Previously, analysts were restricted to specific tasks, such as recruiting, compensation, and so on. The restructuring gave analysts responsibility for *all* personnel matters in a particular department. This increases variety and wholeness and enhances opportunities for feedback, since department officials now can contact the analyst responsible for their department directly.[5]

Public sector enrichment has not been limited to office employees. In Rocky Mount, North Carolina, Sanitation Department drivers were given quality control responsibilities for their own routes. Any citizen complaints are referred directly to the driver of the route, who is responsible for rectifying them.[6] Note that this is an example of a limited form of enrichment —task variety and wholeness were not affected by this change, only responsibility and feedback were added.

A similar kind of enrichment was devised for parks maintenance supervisors in Little Rock, Arkansas. They had previously been responsible for transporting laborers to and from work sites and supervising their work.

Redesign expanded their responsibilities to include: obtaining and replacing equipment, assigning and supervising specialized tasks to maintenance crews, and inspecting work to see that it meets specifications. (These tasks were previously assigned to a different position.)[7]

Another approach to enriching jobs takes an opposite tactic from those described above. Instead of adding factors to the job, it removes routine aspects of it, leaving only the "higher level" functions. This is usually the result whenever paraprofessional positions are established; for example, for teachers, health care personnel, and police officers.[8] The components that remain in the restructured job are typically those viewed as core dimensions. Since the use of paraprofessionals is becoming fairly common to various government agencies, specific examples are not necessary here. It should also be remembered that a primary advantage of using paraprofessionals is cost savings; they are paid far less than the professionals who had previously spent time doing routine work.

Job Enlargement. Job enlargement is sometimes incorrectly described in a way that makes it appear to be the same as job enrichment. However, job enlargement really means increasing the diversity of a job by adding additional tasks at approximately the same skill level. It is referred to as "horizontal loading," while job enrichment is called "vertical loading." The addition of tasks does not necessarily lead to the employee completing a whole task, however. Increasing autonomy and feedback are usually not part of the enlargement concept.

Two of the more common examples of public sector job enlargement have already been discussed in chapter 8 as examples of redesign. One is the creation of a public safety officer position, where police officers are trained to perform some firefighting functions, and firefighters are trained in some police functions. There are numerous examples of this particular kind of enlargement. The other common example is training building inspectors to perform a variety of types of inspection, instead of having several specialist inspectors. Evidence from communities using public safety officers indicate that most of them experienced savings due to reductions in staff size, and most were satisfied with the effectiveness of the program. In a similar vein, the generalist inspectors were usually judged to be more efficient and/or to result in cost savings.[9]

A number of other job enlargement efforts have involved firefighters, undoubtedly because of the amount of "idle" time they have when not fighting fires. It is common for them to conduct fire safety and building code inspections, for example. In Mesa, Arizona, they perform a safety patrol function to provide any general assistance needed. In Glenview,

Illinois, they operate the printing department, a rather unusual form of job enlargement.[10]

Job Rotation. Job rotation could be viewed as a different approach to job enlargement. Its purpose is to provide variety. It accomplishes this by having employees work at different jobs instead of by adding tasks to their basic job. In addition, the kind of work done during rotation might also add elements of autonomy, feedback, and so on. This is sometimes the goal of the program, but the main purpose is usually to increase diversity. The amount of time spent at a new position varies. It could be a matter of weeks or months, but sometimes it is an assignment of two or three years duration. Eligibility for rotation varies among programs. Some are strictly voluntary, others select employees on the basis of skills, while others rotate all employees in a given unit.

Job rotation can be confined to a single agency, or can involve different agencies within a jurisdiction. At times, it has been practiced on an interjurisdictional basis. Some rotation programs have additional goals of enhancing understanding of the problems of other agencies, or of the jurisdiction as a whole. This is somewhat related to the "wholeness" job dimension, and may also lead to greater cooperation among agencies. In other programs, it is hoped that employees will bring new ideas or techniques back to their original positions.

Rotation is fairly common in police departments, often associated with changes in patrol beats or other assignments, but it can also be geared toward varying the type of work done. A program in Elmhurst, Illinois, enabled patrol officers to rotate through seven detective positions, each focusing on different kinds of investigative work. Sergeants in the program could rotate into investigations, records, and communications, or a special unit.[11] A similar program exists in Pacifica, California, but patrol officers rotate among positions such as detective, court officer, traffic officer, and crime prevention officer. An interjurisdictional arrangement also existed for a while between six neighboring California police departments, with the rotated officers serving as staff assistant to the police chief.[12]

Two examples of programs to add diversity to relatively low-level jobs come from Fayetteville, North Carolina. In the finance department, many of the clerks are rotated to different clerical jobs every three months. This also increases their eligibility for promotion. In the engineering department, draftsmen and surveyors are allowed to exchange positions after training in the new skills.[13] Some programs are designed to increase not only variety but the level of skills used. In Glendale, Arizona, firefighters, waste collectors, and other line personnel can rotate into positions in the personnel department.

Over a three-month period they are assigned increasingly complex tasks, such as analyzing examinations, designing forms, and so on.[14]

A number of rotation programs are designed for managerial and supervisory personnel. In Sunnyvale, California, for example, department directors and supervisors have been assigned to similar positions in other departments for 6-8 weeks. One goal of this type of program is to encourage citywide perspectives on problems among high-level personnel.[15] An interjurisdictional variant on supervisor exchange has been used by Santa Ana, California, where City officials feel there are benefits from exposure to other management styles.[16]

Team Approaches. Team approaches operate by assigning groups of people to work closely together. Rotating jobs among team members is a common variant in this approach. In cases where the latter occurs, variety is clearly added to individual jobs. Without this, enlargement of individual jobs may not occur. However, team efforts usually increase the amount of task identity or wholeness experienced, and teams are usually given additional responsibility for decision making. Since employees are working in groups, feedback from co-workers is to be expected. Teams will also increase the extent to which social needs are filled on the job. Thus this one technique has the ability to increase a number of the core dimensions associated with motivation.

The most common use of public sector teams is team policing. In general, team policing involves permanent assignment of a group of officers to a specific area or neighborhood. The team is typically made responsible for all police activities in the area, including investigation of crime (which is usually reserved for specialists). In some areas, teams are also responsible for community relations and for managerial functions such as planning patrols, scheduling, and so on. Team policing has been used in a fairly large number of jurisdictions (over 70 reported use in 1978), probably because it was recommended as a way to improve service and police working conditions by the President's Commission on Law Enforcement and the Administration of Justice in 1967.[17]

Although teams are most common in police departments, there are some examples of them in other government agencies. In Baltimore, Maryland, inspectors from the housing and health departments have worked as teams to inspect buildings. Similar inspection teams have been used in other cities. In Hempstead, New York, custodial employees work as teams while cleaning public buildings. Health-care teams, usually consisting of doctors and nurses, have been utilized in several locations.[18]

The above sections have presented descriptions of major enrichment methods and examples of their application to public sector jobs. Job enrichment is the most comprehensive of the techniques. The other methods provide alternative ways of supplying some or all enrichment factors to a job. An explanation of when and how to use these methods will be provided later in this chapter.

APPROPRIATENESS OF ENRICHMENT

The first step to take before implementing enrichment is to determine whether the particular job being considered for enrichment is a good candidate for it.[19] Although enrichment methods are broadly applicable, that does not mean they are always needed or that they will always be effective. Therefore, the first step should be assessment of appropriateness for enrichment. This involves answering the following questions:

Does some problem exist (other than lack of enrichment) that is affecting productivity?

Does this job need enriching?

Do the employees who perform this job want enrichment?

Can the jobs, units and/or people affected by this job accommodate to changes enrichment may bring?

Do Other Problems Exist? Asking this question seems obvious, but it might not be considered by someone enthusiastic about "trying out" an enrichment project. The first thing to determine is whether lower-level needs (pay, security, and other working conditions) are being met to a satisfactory degree. If employees are unhappy about basics like pay, for example, introducing enrichment is highly unlikely to be successful. Determining satisfaction with basic needs might be accomplished through a questionnaire or interviews with employees, or it might be ascertainable from immediate supervisors. A diagnostic survey that covers this and a variety of other information useful in deciding whether to initiate job enrichment has been developed by Hackman and Oldham, but is too lengthy to reproduce and discuss in full here.[20] A sample of their questions related to satisfaction of lower-level needs is provided in Table 10-1. Administration of this or a similar questionnaire to employees whose jobs are being considered for enrichment will indicate whether these needs are perceived as being met satisfactorily.

In a similar vein, it should be determined whether there are other factors that might be causing low productivity; for example, old equipment that keeps breaking down; contractual agreements that limit the amount of work done, and so on. Again, enrichment will not help if low productivity is due to

Table 10-1. Sample Questions to Determine Whether Lower Level Needs are Met

Write a number in the blank beside each statement, based on the following scale: How satisfied are you with this aspect of your job?

1	2	3	4	5	6	7
EXTREMELY DISSATISFIED	DISSATISFIED	SLIGHTLY DISSATISFIED	NEUTRAL	SLIGHTLY SATISFIED	SATISFIED	EXTREMELY SATISFIED

_____ 1. The amount of job security I have.

_____ 2. The amount of pay and fringe benefits I receive.

_____ 3. The amount of personal growth and development I get in doing my job.

_____ 4. The people I talk to and work with on my job.

_____ 5. The degree of respect and fair treatment I receive from my boss.

_____ 6. The feeling of worthwhile accomplishment I get from doing my job.

_____ 7. The chance to get to know other people while on the job.

_____ 8. The amount of support and guidance I receive from my supervisor.

_____ 9. The degree to which I am fairly paid for what I contribute to this organization.

_____ 10. The amount of independent thought and action I can exercise in my job.

_____ 11. How secure things look for me in the future in this organization.

_____ 12. The chance to help other people while at work.

_____ 13. The amount of challenge in my job.

_____ 14. The overall quality of the supervision I receive in my work.

Source: J. Richard Hackman and Greg R. Oldham, *Work Redesign,* Addison-Wesley, Reading, Mass. ©1980, p. 284. Reprinted with permission.

problems of this kind. Information of this nature should be available from supervisory level personnel.

Is Enrichment Needed? Determining whether a job needs enriching calls for analysis of the job in question. Some jobs are already "enriched"; that is, they contain reasonably high levels of the core dimensions. It would not be particularly fruitful to try to enrich such jobs further when others are in real need of enrichment. Thus many professional, supervisory, and managerial jobs are not strong candidates for enrichment, although rotation and team efforts sometimes involve jobs at this level.

One of the best ways to determine whether a job needs enriching is to rank it high, medium, or low in terms of each of the core dimensions. While this is not a sophisticated ranking system, it will identify jobs that are clearly good candidates for enrichment, or which of a group of jobs is in greater need of enrichment and should be dealt with first.[21] A more complex and sophisticated approach to ranking jobs can be derived by using the full job diagnostic survey mentioned above.

Ranking job characteristics can be done in a more objective way by using some kind of analytic process rather than relying on opinion. One approach would be to use process charts to record the steps involved in performing a particular job. These individual activities can then be analyzed to determine how much variety, autonomy, and so on, they contain and, by summing these, how many core dimensions are present in the job as a whole. Another approach would be to use a questionnaire to determine the extent to which employees feel that core dimensions are present in their jobs. It should be noted that *perception* of the degree to which a characteristic is present may be more important than an objective assessment. A sample of questions that could be used to help rate the job in terms of core dimensions is provided in Table 10-2. Of course, both methods could be used to build an even stronger impression of the nature of the job.

Do Employees Want Enrichment? This question deals with employee satisfaction and motivation. It should be determined whether low levels of satisfaction and motivation exist. This can be done through questionnaires, interviews with employees, supervisors, and so on, and by records of lateness, absenteeism, and turnover. A sample questionnaire is provided in Table 10-3. The important thing to determine here is whether satisfaction and motivation are *not* problems; if they are not, the real problem needs to be determined and an alternative productivity improvement method must be found, as was discussed earlier in this section.

A second aspect of this question is determining whether the employees whose jobs will be redesigned are likely to be motivated by higher level needs. Job enrichment has not been successful with all employees; therefore it is important to determine whether the work force under study is likely to respond favorably to an enriched job. Some studies have identified alienated, urbanized workers as being generally unresponsive to job characteristics associated with enrichment. Other studies indicate that employees must place high value on work in general for enrichment techniques to succeed. More recent studies indicate that the individuals's psychological need for growth is the major factor affecting reaction to job enrichment.[22]

A sample of questions to determine growth needs is provided in Table 10-4. (Growth need questions are numbers 2, 3, 6, 8, 10, and 11.) Since most enrichment efforts involve changing a job category as opposed to redesigning the work done by a particular employee, it should be determined whether

Table 10-2. Sample Questions to Determine Presence of Core Dimensions

Write a number in the blank beside each statement, based on the following scale:

How accurate is the statement in describing your job?

1	2	3	4	5	6	7
VERY INACCURATE	MOSTLY INACCURATE	SLIGHTLY INACCURATE	UNCERTAIN	SLIGHTLY ACCURATE	MOSTLY ACCURATE	VERY ACCURATE

_____ 1. The job requires me to use a number of complex or high-level skills.

_____ 2. The job requires a lot of cooperative work with other people.

_____ 3. The job is arranged so that I do *not* have the chance to do an entire piece of work from beginning to end.

_____ 4. Just doing the work required by the job provides many chances for me to figure out how well I am doing.

_____ 5. The job is quite simple and repetitive.

_____ 6. The job can be done adequately by a person working alone without talking or checking with other people.

_____ 7. The supervisors and co-workers on this job almost *never* give me any "feedback" about how well I am doing in my work.

_____ 8. This job is one where a lot of other people can be affected by how well the work gets done.

_____ 9. The job denies me any chance to use my personal initiative or judgment in carrying out the work.

_____ 10. Supervisors often let me know how well they think I am performing the job.

_____ 11. The job provides me the chance to completely finish the pieces of work I begin.

_____ 12. The job itself provides very few clues about whether or not I am performing well.

_____ 13. The job gives me considerable opportunity for independence and freedom in how I do the work.

_____ 14. The job itself is *not* very significant or important in the broader scheme of things.

Source: J. Richard Hackman and Greg R. Oldham, *Work Redesign* ©1980, Addison-Wesley, Reading, Mass., pp. 280–81. Reprinted with permission.

the *majority* of employees performing a particular job want enrichment. This will result in some people being "overenriched" and some being "underenriched," but this is the normal course of events unless jobs are individually tailored to meet employee needs. Employees with a high need for growth should be early targets for job enrichment; those with a low need

Table 10-3. Sample Questions to Determine Present Satisfaction and Motivation

Write a number in the blank for each statement, based on this scale:

How much do you agree with the statement?

1	2	3	4	5	6	7
DISAGREE STRONGLY	DISAGREE	DISAGREE SLIGHTLY	NEUTRAL	AGREE SLIGHTLY	AGREE	AGREE STRONGLY

_____ 1. It's hard, on this job, for me to care very much about whether or not the work gets done right.

_____ 2. My opinion of myself goes up when I do this job well.

_____ 3. Generally speaking, I am very satisfied with this job.

_____ 4. Most of the things I have to do on this job seem useless or trivial.

_____ 5. I usually know whether or not my work is satisfactory on this job.

_____ 6. I feel a great sense of personal satisfaction when I do this job well.

_____ 7. The work I do on this job is very meaningful to me.

_____ 8. I feel a very high degree of *personal* responsibility for the work I do on this job.

_____ 9. I frequently think of quitting this job.

_____ 10. I feel bad and unhappy when I discover that I haver performed poorly on this job.

_____ 11. I often have trouble figuring out whether I'm doing well or poorly on this job.

_____ 12. I feel I should personally take the credit or blame for the results of my work on this job.

_____ 13. I am generally satisfied with the kind of work I do in this job.

_____ 14. My own feelings generally are *not* affected much one way or the other by how well I do on this job.

_____ 15. Whether or not this job gets done right is clearly *my* responsibility.

Source: J. Richard Hackman and Greg R. Oldham, *Work Redesign*, ©1980, Addison-Wesley, Reading, Mass., pp. 282-83. Reprinted with permission.

should be considered for other kinds of productivity methods or perhaps for a more careful, slower introduction to enrichment.

Can the Job be Changed? One should determine whether a job can be changed in a meaningful way by considering technological and organizational barriers (other than the employees performing the job). The most problematic barriers would be technological; for example, if equipment used for the job is too costly to allow the work to be changed in ways needed for enrichment.

Table, 10-4. Sample Questions to Determine Growth Need Strength

Using the scale below, please indicate the *degree* to which you *would like* to have each characteristic present in your job.

NOTE: The numbers on this scale are different from those used in previous scales.

4	5	6	7	8	9	10
WOULD LIKE HAVING THIS ONLY A MODERATE AMOUNT (OR LESS)			WOULD LIKE HAVING THIS VERY MUCH			WOULD LIKE HAVING THIS EXTREMELY MUCH

_____ 1. High respect and fair treatment from my supervisor.

_____ 2. Stimulating and challenging work.

_____ 3. Chances to exercise independent thought and action in my job.

_____ 4. Great job security.

_____ 5. Very friendly co-workers.

_____ 6. Opportunities to learn new things from my work.

_____ 7. High salary and good fringe benefits.

_____ 8. Opportunities to be creative and imaginative in my work.

_____ 9. Quick promotions.

_____ 10. Opportunities for personal growth and development in my job.

_____ 11. A sense of worthwhile accomplishment in my work.

Source: J. Richard Hackman and Greg R. Oldham, *Work Redesign,* ©1980, Addison-Wesley, Reading, Mass., pp. 286–87. Reprinted with permission.

However, this kind of problem is more likely to occur in manufacturing work than in the public sector. Civil service rules or union contracts might be a barrier if they inhibit changes in job content, personnel assignments, and so on.

The way enrichment might impact work units directly associated with the job being changed is also a factor to consider. If effects of change will disrupt the functioning of other units, enrichment may have to be foregone. Alternatively, by considering these impacts in advance and consulting with affected units, it may be possible to design the enrichment to satisfy the needs of all units to some degree. (A more detailed discussion of this and other problem areas and how to deal with them appears later.) The key point at this stage of analysis is to quickly discover major barriers that would make enrichment impossible. This will prevent wasting more time on a job that can't really be changed.

Applying the four-stage analysis described above should help identify a group of jobs that need enrichment and/or employees who will be better motivated by enriched jobs. The analysis might also identify employees who are not motivated by the higher level needs, but they should not be perceived negatively as a result of this; to assume everyone *should* be motivated by higher-level needs is a value judgment, not a fact.[23]

HOW TO ENRICH A JOB

Once a job is identified as being suitable for enrichment, the obvious next step is to enrich it. This section will explain how to conduct the enrichment process.

The first step is to determine which core dimensions (diversity, autonomy, wholeness, and feedback) need to be expanded. The ranking done to determine whether the job needed enrichment can be used for this. Strong efforts should be made to increase any dimension ranked low, and those ranked moderate should also be considered for expansion, if possible. Thus a job may be ranked as follows:

diversity	low
autonomy	moderate
wholeness	high
feedback	high

The most urgent need in this case would be to increase job diversity, but it would also be desirable to expand autonomy.

Once the factors needed most have been identified, the next step is to decide where and how the principles of enrichment (combining tasks; forming natural work units; vertical loading; feedback), can be applied. This can be done by systematically studying the job as it is currently performed to see where and how these enrichment principles can be applied. This should sound familiar, since it is essentially the same kind of critical analysis described for job redesign. In the enrichment context, job redesign has the goal of greater complexity, rather than simplification.

Critical Analysis. A form that can be used to help conduct a critical analysis is shown in Table 10-5. This form is arranged to help enrich the job in the simplist and most intuitively logical way. This involves adding tasks or responsibilities that are, in practice, associated with the task at hand but which are, for one reason or another, performed by someone other than the

Table 10-5. Job Enrichment Critical Analysis

Job under analysis:

Core dimensions most in need of enrichment:

Major Activity #1:

I. *Combining Tasks/Natural Work Groups*
   What other tasks/activities are related to this?
   Are they part of this job?
   Can they be made part of this job?
   What changes (e.g., technological, organizational) must be made to do this?
   Are these changes feasible? If not, are compromise positions possible?

II. *Vertical Loading*
   Which of the following control mechanisms are associated with this activity and are performed by the employee doing the job?
      Scheduling/priority setting
      Troubleshooting/resolving problems
      Quality inspections
      Error corrections
      Budgetary responsibility
      Providing information for supervisors and/or clients
   Which of the above can be made part of the job?
   What changes must be made to do this?
   Are these changes feasible? If not, are compromise positions possible?

III. *Feedback*
   Which of the following kinds of feedback are channeled directly to the employee?
      Inspection of own work
      Receipt of data, reports, etc., that indicate output, accomplishments, and errors.
      Contact with other employees who use the output of this activity
      Contact with clients outside the department, agency
   Which of the above can be made part of the job?
   What changes must be made to do this?
   Are these changes feasible? If not, are compromise positions possible?

---

person doing the job under study. The form encourages careful consideration of both the changes necessary to bring about redesign and the impacts it will have. In effect, this involves anticipating some potential problem areas and devising methods to deal with them, or finding other satisfactory alternatives. The various components of the form will be discussed here to illustrate how it should be used.

Since most jobs consist of a variety of tasks or activities, the form should note the overall job title and indicate which major activity or task is being analyzed for enrichment. Several activities could be considered in sequence to determine which can be used to help enrich the whole job. Since the job should already have been ranked in terms of core dimensions, those needing enrichment should be noted on top of the form so particular attention can be paid to increasing them. Then the job should be examined in terms of each of the core dimensions.

Section one in Table 10-5 deals with variety and task wholeness. If the job being examined has been simplified or fragmented, components of it are probably being done by other people. For example, one clerk might be filling in the information permit forms while a different clerk accepts the fee, although both steps are logically part of the same job. The person conducting the analysis should identify related tasks or activities, and then determine what changes would be necessary to bring the components together as a complete, more diverse, job.

Changes suggested should be identified in terms of the job being studied (e.g., equipment, training), the unit that will lose the element being moved, and any other affected units. As noted earlier, if enrichment in one unit has a major negative impact on another unit(s), the change may have to be foregone unless a more compatible alternative can be found. For example, the output of one unit may be the input of another. If the former unit is given increased responsibility for work scheduling, the output may not be produced as regularly or predictably as it was before enrichment. This might cause major scheduling problems for the other unit.

In a similar vein, the second section identifies various control mechanisms or decision points related to the job and whether the person doing the job is responsible for them. For example, scheduling work and quality inspections might be assigned to a supervisor, but would lead to greater autonomy if they were done by the employee. The third section is similar in format but seeks to identify what kinds of feedback associated with the particular job are received by the employee doing the work, as opposed to feedback directed to his/her supervisor or some other party. Each of these sections also requires consideration of changes required and impacts on other units.

Brainstorming. An important decision relates to who will perform the enrichment analysis and the redesign stemming from it. The ideal situation would be to have a group of people work on them in a kind of brainstorming format; each contributing as many ideas as possible about potential ways to enrich the job and how to make them workable. Participants should be thoroughly briefed on the concept of job enrichment beforehand. This could be done in a workshop conducted by a staff member from the central productivity office or by a consultant, if one is being used for the enrichment project.

The members of the brainstorming group (which could be called an enrichment task force), should ideally include the following: staff members from the central Productivity Improvement Program (PIP) unit; the consultant (if applicable); someone from the productivity office of the department or agency in which the job is located; the supervisor of the unit in which the job is located; representatives of the employees whose jobs are being redesigned; a union representative (if applicable); supervisors of other units or departments closely linked to this job (e.g., units that depend on its output as their input).

While this may seem like a fairly large group, there are good reasons for including each member. First, it should be kept in mind that creativity is fostered by the diversity of opinion. The parties mentioned above can provide valuable input to the process because of their knowledge of the job; and/or because their work will be affected by the change and they can indicate potential problems and help devise ways to avoid or reduce them. If necessary, however, a smaller group can be used. Input can also be solicited on an individual basis if large brainstorming groups are not a viable option.

Participation in the redesign process also will help build better understanding of enrichment and greater commitment to making it successful. This is particularly useful for two groups of participants; the employees whose jobs are changed and their immediate supervisors. By participating in the process, the employees will gain a better understanding of the rationale for job enrichment, which should help them accept the changes in their jobs. Since they will have input into the redesign process, they should be more satisfied, motivated, and committed to the enriched job.

Supervisors are another group whose commitment is needed for success since their work is likely to be strongly affected by redesign. Many of the new responsibilities added to the enriched job may have been done formerly by supervisors (e.g., scheduling, quality control, etc.). Thus they may feel a loss in their own status. They may compensate for their reduction in responsibilities by oversupervising their employees or being too critical, which would negate the satisfaction generated by enrichment. Thus supervisors must understand the importance of the enrichment program and be committed to its success. They should also be given new responsibilites to replace any taken away, such as training and counseling employees for their enriched jobs, helping them set performance goals and evaluate performance, and so on.[24]

USING ALTERNATIVES TO ENRICHMENT

The enrichment analysis/brainstorming format just described centers on basic job enrichment; that is, enriching an individual job. However, it may be decided during this process that this approach is not feasible. In this case, the same analytic format should be applied to the alternatives of job enlargement, rotation, and teams. The intent is to determine whether the technique can be used; what changes are necessary to do so; to identify potential problem areas and ways to overcome them; and to identify impacts external to the changed job(s). Since each of these variations is slightly different, the unique characteristics of each will be briefly noted here.

Using Job Enlargement. Job enlargement should be easier to design and implement than job enrichment because it is, in effect, a partial enrichment, seeking to add only diversity and wholeness to the job. Thus the first section of the enrichment critical analysis form can be used to help design the enlarged job.

Employees without strong growth needs may find enlargement less threatening than enrichment and benefit from increased satisfaction due to greater diversity alone. However, employees with strong growth needs may not find enlargement alone sufficiently satisfying or motivating.

Job enlargement may be more acceptable than enrichment in some situations because it involves less organizational change. It involves rearranging job assignments, but it doesn't affect organizational behavior patterns such as responsibility for scheduling or quality control. In general, there are fewer external impacts, which eliminates one source of potential problems and/or resistance.

Using Job Rotation. Job rotation is different from other techniques discussed because it does not involve any real job changes. The key to a rotation program is to identify employees/jobs to be rotated and determine the length of time spent at each assignment. The simplest kind of rotation would involve only jobs at approximately the same skill level, meaning that employees being rotated would need little training to "fit into" their new assignment. As a result, any decrease in productivity resulting from adjustment to each job rotation should be minor. This would also allow for assignments of relatively short duration (weeks or months).

A more ambitious and difficult type of rotation would assign employees to jobs requiring significantly different skills than they regularly use on their own job. This implies a need for more substantial retraining at each new assignment and a productivity drop until new skills are learned. This suggests that long assignments (six months or more) are needed to avoid continuing low productivity levels as employees are constantly "in training." The latter kind of rotation is more like enrichment, while the former is more like enlargement, since it mainly adds diversity.

Job rotation may not be welcomed by supervisors/administrators who will have to provide training and may experience lower productivity or more errors from employees new to the job. However, this should be less of a problem in rotation programs with longer assignments at each job. Some employees also might resist rotation because they are more comfortable doing the same kind of work and remaining in familiar surroundings. Such employees might still welcome enlargement or enrichment of their own jobs.

Using Teams. Designing work for teams can be done by using the same methods used for individual jobs.[25] Since a number of people will be doing the work, a whole job is the most logical assignment for teams. This will also help build commitment due to perceived significance of the job. Teams should be given substantial responsibility for decision making, scheduling, quality control, and so on, both because there are more people available to share these tasks and because this will help them function as a cohesive unit. However, care should be taken to insure that jobs of all team members are enriched, rather than simply transferring the status quo from an individual work basis to a group work basis.

Team efforts usually include some degree of job rotation among team members, which is determined by the team itself. Therefore, the team should consist of people with a variety of skill levels, both to allow them to perform all tasks necessary and to permit rotation. Unfortunately, employees with higher-level positions who are assigned to teams (e.g., detectives on police teams or doctors on health care teams) may perceive this as a reduction in status and may not work well within the team, causing its overall performance to be less than it could be. This could be avoided by not having too broad a range of positions on any team, or else working closely with the team to build cohesion and dispel negative feelings.

A general advantage of teams is social interaction between group members, which provides a supportive atmosphere for dealing with the new job responsibilities. It also adds peer pressure as a factor influencing individual output, which is beneficial if the team is committed to high levels of performance. It may, therefore, be advisable to employ group incentives to encourage a group norm of high performance.

Regardless of the enrichment approach finally chosen, the change must be well designed. A combined critical analysis/brainstorming approach should generate many creative ideas which will lead to maximizing the amount of enrichment in the redesigned job.

POTENTIAL PROBLEM AREAS

Selecting the Wrong Job. The most serious potential problem for an enrichment program is selecting the wrong job for enrichment. This includes a job that doesn't need enrichment, or one whose employees aren't motivated by higher-level needs, or that has other, more serious problems. It also includes jobs or departments where enrichment will conflict with organizational technology and/or philosophy. Technology, in this case, includes the way work is organized and distributed, as well as equipment. If technology is inflexible or expensive to change, enrichment that requires changes in the way work is done will probably be precluded.

In a similar vein, if considerable importance is placed on adhering to rules and regulations, following lines of authority, and so on, changes involving greater flexibility, less predictability, and redistribution of responsibility to lower levels are likely to be resisted by managerial level personnel. Therefore, both technology and organizational philosophy should be considered before embarking on an enrichment program.

Choosing the wrong job should be avoidable by careful analysis. Problems such as those described above should become apparent in the diagnostic process or the redesign stage. If the kinds of change entailed are strongly incompatible with organizational style, it would probably be wiser to approach productivity improvement from a different perspective.

Another roadblock whose existance should be determined before beginning the redesign process is the presence of regulations or agreements that prevent or limit changes in job content. This includes civil service regulations and/or union contracts limiting the scope of responsibility for a particular job title.

Impact on Other Units. The potential impact of enrichment on other departments or agencies can also present a barrier. This can largely be avoided either in the diagnostic or redesign process by trying to identify all such effects and their seriousness. Modifications can then be made to avoid major negative impacts.

A different kind of side effect occurs because tasks or responsibilities added to one job must be removed from another. This may diminish core dimensions and/or status in the latter. Thus some consideration must be given to effects on equity of workload and job identity of *all* affected jobs during the redesign process. It may be possible to alleviate this problem if jobs reduced in some tasks or responsibilities could be merged with others similarly diminished, or if some could be abolished entirely.

Employee Resistance. Some employees may resist enrichment. As discussed previously, there is some tendency to resist change of any kind. Thus, even employees with strong growth needs may be somewhat resistant at first. Two approaches can help in dealing with employee concerns and/or resistance. Educating them in the objectives of enrichment is one, and including them in the redesign process is the other. In addition, it should be made clear that training and counseling will be provided to help them learn to perform their new assignments.

Another problem that may arise is that employees are likely to expect more pay for doing more work. In some cases, employees have refused to participate in enrichment programs unless additional pay was provided.[26] This problem should be anticipated beforehand so a decision concerning pay policy can be reached in advance of employee demands. From one perspective, it is logical and fair to provide more compensation for expanded duties. This seems particularly appropriate if productivity increases, and especially if this leads to savings from staff reduction. However, this will obviously make the program more expensive. As a result, managers frequently take the perspective that the psychological rewards related to esteem and actualization should be viewed as sufficient compensation for additional work performed.

This is not an easily resolved issue, and the resolution should probably be related to the magnitude of the redesign. Considerable expansion of tasks and/or responsibilities that is not accompanied by a pay increase will be viewed as unfair by employees, and this will probably undermine the beneficial impacts of enrichment. For cases that do not involve major changes in duties, one way of dealing with the pay issue may be to offer an increase only if enrichment results in productivity gains within a specified time period.

Another employee problem may result from supervisors who feel a loss in status and in job functions because their subordinates have increased responsibilities. As noted earlier, a combination of actions should help alleviate this problem. Supervisor participation in the redesign process should help build commitment, while special efforts at communication and education should help them understand and accept the philosophy of enrichment. In addition, they should be given other responsibilities to compensate for any reductions due to enrichment.

A final topic to note here is not really a problem, but it might be viewed as one, especially if it is unanticipated. It is more appropriately viewed as a normal feature of the enrichment process. Since enrichment entails taking on new tasks and/or responsibilities, training must be provided to employees. Because there will be a training and breaking in period, it must be expected that productivity will be lower during these times. These should be considered part of the normal costs of undertaking an enrichment program, as opposed to something that can be avoided or as a problem.

SUMMARY

This chapter has described job enrichment methods that can be employed in a PIP. Enrichment is designed to increase productivity by increasing satisfaction and motivating employees to produce more. Instead of relying

Table 10-6. Summary of Enrichment Methods

METHOD	HOW THE METHOD WORKS
Job Enrichment	Redesigns job to increase core dimensions: diversity, autonomy, wholeness, and feedback.
Job Enlargement	Increases diversity and wholeness by adding additional tasks at same skill level.
Job Rotation	Increases diversity by having employee work at different jobs. These jobs may vary in their content of core dimensions, so additional enrichment factors may also be derived.
Work Teams	Increases all core dimensions for the team as a whole by giving responsibility for a whole job. Overall enrichment may exceed the amount of enrichment experienced by individual team members, however.

on outside rewards, however, it increases aspects of the job that satisfy employee needs for growth and esteem. A summary of enrichment methods is provided in Table 10-6.

Enrichment may be viewed as a job redesign process geared toward increasing the complexity of the job in terms of diversity, task identity, autonomy, and feedback. Alternatives to fully redesigning a job to enrich it include job enlargement (a partial redesign), job rotation and work teams. Enrichment is best accomplished by careful diagnosis of jobs to determine if they can be enriched and if enrichment is *needed,* combined with a participatory redesign process. It is particularly useful for lower-level jobs that are routine and monotonous. It can also be applied to lower-level managerial and professional jobs that have insufficient amounts of motivating factors. However, since enrichment methods are not directly geared toward increasing output, they should not generally be relied upon as the primary method used in an improvement program.

NOTES

1. For a discussion reflective of this perspective, see John R. Hinrichs, *The Motivation Crisis: Winding Down and Turning Off* (New York, AMACOM, 1974), pp. 9-36.
2. The description of job enrichment here relies heavily on J. Richard Hackman, "Designing Work for Individuals and for Groups" in: ed. J. Richard Hackman, Edward E. Lawler III, and Lyman W. Porter. *Perspectives on Behavior in Organizations,* pp. 242-256. New York: McGraw-Hill Book Company 1977 and John M. Greiner et al., *Productivity and Motivation: A Review of State and Local Government Initiatives* (Washington, D.C.: The Urban Institute Press, 1981), pp. 233-238. For further information on job enrichment see, for example, Ramon J. Aldag and Arthur P. Brief, *Task Design and Employee Motivation* (Glenview. Ill.: Scott, Foresman, 1979); J. Richard Hackman and Greg R. Oldham, *Work*

Redesign (Reading, Mass.: Addison-Wesley, 1980); John R. Maher, *New Perspectives in Job Enrichment* (New York: Van Nostrand Reinhold Company, 1971); Richard B. Miller, *Participative Management Quality of Worklife and Job Enrichment* (Park Ridge, N.J.: Noyes Data Corporation, 1977); Lyle Yorks, *A Radical Approach to Job Enrichment* (New York: AMACOM, 1976).

3. National Commission on Productivity and Work Quality, *Employee Incentives to Improve State and Local Government Productivity* (Washington, D.C.: U.S. Government Printing Office, 1975), p. 27.
4. Ibid., p. 39.
5. Greiner, et al., *Productivity and Motivation,* p. 318.
6. National Commission on Productivity, *Employee Incentives,* p. 38.
7. Ibid.
8. Greiner, et al., *Productivity and Motivation,* p. 309.
9. Ibid., pp. 302-305.
10. Ibid., p. 295.
11. National Commission on Productivity, *Employee Incentives,* p. 32.
12. Greiner, et al., *Productivity and Motivation,* pp. 288-290.
13. National Commission on Productivity, *Employee Incentives,* pp. 32-33.
14. Greiner, et al., *Productivity and Motivation,* p. 289.
15. Ibid., pp. 289-291.
16. National Commission on Productivity, *Employee Incentives,* p. 33.
17. Greiner, et al., *Productivity and Motivation,* pp. 245-250.
18. Ibid., pp. 255-256.
19. Material in this section draws heavily on Aldag and Brief, *Task Design,* pp. 59-126 and Hackman, "Designing Work," pp. 246-248.
20. Hackman and Oldham, *Work Redesign,* pp. 275-315.
21. Hackman, "Designing Work," pp. 246-247.
22. Aldag and Brief, *Task Design,* pp. 81-88.
23. For a further discussion of this point see Charles L. Hulin, "Individual Differences and Job Enrichment—The Case Against General Treatments," in: ed. John R. Maher *New Perspectives in Job Enrichment,* (New York: Van Nostrand Reinhold Company, 1971), pp. 159-191.
24. Hackman and Oldham, *Work Redesign,* pp. 152-153.
25. This section relies heavily on Hackman, "Designing Work," pp. 251-255.
26. Greiner, et al., *Productivity and Motivation,* p. 331.

11 IMPROVING PRODUCTIVITY THROUGH GROUP PARTICIPATION: QUALITY CIRCLES, LABOR-MANAGEMENT COMMITTEES, AND TASK FORCES

HOW QUALITY CIRCLES IMPROVE PRODUCTIVITY

Quality circles (also referred to as quality control circles or QC circles), have received considerable attention in the past few years as one of the "Japanese management" techniques associated with impressive gains in product quality and productivity in Japan. Quality circles are an example of an employee participation method that uses a small group format. They involve use of a highly structured approach to organizing and conducting group participation. A brief definition is:

> A quality circle is a group of people who work together, meeting on a voluntary basis to identify, and develop solutions for, problems in their own work unit.

Quality circles are felt to improve productivity in several ways; in particular by increasing motivation. Inviting employees to participate in desision making, and formally considering and acting upon their recommendations, is a way of acknowledging their competence and value. This fulfills some of their esteem needs, and increases motivation and morale. Meeting in groups and working on problem solving increases both job diversity and social contact, which also helps increase motivation. New skills are learned and practiced in the circles, which is an additional factor that increases motivation, self-esteem, and self-actualization. Circle meetings also help create "team spirit."

Quality circles also improve productivity through the identification and solution of workplace problems. Although it is not mandatory that circles work on ways to improve productivity, many of the problems selected are directly or indirectly related to productivity improvement. For example, solving a problem of work bottlenecks or equipment breakdowns, or streamlining the way a job is performed, should directly increase productivity. Solving problems involving employee comfort, morale, or interpersonal relations indirectly helps improve productivity.

The Quality Circle Philosophy. The philosophy inherent in quality circles further explains why they affect motivation and productivity or quality.[1] Quality circles are based on a belief in participation management. This means that management recognizes that the employees performing a job have valuable knowledge about their work. Employees are viewed as being willing and able to contribute usefully to the organization as a whole and to take on responsibilities. They are seen as being capable of growth and development. In short, an important aspect of the quality circle philosophy is to reduce the "we/they" mentality that commonly prevails between managers and employees.

Another key component in the philosophy is that circles are "people building." They not only provide organizational benefits by solving workplace problems, they provide benefits to the people involved in them as well. Training in problem-solving techniques used by circles, as well as in circle operations, is provided. Circle members are expected to help each other master these skills, and to work cooperatively as a team. Creativity is encouraged, and communication skills are developed. Circles also provide an opportunity to take on interesting and challenging work outside of the employee's normal responsibilities. This all leads to enabling participants to develop and use their capabilities more fully.

In addition to fostering individual growth, quality circles also perform a team-building function. Working together in circles generates a sense of commitment to the work group as well as to the overall organization. This is strengthened by the practice of viewing circle recommendations as group efforts, and giving recognition to the circle as a whole. Through the circle process, members learn to cooperate and work together as a team, to communicate more effectively with each other, and to develop better understanding of the perspectives of others. These team skills and attitudes should carry over to improve performance in regular work roles, since circle members are drawn from the same work area and will continue working together outside of circle meetings.

Another important feature of quality circle philosophy is that participation in circles is voluntary. An organization may prepare the foundation for circles to develop, but it is up to the employees as individuals to choose whether or not to participate in them. Since circles are composed of people who work in the same area, a circle for a specific department or work unit can only exist if there is a sufficient number of employees in that unit who are willing to join it. The voluntary nature of quality circles contributes to their effectiveness, since it insures that the people involved in them are really interested and willing to work toward making them successful.

APPLICABILITY OF QUALITY CIRCLES

Although quality circles have been most widely associated with manufacturing industries in both Japan and the United States, they are not limited to that setting. Quality circles have been successfully applied in work situations involving white-collar jobs and direct service-providing jobs. Their use has also been expanded to the public sector. The only limiting factor to their application is that they should be used in situations where people work together in indentifiable work units. The employees in these units do not all have to perform the same type of work, but they must work together to produce that unit's output or service.

APPLYING QUALITY CIRCLES: ROLES AND FUNCTIONS

A brief overview of what quality circles involve will be helpful in understanding their application.[2] As noted above, each circle consists of a group of employees who normally work together in the same work unit (department, division, etc.). Numerous circles can exist within the same organization. Circles may contain from 3 to 15 employees, with about 8 to 10 considered the most appropriate size. Circles generally meet once a week for an hour. Meetings are held as part of the normal workday, not on the employees' own time or on overtime. Circle members select a problem that exists in their work unit for study and solution. They analyze the causes of the problem and identify a workable solution for it. The problem and solution are then described to the organization's management for approval before implementation occurs. If approved, the circle may also carry out the implementation phase if it is within their ability to do so.

Since quality circles are a highly structured approach to employee participation, understanding and setting up the organizational structure is one of the first steps toward implementation. The organization or structure of quality circles is best described in terms of the roles and functions associated with the different parties involved in creating and maintaining quality circles. These are summarized in Table 11-1.

Steering Committee. Once a decision is made to institute quality circles in an organization, a steering committee should be formed to guide and

Table 11-1. Quality Circles: Roles and Functions of Participants

ROLE	FUNCTION
Steering Committee	Guides and coordinates all circles
Facilitators	Implement new circles and provide training. Perform coordinating and supporting role for existing circles.
Leaders	Organize and direct meetings; train members.
Members	Work together to identify, analyze and develop solutions for problems in the work unit.

coordinate the process. In the Productivity Improvement Program (PIP) context, a steering committee would generally be formed at the agency or department level in each participating agency or department. In small cities, a citywide steering committee, operating out of the central PIP office, could be formed instead. The steering committee usually consists of representatives of all major functional areas of the organization (generally chosen from middle- or upper-level management), a union representative (if applicable), and the facilitators (whose role is explained below). A representative from the central PIP office could also sit on the steering committee during the early phases of circle formation and implementation.

One of the major functions of the steering committee is to determine the policies that guide circle operations. Setting policy usually means determining whether circles are to direct their efforts toward specific types of problems (e.g., quality improvement, waste reduction, etc.), and/or determining whether certain topics are "off limits" (e.g., wages and benefits). In general, items covered by union contracts or the civil service are off limits. Other policy decisions may include whether or not to give rewards or other forms of recognition, determining how presentation of circle recommendations should be made, and so on. The committee usually prepares a "policies and procedures" document for the organization. In the PIP context, the central PIP unit may choose to set policies for all circles to insure citywide consistency. An alternative approach would be to determine some policies centrally, while letting department steering committees set others.

In its guiding and coordinating roles, the steering committee arranges for training in quality circle methods necessary for circles to begin operating. It also monitors the progress of existing circles, and plays a troubleshooter role when needed (e.g., by locating outside expertise, if necessary). It evaluates and provides feedback on the performance of the circles. It also helps coordinate and follow up on recommended changes that have been approved by management. The steering committee is responsible for publicizing the circles and their accomplishments within the organization. It is also responsible for program expansion.

Facilitators. Most of the actual work needed to carry out the steering committee's functions is performed by the facilitators. While there is generally only one steering committee in an organization (unless it is extremely large), there can be more than one facilitator. Facilitators are members of the steering committee, and can be viewed as its "action arms." They carry out the work needed to introduce and implement quality circles in the organization. Facilitators are assigned to "facilitate" the efforts of one or more circles, and, therefore, they attend the regular meetings of those circles. Since they also sit on the steering committee, facilitators report back to the committee on how their circles are performing.

In small cities, facilitators could be members of the central PIP staff or other centralized departments (e.g., personnel). They would work with circles in various departments or agencies as needed. In larger cities, it would be more appropriate to select one or more facilitators from the staff of each agency or department that institutes quality circles.

Facilitators are responsible for recruiting and providing training in quality circle processes to circle leaders. This means that facilitators themselves must receive training first. This can be done through attendance at quality circle training programs, or by bringing in consultants. After performing the training function, facilitators work closely with newly created circles and their leaders during the early stages of the circle's existance. Productivity Improvement Program staff members might also work closely with facilitators and steering committees during this stage.

As noted, each facilitator is responsible for facilitating, or supporting, the work of several circles. This involves being available at all circle meetings to provide help and guidance as needed. This also enables facilitators to insure that circles are following appropriate procedures and using analytic techniques correctly. If a circle is not functioning properly, the facilitator should step in to alleviate the difficulty through guidance or counseling, or by providing additional training review sessions, if needed. Facilitators also provide feedback to the circles on their performance on a regular basis.

The facilitator is responsible for providing circles with what they need to help them work on the problem they have chosen to solve. The facilitator may have to identify outside experts and arrange for them to consult with the circle. In some cases, the problem may require arranging meetings between people from other departments within the organization and circle members. If the circle needs information or other resources, the facilitator arranges to obtain them, also. Some of the outside expertise or resources needed may be available from the central PIP staff.

Facilitators also perform administrative and coordination functions. They keep records of circle meetings and keep the steering committee, management (particularly management of the units where circles exist), and the central PIP office, informed about circle progress. They also arrange the scheduling for presentations to management and work on the implementation of changes that receive management approval. Facilitators generally are responsible for promotion and publicity activities (e.g., write the newsletters or memos that provide information on circle activities, plan any circle recognition activities, such as award dinners, etc.), and any further educational activities (e.g., conferences on circles for the organization as a whole). However, if quality circles are part of a PIP where publicity for all improvement efforts is handled centrally, this function could be removed from the facilitator's role, or they might act as publicity liason for the central staff.

The role of the facilitator can vary somewhat in different organizations. In general, the role is a diverse one, requiring that those chosen for it can perform a wide range of activities successfully. Good communication skills and the ability to work well with different types of people are important characteristics for facilitators to have. Experience or skills in providing training is also helpful.

Leaders. The next role in the circle hierarchy is that of the circle leader. Each circle has a leader, who is responsible for conducting (or leading), meetings of that circle. The circle leader is generally the supervisor (or person with similar authority), of the work unit from which the circle originates. Using supervisors as circle leaders allows quality circles to support the normal hierarchy of authority in the organization. Otherwise, circles might be perceived as setting up a competing organizational structure. However, in some organizations the choice is made not to use supervisors as leaders, or to use them only for the first year of circle operation, and then allow circle members to elect the next leader.

The leaders perform functions that are similar to those of the facilitators, but leaders have more immediate responsibility for their circle's operation. The leader should:

- arrange the time and place of meetings
- prepare the agenda
- direct the progress of the meeting (e.g., keep discussion orderly and on the topic at hand)
- make sure that circle procedures are followed and methods are used properly
- encourage participation of all circle members

- discourage monopolization of the meeting by any member(s)
- see that minutes of circle meetings are taken and distributed
- follow-up on progress of projects or assignments
- work with the facilitator (e.g., evaluate circle performance, work on solving problems affecting it)
- generally provide encouragement and support to members

In addition to performing these functions, leaders are usually responsible for recruiting and training circle members (in some organizations, facilitators do this in addition to training leaders).

Although there are many tasks associated with directing or guiding quality circles so they function smoothly and effectively, leaders must perform them without dominating their circles. Thus their training must provide them with skills in communication, leadership, and group dynamics as well as in circle processes and methods.

Members. The final role is that of the circle member. Members are the heart of the quality circle process. They are responsible for doing the work of the circles. The functions they perform are these:

- They attend and participate in circle meetings
- They identify problems in the work unit
- They analyze and develop solutions for the problems selected for study
- They make a presentation to management on the recommended solution
- They help implement the solution

Members are expected to help each other, follow circle guidelines, and work cooperatively to achieve circle objectives.

As noted earlier, circle membership is voluntary; no one should be required to participate in quality circles. If more people want to join a particular work unit's quality circle than is practical, time limits on circle membership can be imposed (e.g., a one-year term) to give more people the opportunity to become members. Those who volunteer to become members receive training in the quality circle concept, processes, and methods before their circle becomes operationalized (or before joining an existing circle).

APPLYING QUALITY CIRCLES: PROCESSES AND METHODS

The above discussion identified the participants in quality circles and their functions. This section will provide more information about what happens in the problem-solving process, the rules that guide the process, and the methods used in it.

Meetings. Circles normally meet on a regular schedule (once a week, for one hour) to encourage members (and others), to regard circle work as an accepted aspect of work life. Circles meet during normal working hours (i.e., on "organization time" rather than after hours or on lunch breaks, etc.). A separate meeting area that provides a "meeting room" atmosphere and removes circle members from workplace distractions is usually designated for circle meetings.

Circle members are expected to attend all meetings; lateness or absenteeism is discouraged. Circle leaders are responsible for working to change the behavior of members who violate these norms. Members are also expected to be active participants and to perform a fair share of work on projects that may be assigned to individuals or subgroups. Leaders and/or facilitators may have to make efforts to encourage greater participation on the part of some members, and/or to limit monopolizing tendancies on the part of others. Such group leadership skills are part of their training.

Circle members usually select a name for their circle at the first meeting. Names, or acronyms, often (but do not have to), reflect the type of work done in that unit, or incorporate unit identity with the problem-solving, productivity, and/or quality-improving nature of circles. While naming a circle may seem to be a trivial point, it serves the same functions as naming a sports team. It helps create an identity for the new circle, which encourages members to feel a sense of "belonging" and commitment to the group. In short, it helps build team spirit. Circle names are also helpful for purposes of publicizing circle accomplishments (e.g., in newsletters, on awards or certificates, etc.).

Problem Selection. The first real task a new circle faces is choosing a problem to "solve." This process also is repeated after each round of problem-solving is completed. There are usually few restrictions on the type of problem circles can choose to work on, which are stipulated in the policy guidelines prepared by the steering committee (e.g., wages, grievance matters, etc.). Circles also cannot select problems in work units other than their own. The organization may suggest that circles work on particular types of problems, such as productivity or quality improvement. In general, however, conventional practice is to allow circles considerable freedom to select problems for study. This may result in some circles dealing with problems that do not appear to be productivity related, such as making the unit's work area more attractive or comfortable, and so on.

Allowing circles to choose their own problem serves important functions, however. It convinces them that management is really committed to employee participation, and that circles can provide benefits for members, not just for the administration. This encourages commitment to the circle process, which should eventually result in selecting problems that are more directly related to productivity. Even those problems that seem to be unrelated to productivity improvement can indirectly affect it by increasing employee morale and job satisfaction.

The first stage of the problem-selection process follows some of the standard procedures for quality circle operations. A long list of potential problems is generated in a circle brainstorming session. The purpose of brainstorming is to maximize the number of ideas generated. To encourage this, all suggestions are accepted without comments, criticism, or evaluation; people may build on previous suggestions; each person speaks in turn, presenting one idea at at time until ideas are exhausted; and interruptions are not allowed.

Ideas generated during brainstorming are recorded on a flip chart or blackboard so they can be referred to during the actual problem-selection process. In this step, the circle must decide which of the many potential problems they will choose to work on at this time (the list can be saved for the next round of problem selection, however). There are different ways to do this. The group may discuss the problems and decide on one by consensus, or by voting. Alternatively, the circle may choose to identify criteria and use a ranking system to select the problem. Criteria commonly used include such issues as ease of solution; potential resistance to change; magnitude of improvement expected; time needed to implement. These can be ranked (e.g., on a scale of 1 to 3 or 1 to 5). If desired, the criteria can be weighted to indicate their relative importance.[3] In some cases, the circle may decide that information gathering is needed to help make the selection (e.g., to identify the most severe and/or frequent problems).

Problem Analysis and Solution. The next stage of circle activity is to analyze the problem selected and agree upon a solution to recommend. This process involves use of most of the analytic methodologies common to quality circles.

Problem analysis typically requires some information gathering to use to determine the magnitude and nature of the problem; to separate real problems from perceived problems; and to help identify the causes of the problem. The types of information commonly collected include: where the problem exists; how often it occurs; variations in problem severity and how often each occurs; conditions related to problem occurence and so on. Such information may be available from records that the organization already keeps, or it may be necessary to take samples of work unit output, or to interview employees, to obtain the necessary data. Circle members volunteer for, and perform, any data collection tasks that are required. Techniques for gathering data, using sampling methods, and displaying statistical information effectively (e.g., preparation of line graphs, histograms, Pareto diagrams), are taught in the quality circle training sessions.

After information is collected, the circle begins analysis of the problem and its causes as a preliminary step to developing solutions. One of the techniques used in this step is Pareto analysis, based on the familiar Pareto "80-20" rule" (e.g., 80% of the mistakes are made by 20% of the workers; 80% of sales are made by 20% of the salespeople, etc.). This is also referred to as the "vital few" and the "trivial many." Pareto analysis uses histograms (bar graphs) combined with a line graph to display how frequently a particular cause is associated with problem occurrance, or to show the relative frequency of particular types of problems.[4]

For example, if the problem under study is errors on application forms in a social service agency, records might be kept for a period of time to indicate which kinds of information contain the errors. A Pareto diagram would use histograms to show what percentage of errors occur in each category of information. Categories are arranged in order of most significant (on the left side of the graph) to least significant (on the right). A line graph imposed on top of the histogram shows the cumulative percentage of the problem accounted for by different combinations of information categories.

A simplified example is provided in Figure 11-1. Five categories of information from the application form are shown. Family income accounts for 50% of the incorrect or missing information, and family size for 25%. In combination, these two types of information account for 75% of all errors on this form, as shown by the line graph. Addresses account for another 15% of errors, and length of residence and social security numbers for 5% each. Use of information gathering and Pareto analysis in this case shows that the problem of errors on application forms is concentrated in two categories. Thus the "real" problem is less widespread than was originally perceived. Pinpointing the nature of the problem in this way is also helpful in designing appropriate solutions.

Another form of analysis commonly used in quality circles is the cause and effect (or "fishbone") diagram.[5] (It is called a fishbone because the basic diagram resembles a fish skeleton.) The diagram shows the problem as the "effect" on the right side of the page. Major categories of potential causes of the problem are listed, generally machinery, materials, methods, and "manpower" (or people). Circle members then brainstorm (following regular brainstorming rules), to fill in potential causes for this problem under each of the major categories.

An example of a simple cause and effect diagram is shown in Figure 11-2.

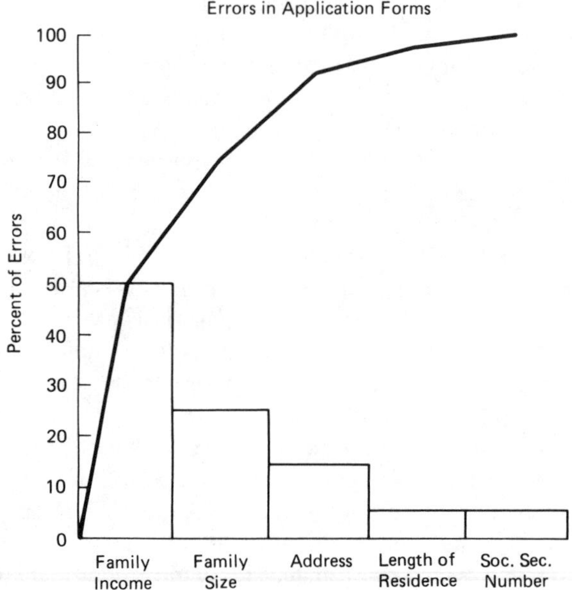

Figure 11-1. Example of Pareto Diagram.

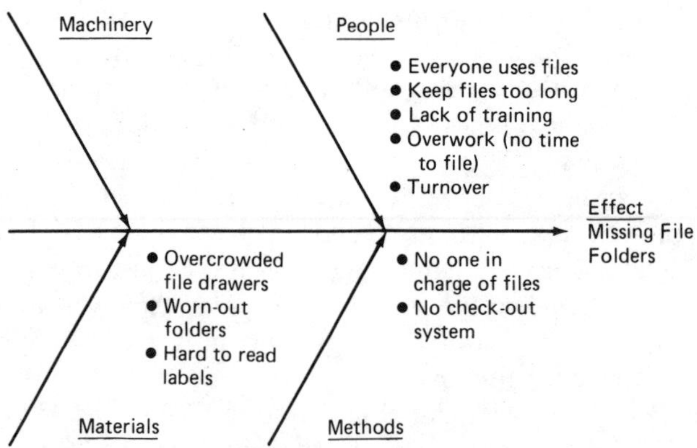

Figure 11-2. Example of Cause and Effect ("Fishbone") Diagram.

In this example, the problem under study is that file folders are not available, or are difficult to locate, when needed. Since machinery is not involved in this case, no causes are listed under that category. Among the possible materials-related problems are overcrowded file drawers, worn out folders, and hard-to-read file headings. Possible problems related to people include:

everyone uses the files; people keep files too long; lack of training in proper filing methods; overwork (lack of time for filing); and high turnover. Under the methods category, probable causes are that no one person is in charge of files, and there is no check-out system for them.

The goal of cause-and-effect analysis is to generate as many probable causes of the problem as possible. These causes are then critically discussed by the group to identify those that seem most likely to be the real causes. An alternative approach is to have members vote for the causes they think are most likely to be responsible for the problem. Once the list is narrowed down to a small number of causes, circle members decide how to verify which causes are really creating the problem. Verification may require information gathering of different kinds (e.g., observation of work practices, interviews, etc.), to single out the major cause or causes of the problem.

After using Pareto analysis and/or cause and effect diagrams to determine the nature and cause of the problem, the circle is ready to develop a solution to it. Brainstorming is used again to generate as many potential solutions as possible. The list is narrowed through a series of group discussions on the potential effectiveness of the solutions and the feasibility of implementing them. Under the latter heading, circles consider costs of implementation, impacts on the way work is done, effects on employees, management reaction, and any other potential restraining factors. In short, the circle carefully considers the relative pros and cons of each solution before making a final selection. Where appropriate, a "test run" of the proposed solution should be made to be sure that it works.

Management Presentation. After the circle has agreed upon the solution to their problem, the next step is a presentation to management to recommend adoption of their suggestion. The management presentation is treated as a formal, and important, event by quality circles. Management is not required to accept all recommendations, so the circle must present a convincing case for their solution to "sell" it.

Circle members generally present the information they have gathered and the analysis they have performed (e.g. Pareto analysis, cause and effect diagrams), as part of the presentation. They describe their recommended solution and the reasons why they are recommending it. As a rule, portions of the presentation are given by different circle members, rather than using a single spokesperson to make the entire presentation. Circles often use one or more meetings to prepare materials and rehearse their presentations.

Presentations are not important just because they are where solutions are accepted or rejected, but because they provide an opportunity for recognition of the circles and their work. Management seriously listens to, discusses, and considers for adoption, the ideas of its employees. This alone is an important way of recognizing employee capabilities. It is also used as an opportunity to publicly praise circle members for their efforts and, hopefully, to accept their recommendations. Thus presentations are an occasion for considerably increasing the self-esteem of circle members.

Solution Implementation. The final stage of the quality circle problem-solving process is to implement the proposed solution. The degree of circle involvement in this process varies according to what is involved in the solution. For example, if the solution requires purchasing and using different kinds of equipment or supplies, there is not much room for involvement of circle members. If the solution requires using a new method that the circle designed (e.g., a "check-out" system for file folders so those that are removed from the files can be located by other staff members who need them), then circle members should explain the process to other employees in the work unit and help perform whatever implementation steps are needed.

IMPLEMENTING AND MAINTAINING QUALITY CIRCLES

Since quality circles are voluntary, their implementation primarily involves making the option of joining circles available and encouraging participation in them. This section will describe major aspects of implementation and maintenance of quality circles.

Preliminary Steps. Once it is decided to implement quality circles in a particular department or agency, one of the first steps necessary is to create the steering committee to guide the process. The steering committee must also determine the operating policies or guidelines for the circles at this stage. As noted earlier, the steering committee could be operationalized at the citywide level in smaller cities. However, it is more common for the steering committee to be part of the agency or department that is implementing quality circles.

The committee then seeks volunteers for the role of facilitator, and selects one or more persons with the qualities needed to perform the varied functions associated with this role (described perviously). Enthusiasm for, and commitment to, the quality circle concept should be an important characteristic of the facilitator. The steering committee must then arrange for quality circle training to take place. The central PIP staff should work with (or be available to assist), the departmental committees in performing these steps.

Training. Since circles follow a standardized set of procedures, and use specific analytic methods, training in these procedures and methods is the most important aspect of implementation. As noted above, many of the participants in the circle process are responsible for training those below them in the circle hierarchy. The initial training program that starts the process is for facilitators. One or more should be trained, depending on organization size and how many circles are expected to be operationalized. More facilitators than are needed initially can be trained in anticipation of creating additional circles in the relatively near future.

Facilitators can be sent to training programs offered by consultants, associations, universities, or other organizations or government units that operate training programs for their own circles and for "outsiders." Alternatively, consultants can be brought in to do the training. Large organizations often develop their own centralized training programs. The central PIP office might offer facilitator training for all city departments or agencies. (Of course, before this can be done, those in charge of in-house training must receive training themselves, unless new people are hired to do this.) Training facilitators usually involves a three- or four-day program. Some programs are designed to train circle leaders at the same time as facilitators.

After facilitators have been trained, they generally perform the training for circle leaders (who are the supervisors of the various work units). This training is typically covered in one day (eight hours). Some organizations provide additional training sessions for leaders periodically (e.g., quarterly), on topics such as communication skills, group dynamics, and leadership skills. Regular luncheons featuring outside speakers discussing different aspects of quality circle leadership and operations can also serve to further enhance the skills of circle leaders.[6]

After circle leaders have received their basic training, they can seek volunteers for quality circle membership and training in their work units. Volunteer solicitation is usually done by providing information on quality circles and asking interested employees to volunteer. This can be done by making brief presentations to all employees or to individual work units; by sending informational materials to all employees; or by having supervisors individually contact employees in their work units. Once circle members have been selected, circle leaders (under supervision of the facilitators), provide a training program of approximately eight hours duration. This can be divided into weekly, hour-long sessions (in effect, the first eight meetings of the circle), two half-days, or as a full-day program.

In addition to providing training for circle participants, sometimes training is provided for middle and top management as well. This is primarily informational in nature and is designed to minimize concerns and build support for the quality circle program. This type of program is generally brief (one to four hours), and can be provided by outside consultants or by the facilitators after their training is completed.

Pilot Projects. It is always advisable to introduce any kind of organizational change on a "pilot project" basis. Quality circles are no exception to this rule. Fortunately, they are particularly suitable to this kind of introduction. Since the circles in the various work units function independently, there is no need to launch them all at the same time. The gradual addition of new circles can be controlled by phasing the recruitment and training of circle leaders and members in the various work units. As is usually the case, the areas chosen for pilot projects should be those that are most likely to be successful. Thus, work units where the employees are enthusiastic about the idea, and where the supervisor (who will be the circle leader), is supportive of employee participation and the quality circle concept, and has the qualifications for circle leadership, should be selected.

A phased introduction can also help circles function better. Since facilitators would be responsible for fewer circles, they can give more time and attention to each circle, and are more likely to discover and deal with any problems in their early stages. This increases the likelihood that the circles will get off to a smoother start and their members will learn circle methods and procedures more thoroughly. As a result, circles are likely to function better during their future operations as well. It is also useful to encourage circles to be careful about selection of the first problems they work on. Choosing an overly difficult or controversial problem increases the amount of work needed, and reduces the likelihood of success. It is better to start fairly small, and let successful resolution of the initial problem build member confidence, as well as skills. Harder problems can be tackled with greater chance of success after circles have had some experience with easier ones. This could be viewed as a kind of phased introduction to problems in each circle that is consistent with the overall phased introduction of quality circles.

Publicity. Publicizing the various productivity improvement efforts of different departments or agencies (and their successes), has already been mentioned as a normal component of the PIP. Publicity is also regarded as one of the regular processes of quality circle operations. Publicity is obviously needed during the introductory stage, to help familiarize people with the concept of quality circles and how they will be operationalized in that organization, and to generate enthusiasm (and volunteers), for them. This kind of introductory publicity can include distribution of informational materials and letters to all employees, and/or meetings in various departments or divisions to introduce the quality circle concept and answer any questions about it.

Publicity does not end once the first circles are operationalized, however. It is treated as an on-going aspect of the quality circle process. Publicity is viewed as one of the forms of recognition that circle members receive that helps build their self-esteem (and their motivation). It also maintains general interest in quality circles by keeping everyone informed about their activities and accomplishments. This can help generate interest in work units where circles are not in operation, which can pave the way for expansion of circles into those units. Publicity can also help spread ideas about problems to work on, or successful solutions to common problems. The kind of continuing publicity described above is typically handled in a newsletter format (often on a monthly basis), which provides brief updates on each circle's activities.

In addition to printed publicity, other forms of recognition for quality circles are fairly common. Some organizations hold annual award dinners (or similar events), for all circle members. Specific forms of recognition are sometimes given to members of circles that made particularly impressive contributions (these can range from token prizes to more substantial gifts or cash awards). Some organizations choose to give some tangible form of recognition to everyone involved in circles (e.g., certificates, plaques, or T-shirts).

Since there is usually a substantial amount of publicity associated with quality circles, it is probably best to handle it separately from the other publicity activities of the PIP, although circle activities should also be included in general PIP publicity. The steering committee for each department or agency that has a circle program can name a publicity committee (or person), to publish quality circle newsletters for that department or agency. These newsletters can also be sent to the central PIP staff, who can use them as the basis for QC updates in the more broadly focused (and circulated) PIP newsletter (or whatever type of publication is used). Thus, more intensive publicity should be directed at organizations involved in the quality circle process, and less at those that are not.

Potential Problem Areas. Because of their voluntary nature, quality circles are not generally regarded as presenting major problems. Employees who do not want to be involved do not have to participate. This eliminates one of the serious problem areas associated with other improvement methods. Union resistance should also be avoidable, both because of the voluntary nature of circles, and because circle policies can be written to insure that they do not deal with issues that are union perogatives (or that unions feel sensitive about). Inclusion of a union representative on the steering committee should also serve to alleviate potential resistance.

Lack of acceptance of quality circles by some managers may arise. Quality circles are based on belief in the value of greater employee participation. This is not always compatible with the management style or beliefs of some managers. Efforts should be made to educate all members of the organization's management about the philosophies that underlie quality circles, how they work, and the benefits associated with them. (This is a normal part of the training program in most organizations.) Open support by top management will also help build support among lower-level mangers. Circles should not be introduced into areas where managers are hostile toward them. Members of the steering committee might also work on educating such managers; for example, by inviting them to attend circle meetings to get a better understanding of how they work and to witness member enthusiasm, or to attend a presentation of circle recommendations to management to see the value of the process for problem solving.

Another potential problem area is lack of a sufficient number of circles so that all who want to participate can do so. This can be handled by limiting the duration of circle membership (e.g., to a one-year term), so more people can be involved.

Removing employees from their normal workplace for an hour each week may also create problems. This may leave the work unit understaffed, or create resentment amongst employees who are not part of the circle, but who may have to work harder to cover for circle members during their meetings. Therefore, circle meetings should be scheduled at a time that will cause the least hardship for employees remaining in the work unit. Efforts to alleviate potential resentment can be made during the introductory stage by emphasizing that circles benefit the whole organization, not just circle members, and recognizing that the support of nonmembers is also needed for circle success. Appreciation for this kind of support should also be expressed periodically in publicity materials and, of course, personally by circle members to their co-workers.

A final potential problem area is generating overly high expectations of quality circles.[7] No productivity improvement method is a panacea, and quality circles are no exception. All problems that circles choose to work on will not make major contributions to productivity improvement. Some may not affect productivity at all, and circles do not always come up with successful resolutions to the problems they select. Sometimes circles fail to function properly and are disbanded. These problems should be recognized in the introduction and training sessions, even though the emphasis will, naturally, be on QC successes and achievements. It should also be made clear that circle achievements should not be expected in the short run, but that they represent a long-run commitment to participative management.

QUALITY CIRCLE EXAMPLES

Quality circles have been used in the public sector for only a relatively short period of time. Therefore, not many examples of their accomplishments have been reported. One quality circle program that has been widely publicized was initiated at the Norfolk Naval Shipyard in 1979. It began as a pilot program with nine circles in work units such as production, supply, and maintenance. Examples of some improvements attributed to these circles include:[8]

Revision of tool distribution. Workers had to wait at different locations to obtain different types of tools. The circle analyzing this problem found the average wait was 12 minutes. The distribution process was changed so *all* tools could be obtained at all tool dispensing locations. Waiting time fell to 5 minutes. This was estimated as a savings of $200,000 (based on average hourly wages).

Reduction of unnecessary activity. Workers often had to make numerous trips transporting tools and equipment. One circle designed and built tool carts to carry more items at one time and reduce total trips. Savings were estimated at $1,500.

Developing work methods. One circle revised procedures for moving electrical substations. The change halved the time needed to move them, leading to annual savings of $10,700.

In-house production. Instead of buying a particular part from outside vendors, one group manufactured their own at an annual savings of $6,000.

Quality circles have been applied in various hospital settings. One example from the Brown County (Wisconsin) Mental Health Center involved a circle dealing with the problem of staff time wasted looking for misplaced or missing patient charts. The circle's analysis indicated that staff time spent looking for the charts amounted to an average $66.12-worth of employee time per day. The recommended solution was to install a $12 sign-out chart so staff members could determine who had the patient charts they needed. This proposal was accepted. A follow-up study six months later indicated that time spent looking for charts had decreased to $11.07-worth of time per day.[9]

Another example of recent adoption of quality circles is from District 8 of the Illinois Department of Transportation.[10] (which covers 10 counties in southwestern Illinois). The district office has a wide variety of responsibilities, including highway design, construction, maintenance, and so on. In recent years, the office has faced problems of shrinking budgets and growing morale problems (indicated by high levels of suspensions and grievances). The district implemented a quality circle program, which helped reduce employee dissatisfaction and behavior problems. Suspensions decreased from an average of 27 per year to 9 in the year after circles were introduced; grievances dropped from an average of 30 to 12 (leading to a cost savings of about $5,400).

District employees have approached problem solving seriously, and many of their suggestions have been adopted. For example, one circle designed and fabricated a tractor broom to replace manual labor that had been used to remove fly ash from bridges and intersections after snowstorms. This resulted in a $7,000 savings in labor costs. Approximately 15 other equipment items have been developed by the circles, including a "tire jack" to carry on the 60 tractors/mowers so that flat tires can be repaired without waiting for tire-changing equipment to be brought to the disabled vehicles in the field. Typically an hour or more was lost waiting for equipment for each flat tire, with about 10 flats per day occurring in the mowing season. With the new jack, repairs take about 15 minutes, leading to estimated time savings of 1350 hours in the mowing season.

Circle members also suggested organizing tool bins and color-coding tools to increase efficiency when gathering tools and equipment at the start of each work day. As a result, time spent on this decreased from about 25-30 minutes per crew to about 10 minutes. The 15-minute savings, multiplied by the number of employees and workdays involved, results in 6.8 labor years "saved" over a one-year period by getting work crews on the road more quickly.

HOW LABOR-MANAGEMENT COMMITTEES AND TASK FORCES IMPROVE PRODUCTIVITY

Labor-management committees and task forces are grouped together here because they are similar in structure and functions.[11] They also differ from quality circles in some important aspects. They do not adhere to a strictly defined organizational structure, with specified roles and functions, and they do not require use of stipulated procedures and methods to perform their functions.

Despite their operational differences, labor-management committees and task forces are philosophically similar to quality circles for several reasons. First, they use the same approach to improving productivity: improving employee morale, self-esteem, and motivation through increased participation. Second, they use a small group format to utilize employee expertise to help solve workplace problems. The problems involved may be (but are not necessarily), directly related to productivity improvement. Finally, as is true of quality circles, the format of small groups working on problem-solving increases job diversity, employee skills, and social contact, which leads to greater employee satisfaction and motivation.

APPLICABILITY OF COMMITTEES AND TASK FORCES

Like quality circles, these two types of group participation can be used in any kind of work setting. They have a longer history of use in the United States than quality circles, and have been employed successfully in the public sector. They are not restricted to situations where people work together in identifiable work units. In fact, they are frequently organizationwide in scope and/or composition.

APPLYING COMMITTEES AND TASK FORCES

Both of these kinds of participation can be characterized as follows:

Groups are formed to study, and seek to resolve, issues or problems. These problems frequently affect, or occur in, the entire organization, rather than a single work unit.

Group meetings are held away from normal work activities, and usually follow a regular schedule (e.g., one hour per week, or less often).

Groups can be organized at the agency or department level, at a subunit level, or at the citywide level.

Groups lack the power to enact their decisions, which are in the form of recommendations.

Membership is voluntary, and may require election.

Sometimes training in how to function as a group and/or in aspects of the specific problem area(s) under study is provided.

Although they are similar in the above respects, labor-management committees and task forces differ in their longevity and subject matter. Labor-management committees are on-going groups that meet on a regular basis to discuss current problems or whatever issues the members decide should receive group attention. In this sense, they are quite similar to quality circles. As their name implies, these committees include members from managerial ranks as well as employees. Union representatives can also be included on them.

Task forces differ in that the group is formed to study a particular problem or issue and make a recommendation for action. It is usually disbanded after its function has been served. The task force does not generally select the problem it studies; it is usually identified by management before the task force is created to study it. The kind of topic that could be the focus of study is largely unrestricted, and may or may not be closely related to factors affecting productivity. However, with the growing interest in productivity, at least some task forces are focusing on ways to improve productivity.

EXAMPLES OF COMMITTEES AND TASK FORCES

This section will provide examples of labor-management committees and task forces in the public sector to illustrate the various ways they can be used.

As of 1978, at least 40 state and local governments were using joint labor-management committees.[12] Many of these focused on safety-related issues. For example, a committee in the repair and maintenance shop in the Washington, D.C., Department of General Services has studied a variety of hazardous situations, resulting in gradual introduction of safety equipment (e.g., first-aid kits, safety shoes, helmets) or related improvements (better lighting, removal of fire hazards).[13] In Memphis, Tennessee, joint committees in several departments also focused on health and safety, suggesting changes such as including fire extinguishers on rolling equipment. These committees also investigate accidents in their departments.[14]

In Washington, D.C., the committee in the Water Services Division also is largely concerned with safety and welfare, but they focused on a topic not usually handled by such groups: alcoholism. Although employees could be suspended for drinking, the committee recognized this was not a solution to the problem. The committee devised a plan where union representatives deal with problem drinkers on an individual basis, and a supervisor is assigned to bring them to Alcoholics Anonymous meetings.[15] While it is difficult to appraise the effects of programs such as these, the government units and committees involved appear satisfied with them.

Committees also might focus on productivity improvement issues. This was true of transit worker committees in New York City. An example of a productivity improvement resulting from committee suggestions concerns bus maintenance. Prior to the suggestion, major maintenance problems on buses (e.g., suspensions, brakes) were done on a piecemeal basis as needed. The committee decided that a particular group of "heavy duty" jobs should be performed at one time after 35,000 miles. The work involves 56 hours, whereas it would take 114 hours if done on a piecemeal basis. In addition to the saving in maintenance time, road failures decreased 58% because of this revision.[16]

In Springfield, Ohio, one committee goal was to improve the quality of work life. Committees were organized in a two-tier system, with minicommittees in each department plus a central committee. A variety of quality of work life efforts resulted. The public works department initiated a newsletter to improve department communications. The refuse division established a team approach to refuse collection, with rotation between the jobs of drivers and collectors. In addition, several training programs were organized which allow employees to do more diverse tasks and possibly move to higher job classifications.[17]

As of 1978, task forces were reported in use in 29 state or local governments. Some were formed with very specific goals. For example, the task force in Austin, Texas, was formed to develop performance appraisal procedures; the one in Forsyth County, North Carolina, to identify sources of federal funds; the one in Little Rock, Arkansas, to design and administer an employee survey and to respond to problems it identified.[18]

Other task forces have been designed to be more ambitious in scope. In New Jersey, the state Department of Labor and Industry created 23 problem-solving teams and 10 subcommittees to deal with a variety of personnel issues. The suggestions made by these groups have been viewed positively. For example, a problem-oriented team studying overdue and inaccurate reports from unemployment compensation offices recommended more training for office personnel. This was enacted, resulting in a 70% reduction in time spent checking reports and a 50% reduction in overdue reports. The 10 subcommittees made a total of 123 recommendations, 84 of which were accepted for implementation.[19]

Another large-scale approach to task forces was put into operation in Reading, Pennsylvania. A Municipal Management Corps was formed, including supervisory and nonsupervisory employees who would serve as sources of ideas concerning problems in interdepartmental relations, personnel, and financial administration. Some of the suggestions that have been implemented include a reorganization of the city's accounting office and inclusion of the capital improvements program with the regular budget, and adoption of personnel evaluation and discipline systems.[20]

IMPLEMENTING COMMITTEES AND TASK FORCES

Since these two forms of group participation are not as structured and formalized as quality circles are, their implementation does not follow a standard procedure of selecting people for particular roles and training them in specified processes and methods. In fact, there are no formal guidelines for implementing labor-management committees or task forces. However, many of the steps described for implementing quality circles are applicable, particularly in organizations that are forming several labor-management committees or task forces. That is:

The formation of the committee or task force should be announced, and its functions explained.

Volunteers should be sought, and training sessions provided, if desired (e.g., on working in groups, or on problem-solving methods).

Group leaders may be selected by management or elected by their group.

If there are to be a number of committees or task forces, pilot projects can be used to introduce the concept.

As a rule, the efforts of labor-management committees or task forces are not highly publicized. In the context of a larger PIP effort, they would receive as much publicity as any other improvement methods used, but would not have their own newsletters, and so on, as is usually the case for quality circles.

Most of the same potential problem areas discussed under quality circles are potential problems for committees or task forces as well. That is, some managers do not readily accept more participation on the part of employees (which may be handled by educating them in the benefits of group participation, and by locating groups in areas with receptive managers); unions may be resistant (although committees and task forces, like quality circles, should avoid issues that are viewed as union matters); lack of sufficient opportunities for all employees to participate (which can be handled by limiting duration of service); and possible disruption of work, or resentment by other employees, because group members leave their work units to attend meetings (careful scheduling and recognition of cooperation may alleviate this problem).

A potential problem area that may occur with task forces or labor-management committees that do not select their own problems is the nature of the problem the group works on. This can be problematic for two different reasons. First, the problem chosen may not motivate employees. In general, problems must meet two criteria to do this. They must be seen as being significant. If issues chosen for group participation are trivial, employees will see this as a lack of commitment on the part of management and will be dissatisfied rather than motivated. Second, the issues should impact the working lives of employees themselves, not just the overall organization. An example of a failure to meet the second criterion comes from New York City, where labor-management committees were established during the fiscal crisis to find ways to save money to finance cost-of-living increases. Employees were dissatisfied because they felt the program was not geared toward really generating their input or improving job satisfaction.[21]

The other possible problem related to choice of subject matter is that it might be perceived as being too difficult. The employee members of the Reading Municipal Management Corps all eventually resigned because they felt the tasks assigned were too difficult.[22] Thus care must be taken not to present problems that are too challenging, especially in the early stages of the program. Of course, this problem can be resolved by letting groups select their own problems, but that solution is generally not applicable to task forces.

SUMMARY

This chapter has reviewed two methods that seek to improve productivity through increased participation. They use a similar format: small groups of employees working together to solve workplace problems. Quality circles, however, require a more formalized, structured approach to organization, processes, and problem-solving methods than labor-management committees or task forces.

These methods all improve productivity by satisfying the higher level motivators of employees, thus increasing satisfaction and motivation. In this way they are similar to job enrichment. However, they differ from enrichment because they do not alter job content or work format. Instead, they rely on increased participation, use of problem-solving skills, diversity, and social contact in the small-group, problem-solving meetings, to satisfy these needs. Because of their more structured approach to problem solving (i.e., use of specified analytic methods), quality circles generally provide greater opportunities for skill development than most committees or task forces.

Participation in circles, committees or task forces is voluntary. This is advantageous, since the employees that volunteer are likely to do so because they feel a need for the kind of participation and fulfillment of higher-level needs that these methods provide. Therefore, these methods are likely to be successful in motivating them. Quality circles usually provide more opportunities for participation, since they can be created in any work units that have a sufficient number of volunteer participants. Labor-management committees and task forces are not usually present in large numbers, and may only be operated at an organization-wide level. Thus they provide fewer opportunities for participation.

Although employee participation is the primary avenue for productivity improvement in these methods, the solutions the groups design for workplace problems may also affect productivity. Since not all problems chosen will be directly related to productivity, one cannot expect improvements to consistently stem from the solutions themselves. Groups can be encouraged to focus their attention on problems related to productivity, however, thus increasing the potential effect of these methods on productivity improvement. Thus these group participation approaches might be viewed as "combination" improvement methods, since they can impact productivity in two ways.

Since the forms of increased participation described in this chapter are voluntary, it is not clear how much participation and/or productivity improvement they are likely to generate in any organizational setting. Therefore, it is probably best to use them in conjunction with other improvement methods in the PIP context.

NOTES

1. Based on Robert E. Callahan, "Quality Circles: A Program for Productivity Improvement through Human Resources Development" in: *Management by Japanese Systems,* ed. Sang M. Lee and Gary Schwendeman, (New York: Praeger Publishers, 1982), pp. 80-82, and Sud Ingle, *Quality Circles Master Guide* (Englewood Cliffs, N.J., Prentice-Hall, 1982), pp. 4-6.

2. Material on quality circles is based on: Ralph Barra, *Putting Quality Circles to Work* (New York: McGraw-Hill Book Company, 1983); Callahan, "Quality Circles Program"; Donald L. Dewar, *The Quality Circle Guide to Participative Management* (Englewood Cliffs, N.J.: Prentice-Hall, 1982); Ingle, *Master Guide;* Robert I. Patchin, *The Management and Maintenance of Quality Circles* (Homewood, I11.: Dow Jones-Irwin, 1983).
3. For an example of a system using ranking and weights, see: Barra, *Putting Circles to Work,* pp. 87-88.
4. For more detailed descriptions of Pareto analysis, see: Barra, *Putting Circles to Work,* pp. 175-177, and Ingle, *Master Guide,* pp. 107-109.
5. For more detailed descriptions of cause and effect diagrams, see: Barra, *Putting Circles to Work,* pp. 173-175; Dewar, *Quality Circle Guide,* pp. 383-391; Ingle, *Master Guide,* pp. 110-112.
6. Ingle, *Master Guide,* p. 153.
7. John D. Blair, Stanley Cohen, and Jerome V. Hurwitz, "Quality Circles: Practical Considerations for Public Managers," *Public Productivity Review* 6 (March/June 1982): 16-17.
8. Stephen Bryant and Joseph Kearns, "Workers Brains as Well as Their Bodies: Quality Circles in a Federal Facility," *Public Administration Review* 42 (March/April 1982): 147-148.
9. Leah Abrahams, "Evaluating Quality Circles in an Inpatient Facility." Paper presented at the annual meeting of the Evaluation Research Society, Chicago, Illinois, October 20, 1983, pp. 3-4.
10. Edward J. Harrick, Unpublished Notes, Personal Files of Edward J. Harrick, Department of Management, Southern Illinois University at Edwardsville, Edwardsville, Illinois.
11. Material in this section relies heavily on John M. Greiner, et al., *Productivity and Motivation: A Review of State and Local Government Initiatives* (Washington, D.C: The Urban Institute Press, 1981), pp. 259-284.
12. Ibid., p. 242.
13. National Center for Productivity and Quality of Working Life, *Labor-Management Committees in the Public Sector: Experiences of Eight Committees* (Washington, D.C., 1975), p. 7.
14. Ibid., pp. 42-43.
15. Ibid., pp. 48-49.
16. Ibid., p. 18.
17. National Center for Productivity and Quality of Working Life, *Recent Initiatives in Labor-Management Cooperation,* Vol. 2 (Washington, D.C.: U.S. Government Printing Office, 1978), pp. 53-59.
18. Greiner, et al., *Productivity and Motivation,* p. 259.
19. Ibid., pp. 261-263.
20. Ibid., pp. 261-262.
21. Greiner, et al., *Productivity and Motivation,* p. 274.
22. Ibid., p. 264.

12
IMPROVING PRODUCTIVITY THROUGH INDIVIDUAL PARTICIPATION: MANAGEMENT BY OBJECTIVES AND FLEXTIME

This chapter continues the theme introduced in the previous chapter: use of increased employee participation to improve productivity. The two methods to be described here, management by objectives (MBO) and flextime, differ from those discussed in chapter 11 in several ways. First, they involve participation by individuals, rather than groups. Second, participation is not voluntary. Finally, the focus of the participation differs from the problem-solving orientation of group participation. However, like group participation, these two methods can be viewed as combination improvement methods, since their impact on productivity does not come solely from the increase in participation.

HOW MBO IMPROVES PRODUCTIVITY

Management by objectives, like group participation, is based on belief in participative management, the value of employee input, and the ability of employees to take on additional responsibilities.[1] This is demonstrated in MBO by employee participation in setting their own work objectives. This recognition of employee competence, combined with participation in the objective-setting process, helps fulfill the employee's higher-level needs, thus increasing motivation.

Increasing motivation through participation is not the only way MBO affects productivity. Setting work objectives also leads to increased productivity. Establishing targets helps guide employee work effort, thus making it more concentrated and efficient than undirected efforts.[2] Since employees choose their own targets, they will be more committed to achieving them than if targets were unilaterally imposed by management. This commitment also can help increase productivity.

APPLYING MBO

Management by objectives is a process that takes place between a manager or supervisor and a subordinate employee, who is frequently also at the managerial or supervisory level.[3] Management by objectives sometimes involves a group of employees rather than an individual if work is done by teams, and involves so much interdependence that individual goals are not a really meaningful concept. However, individual participation is more common, and will be the focus of discussion here.

The goal of the MBO process is to reach agreement about the work objectives or targets of the subordinate employee for the immediate future (goals are typically set on a yearly basis), and on the actions that will be taken to reach those objectives. The latter is, in effect, a plan for reaching the objectives. Agreement on the objectives and plan for action is reached through a participatory process in which the employee is expected to provide much of the input.

Later stages of the MBO process include feedback to determine whether the plan is being followed and/or whether goals were achieved. There are usually two levels to the feedback or evaluation process: periodic "progress reports" or performance reviews, and a year-end evaluation. The former might result in goal modification if it appears the original goal was set unrealistically high or low; intervening factors have affected the ability to reach goals; or other goals have become more important. The year-end review is typically the employee's annual evaluation, and may be related to pay raises or promotions in addition to assessment of MBO goal attainment.

Organizational Objectives. Although setting objectives by and for individual employees is a major aspect of MBO, it does not occur in a vacuum. The objectives of the individual employees must fit into, and contribute to reaching, the goals of the entire organization. Objective setting, and plans for reaching objectives, are best viewed in terms of a hierarchy.[4] Objectives for the whole organization (e.g., the department or agency), are determined first. Objectives of the units at the highest organizational levels (e.g., divisions, sections, departments), are determined next. These should contribute to the broader organizational goals.

This process continues down the organizational hierarchy. Objectives and plans of work units within a given section or division should conform with the objectives of that section. At the lowest level, the objectives set by each employee should reflect his/her contribution to the objectives of his/her work unit. The result of this process is that objective-setting at each level has been guided by the objectives set at all levels above it. Thus the employee's objectives contribute to those of the work unit; which contribute to those of the section; which contribute to those of the division; which contribute to the objectives of the entire agency or department.

Participation in the objective-setting process at each level does not have to be restricted to employees at that level. A team approach to goal setting is recommended, particularly for higher levels of the organization.[5] This approach means managers at lower levels of the organization participate in setting objectives at the organization level above them. The "team" consists of managers from the organization level for which objectives are to be set and managers from the level directly below that.

The team approach is used to keep participation at lower levels of the organization meaningful. Without these kinds of teams, a "top down" approach would dominate, with lower level managers simply comforming to the objectives set at higher levels, rather than participating in setting them. Teams are used not only to increase participation opportunities, but to help set better objectives. Since work units at lower levels in the organization are responsible for carrying out the plans to reach the objectives, it is logical that managers at lower levels have input into setting the objectives and making the plans. The team approach to goal setting means that a manager at a given organization level participates in objective setting twice: for his/her own level, *and* for the level above that.

Setting Objectives. Before objectives can be set, two preliminary steps are recommended.[6] The first of these is to identify (or articulate), the role or mission of the organizational unit. This is usually based on the roles and missions statement for the organization as a whole. The purpose of identifying roles or missions is to create a starting point for generating objectives.

The second preliminary step is to identify "key results" areas. These are, in effect, priority areas where managers are expected to concentrate their attention. They are often determined at the top organization level to guide objective setting at lower levels. Lower-level managers are generally expected to include any key results concerns that are relevant to their work unit in their list of objectives. Key results areas can be externally or internally oriented; that is, they can be explicitly related to services provided to the public or other departments, such as improving service quality or response time. Or, they can focus on internal matters such as productivity, cost, staff development, turnover, and so on. Higher level managers may also choose to identify indicators for key results areas in advance. Indicators identify how key results are to be measured. For example, productivity could be measured by output/input ratios: staff morale by turnover and absenteeism figures, and so on.

Once roles and missions and key results areas have been identified, objectives can be set. Since objectives are the main concern of MBO, it is important to pay attention to the type of objectives established in the process. In order to be most useful in terms of guiding behavior and motivating employees, objectives should be:[7]

Clear and specific. Objectives expressed in vague or subjective terms; for example, "improve performance," "respond in shortest possible time," are not useful in directing action.

Realistic. This means they must be achievable in relation to the responsibilities of the employee and the resources available to reach them. However, they should not be too easy. Harder objectives are more motivating than easy ones, as long as they are not so difficult as to be unattainable.

Compatible with other organizational goals. The objectives of any one person or unit must fit into a hierarchy of goals established for the entire department or agency.

Measurable (or otherwise verifiable). This is necessary in order to both guide action and provide feedback.

Prioritized. Employees should explicitly determine which of their goals are most important.

Typical objectives might be expressed in terms of amount of work or activities to be performed (e.g., to process 100 cases per week); in terms of effectiveness (e.g., to place 50 applicants in jobs per month); in terms of quality (e.g., an error rate of less than 3%); or in terms of projected completion dates or cost targets. Some combination of all of these types of goals is likely to be found in the average MBO-generated list of objectives.

Plans and Controls. Setting objectives is important because they represent the desired achievements of work units or employees. However, objective statements alone are not sufficient because they do not specify *how* objectives are to be reached. The means for attaining each objective are spelled out in plans that should be developed by the same people involved in setting the objectives. These plans might be referred to as action plans or implementation plans.

Designing action plans requires practicing many of the responsibilities generally attributed to management: planning, programming, scheduling, allocating resources, and organizing. These are applied after objectives have been determined in specific, measurable terms (e.g., to increase productivity of street repair crews by 10% by July 1; to reduce average downtime of emergency vehicles by 5% by September 1; to reduce processing time for applications for social services to five working days by March 1, etc.).

The planning and/or programming stage involves deciding *how* the objectives are to be reached. It may involve initially considering a variety of possible ways to reach the objective (which could be generated by a brainstorming session). This list would then be narrowed down to a single sequence of actions (or a program), that will be implemented. For example, it may be decided that additional training is needed for maintenance employees in order to reach the objective of improving productivity of vehicle maintenance operations and reducing vehicle downtime. Additional training could be provided in several ways: such as sending employees to classes at the community college; hiring instructors to hold training sessions in the repair shop; developing and distributing training manuals. However, one plan of action (which could involve more than one of the suggested alternatives), must be selected for implementation.

Selecting the action plan requires evaluating the alternatives and choosing the one that seems most workable (under existing conditions and constraints). Criteria for narrowing the list of alternative actions could include: effectiveness in reaching the objective; cost; time (needed to implement the plan and/or before it will show results); and feasibility (which could include consideration of any existing constraints). Each alternative should be evaluated in terms of each of these criterion to help determine which alternative to select.

Once an alternative has been chosen for implementation, it should be broken down into a sequence of steps necessary to carry it out. This can be done by using a process chart (as described in chapter 8), or by simply listing the necessary actions in sequence. A schedule or timetable should be prepared to indicate when these steps should be taken and/or when they should be completed. Sequencing and scheduling are needed because some actions necessarily follow a sequential order (i.e., one cannot begin until the previous one is completed); some similar actions might be performed together to save time (e.g., actions requiring use of certain types of equipment, or travel to a particular facility); some actions depend on use of personnel or facilities that are only available at specific times. The complexity of sequencing and scheduling varies, not surprisingly, with the complexity of the action plan for which it is developed. For relatively simple plans, a list of activities and projected dates or time periods for their accomplishment is often sufficient. Complex action plans might benefit from use of milestone charts or PERT charts for scheduling.[8]

The next stage of planning involves allocation of resources necessary to carry out the action plan. This includes budgeting, but should also include nonmonetary resources such as materials, equipment, facilities, and staff time.

The final planning step is assigning responsibility or accountability for accomplishing the various steps of the plan. This refers to managerial or supervisory responsibility, in addition to assigning personnel to perform the action steps. Those who are given responsibility for carrying out specific steps in the plan should, of course, have sufficient authority over resources and work processes to carry out their responsibilities. At lower levels in the MBO hierarchy, objectives may be set by individuals for themselves, so delegation is not an issue.

Successfully reaching objectives requires more than action plans. It requires exercising control over these plans to see that they are carried out. Since MBO is based on a philosophy of participative management, the control aspects are largely viewed in terms of self-control. That is, those who are given responsibility for specific steps of the action plan are also responsible for monitoring their performance (and that of their subordinates), and taking corrective action, if necessary, to keep the plan on schedule.

The self-monitoring, self-control aspect of MBO is a major reason for being sure that action plans and schedules are detailed and specific. A manager (or staff member) should be able to readily compare actions accomplished at a particular point in time to the objectives for that time period to see if he/she is "on target." In order to do this, two things are necessary. First, measurable indicators must be identified for each objective. Second, the manager or employee should either be responsible for collecting the "feedback" data on these indicators, or he/she should be sent such data directly, if it is collected by someone else. Reports should not be sent to the manager's superior first (which is the more traditional pattern), since that removes responsibility for monitoring and control. In some cases, when the corrective action needed requires approval from superiors (e.g., because it requires additional funding), regular channels should, of course, be followed. However, reliance on self-monitoring and control as much as possible is the objective of MBO.

Evaluation. Although self-monitoring is stressed, evaluation by higher level managers is also a feature of MBO. As previously noted, periodic (e.g., quarterly), "progress report" evaluations or reviews are held. These are generally scheduled when the original MBO plan is developed. These provide an opportunity for higher level managers to give feedback to their subordinates. They also provide an opportunity to modify objectives and/or action plans if the original ones appear to be unrealistic at the time of the review, or to set new objectives after the final review of the project.

The second type of evaluation common in MBO is to consider the employee's MBO-related performance as part of his/her annual performance evaluation. While the purpose of the periodic evaluations is largely to insure that the project is progressing as it should, the year-end evaluation is usually focused on reviewing the employee's performance in managing it. Employee performance in setting objectives and developing the action plans may also be evaluated. Although the annual MBO review may be one of the factors used to determine distribution of rewards (e.g., promotions, wage increases, etc.), it also provides important feedback to the employee on his/her managerial performance. This is helpful in terms of developing individual capabilities, and should also be useful in improving performance on the next round of MBO projects.

MBO in Practice. Having explained how MBO should work, some clarifications should be made about the MBO process in practice. Many MBO efforts in the public and private sector are not designed to include participation by lower-level employees. They typically involve only supervisory and managerial personnel. However, some lower-level managers include their line employees in the objective-setting process for their work unit. While MBO theoretically can be used to generate participation by all employees, practice does not always bear this out.

The mutual goal-setting process sounds as if it involves considerable amounts of personal consultation between management and subordinates. In practice, it often relies a great deal on memos or reports identifying: department or agency objectives to be used as guidelines for setting employee objectives; descriptions of employee objectives and activities planned to achieve them; and periodic progress reports and feedback on them. Of course, these are combined with personal contact in the goal-setting process, including discussions based on the written objectives. However, the extent of interaction can vary with the organization and how the administration and the particular manager view MBO.

However, even if the reality of MBO as practiced in many organizations involves less participation than the ideal, it can still have positive impacts on productivity for other reasons. The objective-setting process can help improve overall productivity by clarifying objectives and priorities at all organizational levels. This should help guide the efforts of all employees, including those who are not involved in, or motivated by, individual goal setting. Improving the targeting of work efforts to conform more closely to organizational objectives could be viewed as increasing productivity even if there was no increase in participation and motivation.

EXAMPLES OF MBO

Like job enrichment, MBO has been highly publicized and widely used in the private sector, but seems to have been less quickly adopted as a system in the public sector. Management by objectives has been introduced in some places as part of program budgeting systems which require specification of objectives. Use of MBO by municipal governments has increased in recent years. An International City Management Association survey in 1982 indicated that 59% of the municipalities surveyed (or 269 cities), used MBO, compared to 41% in 1976.[9] Because MBO involves individual goal setting, there is little detailed information about its use or achievements in the public sector that is comparable to examples of specific cases provided for other productivity improvement methods. Therefore, this section will primarily discuss some of the impressions about the use and impact of MBO in the public sector.

The respondents in the 1982 ICMA survey appeared to be satisfied with MBO. Of those using MBO, 35% felt it was very effective, and 60% felt it was somewhat effective.[10] An earlier study of a small number of jurisdictions (25) using MBO found that most users felt positively toward the program, although they had not rigorously evaluated their MBO programs. Most felt that improved communication was one impact, both between management and employees and between different levels of management. Other impacts were improved productivity, better decisions, increased satisfaction, and positive attitudes toward the program. A small number of users noted negative impacts such as employee dissatisfaction and excessive paperwork.[11] A 1979 study of 31 cities found that the benefits most widely reported from using MBO were improved communication (reported by 94% of respondents) and increased goal clarity (90% of respondents). It was also felt that use of MBO had improved productivity (13% felt it greatly increased productivity, and 55% reported it moderately increased productivity). Respondents in this survey did not find that MBO generated excessive paperwork or that it was too time-consuming.[12]

One recent example of how MBO can be used in the public sector comes from New York City's Department of Sanitation, where a new director of fleet maintenance and repair introduced MBO (along with other improvements) in 1979. One of the objectives set was to establish preventive maintenance standards comparable to those in private industry, in order to improve reliability of the fleet. The system developed under MBO called for major preventive maintenance every 45 days, and minor PM every 22 days. Formerly, preventive maintenance had been performed once every 21 weeks. With the use of careful monitoring under the MBO system, the PM objective was met, resulting in immediate improvement in reliability of sanitation vehicles. Similarly, the objectives of rehabilitating vehicles not scheduled for replacement to "near-new" condition resulted in greater availability of salt-spreading equipment. The 1980 season started with less than 10% of spreaders out of service as a result of the MBO objectives, compared with over 20% out of service in prior years.[13]

IMPLEMENTING MBO

Implementation of MBO has some similarities to group participation. However, it implies a more significant change of leadership style and decentralization of decision making in order for the participation to be genuine, which means managerial attitudes are crucial to success. Training in the MBO process and concepts of participation may be helpful in developing the appropriate managerial attitudes. Management by objectives is a widely publicized management system that has been highly regarded in the private sector for quite some time. Therefore, it does not appear likely that public sector managers would resist its introduction very strongly.

Management by objectives is also similar to group participation in that it does not involve major changes in work process. However, MBO is a fairly time-consuming process. Time is necessary for employees to develop meaningful objectives and plans for achieving them. Meetings between managers and subordinates will be necessary for purposes of goal setting, progress reports, and final evaluation. Management by objectives also involves paperwork covering those topics in addition to, or in place of, meetings. Extra paperwork has sometimes been a source of complaint about MBO. However, paperwork and meetings do not really qualify as major process changes.

One of the most important factors in a successful MBO program is the goal-setting process. As noted earlier, goals should be clear and specific, realistic, compatible with higher level goals, measurable, and prioritized. It is desirable to have workshops or training sessions for managers and employees to explain these criteria and their importance and to provide guidance in devising goals that meet these criteria. The complexity of many public sector jobs and the difficulty in measuring outputs or results makes training in goal development even more important. At the same time, it makes MBO an even more valuable tool in helping to clarify the purposes and functions of various agencies, departments, and their subunits.

These difficulties, particularly measurement problems, have led some jurisdictions to limit the coverage of their MBO programs.[14] While this is one way of dealing with the problem, training in goal setting seems a better solution. There is usually some way in which goal attainment can be measured, even if it is not ideal. In addition to training sessions, selective introduction may be a useful approach to implementing MBO. It could be introduced one level at a time, so each level can serve as a model for those below it. Alternatively, it can be tried at all levels in one or two departments whose experience can serve as a model for other units.

Although goals are extremely important, care must be taken to avoid overemphasis on *writing* goals rather than *achieving* them. Feedback on progress toward the goals is necessary to make MBO work as an on-going system rather than an annual exercise in paperwork. A somewhat related area involves the possibility of linking MBO to other rewards. It is not clear that MBO alone will continue to motivate if other rewards are not associated with goal achievement. However, if MBO is linked to rewards, it will be necessary to establish quantifiable goals and to design a reporting system and monitor it for accuracy.

Another factor affecting program success is stability in goals and/or priorities. Management by objectives is not particularly effective in an organizational context characterized by frequent change. Since it is designed to be a flexible tool (as reflected in the periodic reviews that allow for goal modification), most ordinary variations in service provision due to changes in political and/or social conditions can be accommodated by the system. However, frequent major goal changes will cause the process to lose meaning.

Management by objectives has the advantage of being applicable to any kind of job. Employees who want satisfaction of higher-level needs will probably perceive the increased participation and feedback as enriching their jobs, and thus may be motivated to improve productivity. Setting clear performance targets may help other employees direct their work efforts better, and thus help improve productivity for that reason. To maximize the effect of MBO on productivity, employees could be required to include productivity improvement goals with their other objectives. Like other participation related methods, MBO can be used in combination with other improvement techniques.

HOW FLEXTIME IMPROVES PRODUCTIVITY

Flextime is frequently categorized as a method designed to improve the quality of working life, and is sometimes perceived as a kind of fringe benefit to improve employee satisfaction. However, it is also appropriate to view it as a participation-related productivity improvement method. It is usually made available to groups of employees, generally entire units or departments (although specific employees may have to be excluded from the system, which will be explained later in this section). However, the participation involved in flextime usually occurs at the individual level. Thus it is more appropriate to classify it as an individual participation method than as a group method.

A simple definition of flextime (or flexible working hours, or flexitime), is that it is a system that allows employees to exercise a certain amount of control over the hours they work. It usually operates by allowing employees to vary the times they begin and end their workday, although there is a set period of time during which all employees are expected to be at their jobs (see p.194). Flextime is another motivation-related technique that has received considerable attention in the 1970s. It originated in Europe in the midsixties, and has been adopted by many private sector companies in the United States and by a number of public sector agencies.

Flextime increases motivation through participation in addition to having the potential to increase other job dimensions associated with enrichment.[15] Flextime allows employees to decide on their own work schedules, which is normally a managerial perogative. Allowing this participation is implicit recognition of employee capability to make appropriate decisions about when work will be performed, thus filling their esteem needs.

Flextime also may increase autonomy by reducing the amount of time that employees and supervisors are simultaneously present. Thus more responsibility for independent performance is delegated to the employee. This also should enable the employee to exercise more autonomy over the sequence of activities and the way work is performed. In addition, the employee may receive more direct feedback from the job itself as a result of relying on his/her own evaluation of a work product in the absence of a supervisor. Flextime may also add job diversity if employees need to "cover" for each other. Some organizations train employees to perform a variety of different jobs for this reason.

The attributes of flextime noted above are related to motivation and productivity improvement through satisfaction of higher level needs. Flextime is also viewed as having the potential to improve productivity in a unique way, which is by allowing employees to work when they are most strongly motivated. It is recognized that individuals have their own psychological and physiological rhythms which affect alertness and energy. Under flextime, people who typically have high energy levels in the morning can arrive earlier and work more hours while they are at their peak performance levels, while "night owls" can arrive later to take advantage of their own body rhythms. In addition, the fact that there are likely to be periods during the day when relatively few people are present, or when outside interruptions (e.g., phone calls) are reduced, creates "quiet times" that are conducive to concentration and greater productivity.

Flextime can also increase productivity through reduced absenteeism and lateness. These are often related to employee needs to take care of personal and family matters. Under flextime, it is usually possible to fit appointments, errands, and so on into the course of the normal working day without losing time from work.

Flextime is credited with a number of benefits to individuals and society in general, such as enabling employees to spend more time with their families, and reducing rush-hour traffic congestion. Flextime may also enable an organization to provide better service to clients or the general public. Being open more hours during the day allows people to interact with the organization at times that are most convenient for them, which is generally perceived as an improvement in service.

APPLYING FLEXTIME

Key concepts in flextime are the core time and flexible bands. Core time consists of those hours when all employees are required to be present. This is intended to facilitate communication within the organization as well as with those outside it. The flexible bands are the periods during which employees exercise their option to schedule their work. Employees may arrive or leave at any time during the flexible starting and quitting bands. There may also be a flexible band during the middle of the day for lunch or other activities. Of course, employees are expected to arrange their work schedules so that requirements for total hours worked during a given time period are met (this is one of the variable concepts in flextime, and will be discussed further below).[16] A fairly typical flextime schedule might look like this:

Flexible Starting Time:	7:00 A.M.- 9:30 A.M.
Core Time:	9:30 A.M.-11:30 A.M.
Flexible Midday Band:	11:30 A.M.- 2:00 P.M.
Core Time:	2:00 P.M.- 4:00 P.M.
Flexible Quitting Time:	4:00 P.M.- 6:30 P.M.

Two other major concepts are the settlement period and banking or carryover. The settlement period is the length of time over which a contracted number of hours must be worked. Under regular working conditions, an employee works for 8 hours a day and 40 hours a week. If there is a one-day settlement period under flextime, the employee must fit eight working hours into each day. With a one-week settlement period, however, the employee could work only five hours on one day, for example, and spread the remaining three hours over other days.

This concept of carryover refers to accumulation of debit or credit hours which are carried over to later settlement periods. For example, an employee might choose to work 50 hours one week in order to take 10 hours off the next week. As a rule, time off is not allowed during core periods.

Thus, depending on the system used, one could find variations in working hours like these on any given day:

Employee A: Arrives at 7, takes 1-hour lunch break, and leaves at 4.

Employee B: Arrives at 9:30, takes 1-hour lunch break, and leaves at 6:30.

Employee C: Arrives at 7, takes 2½-hour lunch break, and leaves at 5:30.

Employee D: Arrives at 9:30, takes 2½-hour lunch break, and leaves at 4.

Note that the first three employees worked an eight-hour day, while the fourth worked four hours. This creates a four-hour debit, which would only be permissible under a system that had a week or more for its settlement period and/or allowed banking.

The factors that most affect the degree of flexibility available to employees are the length of each flexband, the length of the settlement period, and the ability to bank hours. Short bands result in relatively little flexibility. Thus the word *flextime* can cover a range of degrees of flexibility. Under some systems, there is no midday flexband, just a regular lunch break. Therefore, the employee's arrival time automatically determines departure time (assuming a one-day settlement period without banking). In some organizations, employees are expected to specify, and adhere to, a particular schedule of starting and quitting times. Jobs that are characterized by teamwork (e.g., refuse collection, road repair) will necessitate group decisions about working times, even if they are in organizations that have adopted a liberal flextime system.

It should be fairly obvious from the description of how flextime operates that some form of time keeping system will be necessary to monitor the hours worked and any debit or credit hours banked. Time systems could include traditional methods such as time clocks or having individual employees or supervisors maintain written time sheets. New methods may be more appropriate for flextime, however. There are mechanical time meters designed specifically for flextime which monitor the number of hours worked as opposed to just the times of arrival and departure (the standard time clock approach). The system involves an individual time counter for each employee that is activated by insertion of a badge, key or similar device, and which keeps accumulating hours until the device is removed.

EXAMPLES OF FLEXTIME

A considerable number of federal government agencies have used flextime. By 1980, it was used by about 100 agencies, with about 200,000 employees working under some kind of flextime system.[17] Studies of the federal experience with flextime account for much of the available information on its public sector use. The Social Security Administration introduced flextime in eight large bureaus and offices in 1974 and 1975 and reported on its experience in 1976. It was found that there was a slight reduction in use of sick leave and a substantial reduction in lateness. A survey of employees and supervisors revealed an increase in job satisfaction and a preference for flextime over the previous system. Most employees felt there was an increase in their work quality and/or accuracy. Unfortunately, very few objective measures of productivity were available, and those indicated little or no gains.[18]

The U.S. Geological Survey also began using flextime in 1975, and reported on objective measures of its impact in 1976. Productivity was estimated in terms of output only, with the following results: a 14% increase in map production at the Special Mapping Center; a 13% increase in vouchers processed in the Branch of Financial Management; a 6% increase in reports produced by the Water Resources Division. In addition, there was a 7% reduction in use of sick leave.[19]

A survey of federal agencies reporting on the impacts of flextime found that 11 organizations using measured or objective data to represent productivity changes showed gains in 15 out of 17 measures. Subjective data on perceptions of productivity, work quantity and/or quality indicate 14 of 17 organizations reported positive impacts, while the other 3 reported no change or inconclusive results. Surveys of employee satisfaction and morale showed improvements in all 17 agencies. Objective data on absenteeism indicate a decrease in sick leave use in 10 out of 12 organizations, no change in one and an increase attributed to other factors in the other. Eight organizations reported on lateness, with two reporting substantial decreases and six reporting elimination of tardiness.[20]

A survey of studies of public sector (mainly federal) use of flextime found few attempts to measure productivity objectively. However, it did find reductions in sick leave or absenteeism reported in 16 studies, while tardiness was reduced in 11. Most studies also had subjective data indicating that both productivity and morale increased as a result of flextime.[21]

Although most reviews of flextime indicate reductions in absenteeism, a later analysis of the program in SSA found an increase in use of sick leave, annual leave and other forms of absence. This finding is not easily explained, but it may mean that the initial ability to spend more time on nonwork interests that flextime allows is so satisfactory to employees that they ultimately increase use of leave in order to expand it even more. This would seem particularly likely for those who derive little satisfaction from their jobs. Flextime may have the effect of encouraging such people to spend more time away from work.[22] This finding may be interpreted as an indication that long-term behavioral effects of flextime may vary from short-term effects. However, it should be emphasized that the negative impact on attendance was only noted in one study, while most others found improvements in attendance.

There is less documentation available about state or local use of flextime than federal, although it has been applied in a variety of agencies in different locations. For example, flextime was introduced in Inglewood, California in a pilot project in 1973 and was later expanded to cover 40% of city employees (other than police and firefighters). One beneficial impact of the program is improved service; the public can transact business with city government over an expanded time period (7:30 A.M. to 6:00 P.M.). Overtime has also been reduced as a result of the program.[23]

An example of a flextime failure comes from Los Angeles, where it was implemented in the city personnel department in 1971 under the assumption that different arrival times would allow sufficient coverage and provide an extended service period to the public. However, most employees arrived and left early, resulting in inadequate coverage, which led to program termination. However, this could have been avoided by reaching agreements with employees to assure adequate coverage, which was the approach taken by the California Department of Motor Vehicles when a similar problem was experienced.[24] Of course, this reduces employee flexibility somewhat, but seems preferable to program termination.

IMPLEMENTING FLEXTIME

Flextime involves more process change and less attitudinal change than other participation methods. The latter occurs because employee participation is typically viewed primarily in terms of when to start and stop work. Therefore, efforts to change attitudes and to train employees in participatory techniques are not necessary for flextime.

Because flextime involves more work process change, careful consideration must be given to its implementation. The major decisions to be made involve the degree of flexibility (or participation) employees may exercise; the length of the workday; and who will be allowed to participate in the program. Choices in these areas will be influenced by the perceived impacts flextime will have internally and externally. Therefore, potential impacts should be considered carefully before implementing flextime because their extent and importance vary by organization. Prior analysis of these impacts will allow the program to be designed to minimize negative impacts.

Flextime could have a major impact on communication and coordination among units or employees that normally interact in the process of their jobs. Core time is designed to meet needs for contact within the organization. Therefore, the length of core time should be set to meet the perceived need for intraorganizational contact. High organizational interdependence implies need for longer core times and less employee flexibility.

If most need for interaction is limited to particular groups, excluding them from the program is another solution. Supervisory level personnel are one such group, since they need to be available to deal with problems. However, coordinating schedules of all supervisors so some are always present during the expanded day could allow supervisory participation in flextime. Alternatively, more responsibility can be delegated to employees. This is viewed as one of the motivating features of flextime. In general, excluding employees from flextime is not a desirable solution because it may lead to later resentment, which could result in decreased job performance. It would be preferable to devise some other method of accommodation, if possible.

A somewhat related problem is the need for coverage, either of particular jobs, or of work areas so someone is present to answer telephones, handle visitors, provide information, and/or perform key functions. To accomplish this, it may be necessary to limit employee flexibility somewhat by having them coordinate working schedules to maintain coverage. This, combined with some additional training, if needed, should allow the most basic or urgent needs to be met outside of core hours, while other tasks can wait until the appropriate employee is present. A less desirable solution would be to have long core times and short flexbands, which would reduce the likelihood of a particular employee being absent when needed.

Although flextime is often perceived as a low-cost program, it does entail some additional overhead costs that are usually related to the extended day involved. These are mostly in terms of costs of light, heat, or air-conditioning, but might also include payment for extra hours of work by auxiliary personnel such as cafeteria employees, switchboard operators, or security personnel. Another cost is for a time-recording system and perhaps additional time for record keeping.

External impacts are the other major area of concern that should be considered when planning a flextime system. The external populations affected can be categorized as clients or the general public served by the organization and all others who interact with it, such as members of other public agencies, suppliers, and so on.

It is generally felt that extending the working day provides better service to the public because they will have a greater opportunity to contact the organization at their convenience. Of course, there must be adequate coverage of jobs that involve public contact for this to be true. As noted above, this kind of problem caused flextime to be removed from a Los Angeles agency. Careful coordination of schedules or reduced flexbands could be used to provide sufficient levels of public service during all hours. Another alternative would be to limit public contact to "normal" working hours, but this would remove the chance to increase public satisfaction.

Flextime can have a variety of impacts on the organization and the public that can be undesirable. Most of these problems can be avoided by careful design of the flextime system. In order to do this, however, an effort to identify all potential impacts of the system must be made in advance. Using a "pilot study" approach in one of two departments to see if there are any unanticipated effects might also be considered.

The extent of flexibility possible, or even use of flextime at all, might be affected by laws or civil service regulations that stipulate the number of hours that can be worked during a day or week and/or require overtime pay for work in excess of 8 hours a day or 40 hours a week. These are fairly common, although they do not usually apply to all levels of personnel or all types of occupations. Flextime schedules may need to be designed to comply with such regulations to permit use of flextime. In order to avoid regulations requiring overtime pay for federal employees after 8 hours a day, the Federal Employees Flexible and Compressed Work Schedules Act of 1978 was passed to allow a three-year trial period for flextime experiments regardless of legal restrictions. A similar experimental approach might be used at other government levels to at least temporarily bypass legal restrictions without going through the process of changing the laws.

Another potential barrier to flextime use involves its impact on overtime. It is often suggested that employees can use flextime to better coordinate working time with volume of work; for example, by staying later on days when work is heavier, or working until a task is completed. This essentially implies that overtime will be reduced in a flextime system, and in fact, this has been reported in a number of studies of flextime use. While this is beneficial to the organization using flextime, it is not a feature that employees and/or their unions are likely to welcome. In fact, they may oppose the system because of reduction in overtime, especially if overtime has been a regular portion of the paycheck. Of course, the problem can be avoided by setting eight hours as a daily limit and paying overtime for hours beyond that, if necessary.

Flextime has the advantage of being usable in many job situations, although the work performed should be considered before applying it. Flextime is felt to increase productivity primarily by allowing employees to participate in deciding on their hours of work. This is not likely to be viewed as threatening by even those employees who are not generally interested in job enrichment. Flextime can also provide other enrichment opportunities, such as diversity and more autonomy.

Flextime may also improve productivity by enabling employees to work when they are at their peak performance levels. It can reduce absences or lateness caused by employees attending to personal matters during working hours. In general, however, its major impacts are due to increased motivation and/or satisfaction.

SUMMARY

Management by objectives and flextime are two methods that use increased employee participation to improve productivity. They are similar in that this participation is undertaken by employees as individuals, rather than by groups of employees (as in quality circles, committees, and task forces). However, they differ in most other respects.

The focus of participation in MBO is on setting specific job-related objectives that the individual employee or, more likely, manager, agrees to work toward during a specified period of time. The employee participates in the objective-setting process, and in developing plans to achieve the goals. He/she also has increased responsibility in terms of monitoring his/her progress and taking corrective actions as necessary. These forms of increased participation and responsibility work to improve productivity because they increase motivation by satisfying higher level needs.

Even if it did not affect motivation, MBO would be likely to improve productivity because it provides better direction for employee work efforts. The objective-setting process provides a clear picture of goals and priorities at all levels of the organization, and specifies actions to be taken to achieve them. This alone can have a positive impact on productivity.

Flextime differs in that the focus of participation centers around decisions about what hours the employee will work. Flextime is often viewed in terms of improving the "quality of working life." It is sometimes seen as improving productivity by increasing employee satisfaction, largely because flexible hours makes it easier to cope with, or enjoy, nonwork aspects of life. However, the ability to make decisions about work schedules does increase participation, even if it is in a narrowly defined area.

Flextime also increases participation and responsibility as an indirect result of the new work schedules. Employees often must take on more responsibility because supervisors and other employees are not always present during their work hours. They may also experience more job diversity and develop new skills because they need to "fill in" for absent co-workers. Flextime may also affect productivity in ways that do not result from increased employee motivation. These include enabling employees to schedule work hours to coincide with their peak energy periods, and reducing lateness and absenteeism by giving employees more flexibility to attend to personal needs on their own time.

In short, both MBO and flextime can be viewed as improving productivity through a combination of effects, not just through increased employee participation. In these ways they resemble quality circles, labor-management committees and task forces. However, they differ from these three methods in that participation occurs on an individual, rather than a group basis, and in that participation is not of a voluntary nature. Like other improvement methods using increased participation, these two methods can be used in conjunction with other improvement methods in the PIP context.

NOTES

1. The material in this section relies heavily on John M. Griener et al., *Productivity and Motivation: A Review of State and Local Government Initiatives* (Washington, D.C.: The Urban Institute Press, 1981), pp. 119-151, and Kae H. Chung, *Motivational Theories and Practices* (Columbus, Ohio: Grid Inc., 1977), pp. 215-240.
2. Greiner, et al., *Productivity and Motivation,* p. 120.
3. Description of MBO practices are based on: Greiner, et al., *Productivity and Motivation,* pp. 119-151; Dale D. McConkey, *How to Manage by Results*, 3rd ed. (New York: AMACOM, 1976); Dale D. McConkey, *MBO for Nonprofit Organizations* (New York: AMACOM, 1975); George L. Morrisey, *Management by Objectives and Results in the Public Sector* (Reading, Mass.: Addison-Wesley Publishing Company, 1976); Anthony P. Raia, *Managing by Objectives* (Glenview, Ill.: Scott, Foresman, 1974).
4. McConkey, *MBO for Nonprofits,* pp. 48-49.
5. Ibid., pp. 46-48.
6. For a more detailed discussion of these steps, see Morrisey, *Management by Objectives and Results,* pp. 25-64.
7. Greiner, et al., *Productivity and Motivation,* p. 122.
8. For a discussion of these tools, see Morrisey, *Management by Objectives and Results,* pp. 122-128.
9. International City Management Association, *The Municipal Year Book 1984* (Washington, D.C.: International City Management Association, 1984), pp. 207-209.
10. Ibid., p. 209.
11. Greiner, et al., *Productivity and Motivation,* pp. 143-151.
12. Perry D. Moore and Ted Staton, "Management by Objectives in American Cities," *Public Personnel Management* 10 (Summer 1981): 226-230.
13. Ronald Contino and Robert M. Lorrusso, "The Theory Z Turnaround of a Public Agency," *Public Administration Review* 42 (January/February 1982): 68.
14. Greiner, et al., *Productivity and Motivation,* p. 167.
15. The discussion of the effects of flextime relies heavily on Simcha Ronen, *Flexible Working Hours: An Innovation in the Quality of Work Life* (New York: McGraw-Hill Book Company, 1981), pp. 28-33 and 57-63.
16. For more details on variations in flextime, see, for example, George W. Bohlander, *Flextime —A New Face on the Work Clock* (Los Angeles, Calif.: University of California-Los Angeles, 1977); Ronen, *Flexible Working Hours;* J. Carroll Swart, *A Flexible Approach to Working Hours* (New York: AMACOM, 1978). The material in this section is based on these.
17. Ronen, *Flexible Working Hours,* p. 123.
18. Swart, *A Flexible Approach,* pp. 178-180.
19. Ibid., pp. 187-188.
20. Ronen, *Flexible Working Hours,* pp. 125-144.
21. Robert T. Golembiewski and Carl W. Proehl, Jr., "Public Sector Applications of Flexible Workhours: A Review of Available Experience," *Public Administration Review* 40 (January/February 1980): 76-83.
22. Glenn W. Rainy, Jr. and Larence Wolf, "Flex-time: Short-Term Benefits; Long-Term . . .?," *Public Administration Review* 41 (January/February 1981): 61.
23. Swart, *A Flexible Approach,* pp. 171-172.
24. Bohlander, *New Face on Clock,* p. 68.

13
IMPROVING PRODUCTIVITY THROUGH MORE EFFICIENT RESOURCE USE: NEW TECHNOLOGY, ORGANIZATIONAL RESTRUCTURING, AND RESOURCE REALLOCATION

HOW NEW TECHNOLOGY IMPROVES PRODUCTIVITY

The term *new technology* refers to both newly developed technology or initial adoption of technology by a department or agency. Technology, as used here, refers to any form of capital equipment, including computers. New technology is credited with considerable portions of all productivity improvement in recent decades. It improves productivity by changing the tools or equipment used in order to increase staff efficiency. New technology basically trades capital for labor. In some cases, capital is completely substituted for labor, and automation results. This is more likely to occur on assembly lines than in the public sector, however. More commonly, capital partially substitutes for labor. It can reduce the amount of time and effort required to perform tasks requiring physical strength and/or effort, or to perform repetitive tasks of either a mental or physical nature. Reducing the time and effort required to perform a task enables employees to produce a greater volume of output in a given period of time. It may also reduce the number of employees required to perform a particular job. Alternatively, reducing the amount of time needed for some activities creates more time to be used in other productive ways. Technology might also change the way some activities are conducted. For example, teleconferences could be used instead of bringing people to one place for meetings.

APPLYING NEW TECHNOLOGY

Because of the distinctive characteristics of computers, this section will discuss application of technology in terms of two separate categories.

Technology that does not involve computers will be referred to as equipment, and will be discussed first.

Equipment. Equipment can be categorized in terms of size. Machinery, vehicles, or other large-scale items, whether stationary or mobile, can be viewed as heavy equipment. Smaller items, many of which are portable, can be classified as light equipment. In the public sector, an example of heavy equipment is a refuse collection truck that is designed to pick up, empty, and put down refuse containers by use of a mechanical lift instead of a person. Examples of light equipment include a wider fire hose that allows a greater volume of water to flow through the hose; and adapters on fire hydrants that allow quick connections of hoses to hydrants.

Application of new equipment is fairly simple. It requires purchasing the equipment and using it. (Learning about, or developing appropriate technology, which precedes its application, will be discussed under implementation.) New technology applications often occur quite routinely during the normal equipment replacement/materials purchasing processes. Some more complicated forms of equipment may require training employees in use of the equipment. It may also require job redesign if the equipment alters the way the task is performed. The extent of redesign needed will vary with how substantially the equipment affects the way work is performed.

Computers. The kind of technology that has received the most attention in the recent past has been computers. Computers could be characterized according to variations in their technology, but this involves more technical detail than is appropriate here. It is more useful to categorize computers and/or the programs or packages used in them in terms of the nature of the functions they perform. In broad terms, these are:[1]

Record keeping and restructuring—involves storage and updating of statistics, reorganizing or summarizing them, and retrieving particular classes of data.

Analytic activities—sophisticated manipulation of data such as computer mapping, regression analysis, forecasting models.

Calculating and printing—includes activities such as preparation of utility bills and payroll checks.

Office automation—word processing systems that store typed copy and permit revisions to be made without complete retyping and that produce multiple typed "originals" of letters and reports.

Process control—monitoring data about the operations or status of a system to allow automatic or human correction or control, for example, traffic signal control.

Operational support—helps conduct operations such as scheduling work and facilities, inventory control, licensing, dispatching, library circulation.

To the extent that computers automate certain clerical, secretarial, and/or duplicating functions, their effect on productivity is similar to that of other labor-saving equipment.

Computers can affect productivity by improving control and use of resources (e.g., inventory or budget control, deployment of emergency vehicles, etc.). Another way computers can improve productivity is through the collection and analysis of data that provides better information for decision-making and planning purposes. In addition, computers can affect the quality and quantity of service provided. Computer use increases speed and accuracy, two important aspects of service quality. They may also enable expansion of service with existing staff levels (e.g., by serving more people, and/or by providing additional kinds of services). Such expansion might not be possible without computers to free staff time by performing some kinds of work more quickly.

EXAMPLES OF NEW TECHNOLOGY

Not surprisingly, much of the new technology adopted in the public sector is concentrated in services that are capital intensive. Refuse collection is a prime example of this. There have been a variety of innovations in refuse collection trucks in recent years. One of the early innovations was developed in Scottsdale, Arizona in 1965. Called "Godzilla," the truck had a lift mechanism that would pick up a specific type of container and empty it into the truck. By eliminating the need for manual loading, crew size can be reduced to one: the driver. Higher pay and better working conditions (an air-conditioned, stereo-equipped truck), could be offered to the driver because of savings from reduced crew size. The system was put in operation within two years from the time it was proposed. Crew size was reduced from five employees to one, and collection costs were reduced 45%.[2] Other variations of trucks designed for mechanized refuse collection have since been developed and utilized in a variety of localities.

Refuse collection operations can also be improved with technology that is less expensive than new trucks. In Naples, Florida, rear-view cameras were installed in 1980 to assist drivers of front-loading trucks in backing or moving their vehicles. Cameras mounted to the front of the collection trucks eliminates the need for flagmen, who had formerly been used to provide directions for the truck drivers. The cost of the camera is $1250, compared with $8018 for a flagman.[3]

Fire departments have also been the target of a variety of innovations. The concept of "slippery water" was developed by the RAND corporation in New York City in the late 1960s. A chemical added to water reduces friction and lets the water flow more quickly. This allows use of lighter, more maneuverable, hoses. Large diameter hoses have also been developed to allow greater water flow, thus reducing the number of hoses needed. Another advance in firefighting technology is the Probeye®,[4] an infrared scanning device that helps locate victims or detect hot spots inside a burning building. Smaller versions of the standard firefighting pumper have been developed to respond to minor fires or other service calls. These minipumpers can reduce maintenance costs and prolong the life of the standard vehicles.

Of course, new equipment is not limited to these two departments. In Milwaukee, the Department of Public Works installed an innovative system in their sewers that uses television cameras to locate leaks, and then seals them with a spraying system inside the sewer. This saved the city $325,000 in 1974. The city also installed electric pumps that are automatically activated by high water levels resulting from storms. These are expected to save $50,000 annually by replacing emergency pumping crews. Nassau County, New York, has used new technology in its highway operations. By using a "superstriper" to paint center stripes on highways it has reduced painting crew size from 12 to 3 people.[5]

Computers have been used in a variety of ways in the public sector. In Dallas, computers perform around-the-clock remote surveillance and control over city buildings. This enabled elimination of 10 positions in the early stages of the program, and was expected to lead to annual salary savings of $132,000. Nassau County has computerized its sewer permit system at an annual savings of $75,000 in personnel costs. It has also automated its Public Works inventory system. This enabled identification of obsolete stock, which was sold for $32,680.[6]

Skokie, Illinois recently computerized its water meter reading system. Formerly, employees had to enter homes to read meters. Return cards were left for residents to take their own readings if there was no one home, and estimates were used for billings if the cards were not returned in time. The readings recorded were manually entered into the computer for billing. Under the new system, an electronic device is placed on the water meter. Wires are run to the outside of the house where a device is attached that the meter reader touches with a "probe" to record the account number and meter reading on a cassette tape. The tape is returned to the computer room, where a diskette is made and placed in the computer to create a bill. As a result, there are no customer-supplied or estimated billings, and no incorrect readings. Keypunching of meter readings is also eliminated by use of this innovation, and readings are performed more quickly because entry into the house is no longer necessary.[7]

Computer models are often used to help in scheduling or resource allocation. One that has been widely used was developed by Public Technology, Incorporated to help determine where fire, police, and/or ambulance stations should be located. Models can also be used, for example, to help determine allocation of patrol cars, or to schedule vehicle maintenance, street repair, and so on. Of course, most computer use in local government is of a more routine nature. About 75% of computer applications are for record-keeping, calculating, and printing tasks, with the other 25% divided among the more sophisticated applications.[8]

IMPLEMENTING NEW TECHNOLOGY

Most of the problems associated with adoption of new technology are related to feasibility of adoption rather than to actual implementation. Therefore, barriers to adopting new technology will be the primary focus here.

Developing Technology. One of the first barriers to using new technology is the need to develop technology suitable for public sector needs and/or to become aware of existing technology. Several developments in recent years have been directed toward reducing these problems.

There are some national organizations that either provide information about technology and/or try to develop it. Public Technology, Incorporated, is an example of the latter. It was developed in the early 1970s by the International City Management Association to help develop technology for local governments, such as the computer model to select sites for service facilities noted above. It has also developed other routing or scheduling models. In addition, PTI has helped bring about technological developments by private sector companies, including the Probeye,® an automatic nozzle for fire engines, a new breathing apparatus for firefighters, and a longer-lasting road patching material.[9]

Some jurisdictions have used the tactic of developing their own technology. Under the Lindsay administration's productivity program for New York City in the late 1960s, the City established and partially funded a "think tank," the New York City-Rand Institute. Rand worked on both process and product innovations, including the development of slippery water mentioned earlier, before it was disbanded. A somewhat similar approach was used in Tacoma, Washington where the city manager, William Donaldson, began a technology transfer program in 1971. A relationship with Boeing Aerospace was developed in which Boeing contributed professional staff time to work with city departments to develop new technology to meet their needs (and which would presumably be marketable elsewhere). A number of products were developed, mostly related to fire and mass transit services, although not all were adopted or fully refined.[10] Although undertakings of similar scope are unlikely to be widely employed, smaller-scale efforts to develop technology or form alliances with other organizations for that purpose may be an attractive option to some jurisdictions.

Finding Out About Technology. Awareness of existing technology is also crucial to adoption. Government officials can learn about new technology through conferences, publications, and bulletins made available by agencies or organizations such as The Urban Institute, HUD, the National Science Foundation, the International City Management Association, and the various Productivity and Quality of Working Life Centers that have developed in recent years,[11] which may cover new technology in addition to other productivity improvement or administrative issues. Manufacturers of equipment are a fairly obvious source of information, either through their sales representatives, product literature, and/or advertising. Contacting nearby jurisdictions to learn about their experience with and/or knowledge of new technology may also be a useful approach.

Technology itself has been used to help keep local governments informed of new technology (and other approaches to productivity improvement). Control Data Corporation's computer program, LOGIN (Local Government Information Network), is used in a number of cities. One can ask about specific services or functions and receive information about what other cities are doing to improve productivity or service delivery in that area. Member cities are expected to put information about their own efforts into the system's data bank for use by other members.[12]

Other Implementation Matters. Another major barrier to adopting new technology is cost. Since a broad range of items is included in equipment and/or computerized technology, there is also considerable variation in cost. However, many capital items are quite expensive, or will only generate savings if used for large quantities of work, which suggests that some form of benefit cost analysis should be performed before purchasing them. In calculating costs, the operating and maintenance costs should be considered, as well as the purchase price. One way to manage costs would be to have a leasing arrangement, which is quite common with computer users. Leasing is more expensive than purchasing in the long run, but can make sense, especially if technology is expected to change rapidly. It might also be possible to arrange sharing of computers or other equipment with nearby jurisdictions. Costs of large equipment items may also be made more manageable by financing them through bonds.

The prospect of displacing employees is often an additional barrier to use of technology. In many instances, the technology is clearly designed to replace human labor, (e.g., one-person refuse trucks). Employee and/or union resistance can be expected unless alternatives to layoffs are offered. One solution is to train displaced employees for other government jobs, although placement may be difficult in periods of general staff cutbacks. Another is to phase the new technology in slowly to allow for staff reduction through attrition. Additional compensation is a third way to gain acceptance of an innovation. Unionized sanitation workers in New York City opposed introduction of new trucks requiring a crew of two instead of three workers. The matter went to arbitration, and in December 1980 the arbitrator awarded an extra $11 per shift to each employee working on the new trucks.[13]

While compensation may remove employee opposition, it clearly increases the cost of using the innovation, making it a worthwhile approach only if the savings generated by productivity gains still exceed costs when extra compensation is included. In the New York City case, annualized savings from the sideloaders was estimated to result in a 24% net reduction in personnel costs related to refuse collection. The department was able to add additional personnel to its street cleaning force as a result of reductions in collection crew size, leading to measurable gains in street cleanliness.[14]

The topics discussed thus far really determine whether or not a particular form of new technology is adopted. Assuming the decision to adopt is made, there are a few implementation matters that should be considered. The most important concern, of course, is training employees in using the new technology. Whether training requires a major or minor effort varies with the degree of complexity of the new technology compared to what it is replacing and with the number of employees to be trained. In addition, if employees displaced by the technology are retrained for other government positions, this will also need to be planned and implemented.

Another matter to consider is whether the technology will also have impacts on other units, departments, or members of the public that interact with the unit utilizing the technology. Any such affected parties will need to be informed about how they will be affected and/or about behavior changes that may be required of them. For example, mechanized refuse collection trucks typically are only able to hoist specially designed containers, which means residents must use only those containers for disposal purposes. Therefore, the jurisdiction must make the appropriate containers available and conduct an education campaign to be sure they are used and put in the appropriate place for pick up. Some technology might involve change only on the part of the public. For example, having residents use plastic trash bags instead of other refuse containers would ease the job of loading trucks and reduce time spent at each stop.

New technology has been one of the most common productivity improvement methods. It can be used in many different kinds of work. Computers can also indirectly or directly improve the productivity of a variety of jobs. Technology can have substantial effects on productivity, and is compatible with other improvement methods.

HOW RESTRUCTURING IMPROVES PRODUCTIVITY

There are three types of organizational restructuring that are generally associated with productivity improvement and/or cost reduction. These are: reorganization, contracting for service provision, and intergovernmental agreements. These are sometimes associated with other forms of productivity improvement, such as new technology or job enrichment.

These types of organizational restructuring impact productivity in different ways. Reorganization refers to structural changes within the organization, such as centralization of particular functions. Reorganization is usually associated with increasing the efficiency of resource use. Contracting for service provision is restructuring in the sense that the government unit no longer directly provides the service. It makes a contractual arrangement with a third party that will provide the service instead. Intergovernmental agreements are similar to contracts. They involve a cooperative arrangement between two or more different governments to share the responsibility for providing a service, or to jointly own/use capital equipment or a facility.

Both contracting out and intergovernmental agreements improve productivity by reducing costs. This is generally because there are scale economies associated with providing the service to a larger number of people than served by one government unit. In the case of contracting out, the provider can capture economies of scale by performing the same service for many government entities. Thus administrative costs or costs of specialized equipment or personnel are spread over many users, reducing cost per user. If a single government unit provided the service itself, these resources might be underutilized because of insufficient volume of work, although the jurisdiction would have to pay for the idle time as well as the productive time. Contracting also enables the purchaser to avoid large start-up costs associated with provision of a new service, particularly one that requires purchase of capital equipment.

Contracting is also felt to reduce costs in other ways, not all of which can be substantiated. There is some belief that private firms invariably produce services at lower cost because they operate under the profit motive. Another belief is that personnel costs are likely to be lower because they are not tied to civil service regulations. A more concrete example of cost savings due to contracting is potential reduction in a jurisdiction's centralized administrative costs. For example, personnel and payroll activities are not necessary for employees who are not employed by the jurisdiction.

Cooperative agreements improve productivity in much the same way as contracting does. Instead of finding a service provider, however, the governments involved become their own provider. They pool resources to benefit from economies of scale and to avoid excess capacity associated with individual provision of services. This also reduces duplication of facilities, equipment, and/or personnel among the participating governments.

It should be noted that neither contracting nor intergovernmental cooperation results in productivity improvement in quite the same sense that other productivity methods do. Since service is no longer produced by the jurisdiction, its output per labor hour cannot be viewed as increasing. However, its costs per unit of output should decrease, which is a different way of viewing productivity improvement. In addition, at the service provider level, output per labor hour should be higher than it would be if numerous small jurisdictions produced the service for themselves.

APPLYING RESTRUCTURING

Applying the types of reorganization most commonly related to productivity improvement, centralization and consolidation, has been discussed in the chapter on work redesign. The primary purpose of such reorganization is to eliminate duplication of effort associated with having the same or similar activities performed in numerous departments. It may also lead to lower costs related to large volume production. Large volume may also allow adoption of new technology that would be too costly at lower volumes of output. For example, if a city centralizes its duplicating and printing functions in one office, it may buy newer, faster, equipment which it could not afford to buy for individual departments under a decentralized system.

Reorganization might also be associated with job redesign in terms of either simplification or job enrichment. An example of the former would be a centralized duplicating and printing unit where employees specialize in particular tasks (e.g., mimeographing, collating), similar to assembly-line production. Alternatively, consolidation of several units performing similar functions may lead to enriched jobs. This was the result in previously noted examples where building inspectors, who had been assigned to different departments where each performed only one type of inspection, were trained to do a variety of inspections after consolidation into one department.

Contracting may be used for virtually any service. There is a longer history of purchasing "hard" services such as refuse collection or street maintenance, but a growing number of "soft" or social services; for example, day care, health care, job training, are also provided by contract. Under contract agreements, it is possible to purchase only one or a few aspects of a service while others are performed by a government department. For example, a streets and roads department might purchase traffic signal maintenance services but perform its own street and road maintenance, or a police department might purchase traffic and parking control services but provide all crime-related functions itself.

There are several guidelines that may be used to help determine whether a particular service should be purchased.[15] First, in order to contract for services, there must be one or more providers available (or easily created) to perform them. Second, it has generally been believed that only services whose outputs or activities could be clearly specified or quantified should be contracted so the provider's responsibilities could be unambiguously stated. However, this guideline is no longer strongly adhered to, since many social services do not fit these criteria very well, but are provided under contract arrangements nonetheless. It is still desirable to be as specific as possible about the provider's responsibilities and performance standards expected. Third, services requiring substantial amounts of equipment are generally viewed as good candidates for contracting since this allows the jurisdiction to avoid large capital expenditures.

Intergovernmental cooperation is used here to refer to agreements between jurisdictions resulting in joint efforts to provide services. Contracting between government units could be considered a form of cooperation, but they will be treated separately here. Cooperation, as used here, includes joint purchase and/or sharing of a facility, equipment, and/or personnel.

Areas where cooperation would be helpful can be identified by using job redesign analytic techniques to locate services with underutilized personnel and/or equipment. However, this may not be necessary since many administrators are well aware of units in their jurisdiction where this problem exists. Nearby jurisdictions can be contacted to determine if they would be interested in cooperative arrangements for provision of these (or other) services. Interjurisdictional task forces or committees can be created to help select services for cooperative provision. They can also be responsible for working out agreements concerning allocation of various aspects of service provision responsibility among the participants (see section on implementation).

EXAMPLES OF RESTRUCTURING

Most examples of internal reorganization involve centralization or consolidation. Some have been discussed in earlier sections, such as changing from decentralized building inspections with specialized inspectors to a consolidated approach with generalist inspectors, or consolidating police and fire functions into one public safety unit whose employees are trained for both jobs. While the latter have been successful, they have usually occurred in smaller, primarily residential communities with relatively high income levels.

It seems unlikely that such a program would be successful in jurisdictions with larger populations and higher crime and fire rates. A variation on the public safety unit concept is the Scottsdale Wrangler program, which might be viewed as a mixture of intrajurisdictional cooperation and volunteerism. Wranglers are city employees from any department who pass physical and entry examinations and receive basic firefighting training. They are on call one week out of four, during which time they carry radio pagers and respond to alarms along with regular fire employees (the fire department itself is a contracted service that will be discussed below). This program allows the city to provide greater fire coverage without paying for full-time employees, although the Wranglers do receive additional pay for their week on duty.

Contracting or purchasing public services from the private sector or other government units is fairly widespread. A 1973 survey found that 68 different kinds of services were performed by contract, and this was before social services were widely provided in this manner. Services that are most commonly supplied by contracts are refuse collection/disposal and street maintenance/construction.[16]

As mentioned above, Scottsdale, Arizona supplies fire service through a contract with a private firm, which also serves other communities in the area. The agreement is based on a philosophy of minimum manning, with fire department employees supplemented by the Wranglers to minimize personnel costs. The fire department has also worked on developing or utilizing new technology. It developed a remote-control machine (called the snail) which can drag a hose into a burning building and maneuver it once inside, and devised a combined breathing and communication system. The department also has constructed some of its own trucks, which is less expensive than purchasing commercially produced vehicles.[17]

While many purchasing arrangements involve contracts between a jurisdiction and a private or public sector supplier for a particular service, or possibly a few related services, more extensive arrangements are possible. The so-called Lakewood Plan in Los Angeles County is the primary example of a comprehensive contracting system. Under the plan, jurisdictions within the County can purchase as few or as many services as they wish from a broad range of services the County provides, paying in terms of an hourly charge per type of employee (except for law enforcement and traffic patrol, which are based on annual rates for a car staffed with one or two officers).[18] Thus a municipality would decide to contract for most or all of the services it provides its residents.

Intergovernmental cooperation may be viewed as an alternative to service contracting or as a form of centralization that extends beyond jurisdictional boundaries. Sometimes cooperation is used to allow sharing of equipment that the jurisdictions cannot afford individually. For example, 10 municipalities in the Minneapolis-St.Paul area formed an arrangement to share a central computer installation. Each city has its own data files and access through its own terminals. Computers are a fairly common focus of cooperative agreements.

Another frequent area of cooperation is centralized police and emergency service dispatch (911 systems). Centralization allows reduction in the number of personnel performing dispatching functions, since each jurisdiction no longer needs its own dispatcher. Cooperative purchasing arrangements are also fairly common. By pooling orders for equipment and supplies, a number of small jurisdictions can purchase in sufficient quantity to take advantage of volume discounts. This type of arrangement also reduces the need for purchasing agents in the separate jurisdictions.

IMPLEMENTING RESTRUCTURING

Organizational restructuring has been used here to refer to three separate kinds of change. Internal reorganization, such as centralization or consolidation (either of which may involve job enrichment, new technology, or work redesign), has been covered in other chapters. Therefore, discussion of implementation of these types of organizational change will not be repeated here. Since contracting or purchasing services and intergovernmental cooperation are similar in many aspects of implementation, they will be discussed jointly, with distinctions noted as appropriate.

Selecting Services. The initial concern in implementing a contracting or cooperative arrangement is selecting the service. While it might be desirable to provide any number of services through such an arrangement from the standpoint of reducing costs of service provision, it is generally easier to do so if the service is new to the community. If a service has already been provided, entering a contract or cooperative arrangement means dismanteling the existing service provision structure and displacing employees, which is likely to be resisted by the affected parties, and possibly by other employees and/or the general public. However, it may be possible to deal with the displacement issue by: having the service provider agree to hire the displaced employees; training them for other positions in the same jurisdictions; giving them preference in future hiring; or by a combination of these approaches.

Another potential barrier to contracting or cooperation is lack of willingness to allow parties outside the jurisdiction to control service provision. This can occur for several reasons: removal of the service appears to diminish responsibilities and power of government leaders; it is believed that citizens will object to such an arrangement; it is felt that citizen input or participation will be reduced. This kind of opposition is more likely to occur when services are regarded as "sensitive" and/or are visible and important to citizens, for example, police and fire service.

Although these services are provided by contract or cooperation in many areas, such arrangements are rejected in others. For example, a committee studying possible areas for cooperation among four small towns in Minnesota recommended developing a joint police force. The towns rejected the proposal largely because it meant having an outsider as police chief in towns that were used to having one of their own residents as chief. However, they were willing to cooperate on providing services that were new to the area, such as wastewater treatment and animal control.[19]

A committee or task force format is one approach to making intergovernmental cooperation easier to arrange. Local Councils of Governments, regional planning agencies, state departments of community affairs, or similar bodies could be used to help determine which services are most suitable for joint provision and to assist in planning the service arrangement. A task force of representatives from the governments considering cooperation could be formed to work with the agency. This kind of assistance would be particularly useful for smaller communities.

One approach that can be taken to gain acceptance for use of alternative service delivery structures is to spin off component parts of the service for outside provision. For example, if crime-related police activities are deemed too sensitive for outside provision, less sensitive areas, such as communications and dispatch, traffic control, or laboratory functions might be provided this way. Thus some savings could be realized, and it might be possible to spin off additional functions at a later time if the initial experience is satisfactory.

Before entering a service arrangement, careful comparison of benefits and costs should be made. Comparison should be made between the jurisdiction itself as provider and the potential contractor or intergovernmental arrangement. If there is more than one potential provider, comparisons should be made among them. Long-term impacts should also be considered. The jurisdiction may find itself trapped in a relationship if no competing providers exist, and may face higher costs when the contract is renewed. It is not suggested that the jurisdiction can change such a situation, but merely that it should be considered before entering an agreement.

Contract Agreements and Administration. Once a decision has been made to enter a contract or cooperative arrangement for a particular service, there are two major areas of implementation to deal with: the first is drawing up a contract, which is needed for cooperative arrangements as well as purchase of services. The contract is important because it specifies the responsibilities of the parties involved. While the intricacies of contract writing are too detailed for a full discussion here, some major points will be noted.[20]

The most critical aspect of the contract is the description of the service to be performed. This should include:

- A statement of the goals of the service
- Measurable objectives and tasks to be performed
- The amount and quality of service
- How performance and/or service provision will be measured
- The monitoring and adjustment procedures to be employed

The degree of specificity to which these can be stated will vary with the service involved. Those services involving client interaction and/or exercise of discretion cannot usually be as clearly defined as "hard" services. Of course, other aspects of the contract are also important, including description of the personnel involved, the population to be served, and budgetary information.

The second aspect of implementation is setting up an administrative mechanism or unit to oversee the contract. The oversight responsibilities include monitoring service provision to determine whether quantity and quality standards are being met, as well as handling any complaints regarding service provision. Fiscal oversight would be the other major responsibility of this unit. A traditional concern associated with purchasing services from the private sector is the possibility of graft and corruption related to awarding and/or administering contracts. Therefore, both the contract administration unit and the jurisdiction's central administration should be watchful for this problem.

In the case of cooperative service arrangements, the jurisdictions involved will also have service provision responsibilities. This will require coordination among the jurisdictions and monitoring of service provision in addition to normal service delivery activities.

Organizational restructuring in the sense of internal reorganization fits the more traditional view of productivity improvement by increasing the efficiency of resource allocation. Contracting for services and intergovernmental agreements are not always thought of as productivity improvements since they involve removal of service provision responsibilities. However, this is done with the intention of reducing costs, so they can be viewed as productivity improvement methods from that perspective.

HOW RESOURCE REALLOCATION IMPROVES PRODUCTIVITY

Improved allocation of resources is frequently mentioned as a way to increase productivity. Resource allocation typically refers to one or more of the following: location of facilities; staffing levels and/or deployment; service schedules; and response patterns.

Resource allocation, or *re*allocation, is frequently viewed as an approach to improve service effectiveness rather than efficiency. This is because resource allocation is usually more closely related to responsiveness to citizen demands or needs for service than to the amount of service provided. However, resource reallocation also allows for more efficient use of personnel and facilities, which makes it a productivity improvement method as well.

APPLYING RESOURCE REALLOCATION

One type of resource reallocation involves better deployment or scheduling of employees. This should result in less idle time, and may even reduce the amount of personnel needed to provide adequate service delivery. It can also allow provision of service to growing communities without adding new facilities.

Improving scheduling involves more accurately matching the availability of employees to regular variations in the amount of need or demand for services. Such variations involve consistent patterns in use of service over short-run time periods (e.g., time of day, day of week) or over geographic areas. For example, one might find that city clerical workers who deal with the public are busiest during the middle of the day, or that refuse loads are heavier early in the week, or that more crimes occur in specific neighborhoods.

In order to improve scheduling, current service provision patterns must be studied. If records of a particular service's provision are not routinely kept, employees can keep logs of their activities for a limited time period to identify variations in demand for service. Demand data (e.g., calls for service), can be displayed in graphs or tables. Variations in demand can be compared to staff deployment to see if there is an adequate match. If not, personnel could be reallocated. Work distribution charts (explained in chapter 8) can also be useful for this purpose.

Just as better staff deployment can reduce the need for personnel, better choice of location for facilities such as police or fire stations can result in reducing the number of facilities needed. This also reduces personnel requirements. The location of existing facilities should be analyzed, not just new ones. This is because the need for such facilities may change over time as population patterns change. Thus some facilities should be closed or relocated for more efficient operation. This leads to productivity improvement in the sense of cost reductions. Computer programs have been developed to help relocate service facilities and also to determine service deployment patterns.

It is simpler to explain how resource allocation can be used in a Productivity Improvement Plan (PIP) by giving examples of applications. Thus the following section will help explain how reallocation can be applied.

EXAMPLES OF RESOURCE REALLOCATION

Many examples of public sector efforts to improve scheduling or routing of services and/or location of facilities are linked to computer use. Programs have been developed specifically for site selection of fire stations, and so on, and for patrol car allocation. A variety of different programs exist, and they have been used in numerous localities. They typically require information about the rate, number and/or types of calls for assistance in each geographic area, or a rating of relative service demand or hazard; information about the current location/deployment of facilities or equipment; information about the size of geographic subdistricts and/or a grid or other representation of physical layout.

The programs commonly estimate the amount of travel time between the existing or proposed facility and the origin of a call for service. Some identify the fastest route between points. The patrol car allocation program indicates the number of cars needed on duty in each precinct to provide response within a specified amount of time. The fire station locater has been most widely used, with applications in at least 100 jurisdictions. The first program, developed by the New York City Rand Institute, was credited with allowing the city to eliminate six stations in 1972 at a savings of $4.2 million annually.[21]

Demand analysis does not always have to involve sophisticated models and computer use. One could construct a graph showing the calls for service during the hours of the day and compare this to the number of employees assigned at various times. Personnel availability is often equally distributed among shifts, while demand may be much more concentrated. For example, in New York City the police patrol force was equally distributed among three shifts prior to 1969. Analysis of calls for service indicated that most were received during the evening. As a result, a fourth shift was created to increase the number of officers available during evening hours. Anticrime teams have also been deployed in accordance with crime patterns, resulting in teams representing only 4% of police officers being responsible for 22% of felony arrests in 1973.[22] This type of directed, rather than random, patrol has been adopted in a number of other cities in addition to New York.

A variation on the concept of having different staffing levels at different times of the day is the notion of adaptive response, or varying the amount of equipment/personnel responding to a call for service. Adaptive response originated with New York City's fire department in 1969 because of the large portion of false alarms (38% of alarms received in 1971 were false). In addition, many real fires were not of a serious nature. However, the practice had been to send the amount of equipment needed for a structural fire to all alarms. A computer analysis identified geographic areas and times of day in which alarms were likely to be false or not involve serious fires. The amount of equipment used as standard response in these areas and/or times was reduced from the prior level, resulting in less waste of staff time and increased availability of equipment for real needs.[23]

Another variation on adaptive response involves screening calls for service to assign priorities for response as well as the number of personnel deployed. This is a fairly common approach in police departments. The dispatcher solicits information about the nature of the complaint. Calls about crimes in progress or those recently completed will receive the fastest response with the largest personnel deployment. "Cold" crimes receive a delayed response and might be handled by only one officer. Reports of lesser crimes (e.g., petty larceny, vandalism) might be handled by telephone or by sending a form for the complainant to fill in and return by mail. Hartford, Connecticut began using TeleServe in 1981 in order to free line officers for serious incidents. Nonemergency services are handled over the telephone by this unit. In its first year, it handled over 9700 incidents, shifting 16% of the workload away from line officers.[24]

One approach to improved staffing or scheduling involves use of a mobile or flexible crew or team that can be placed as needed instead of having a permanent assignment. This is particularly helpful when used to supplement staff reductions associated with reallocation. For example, "flying squads" of firefighters have been used in Orange, California and Saint Petersburg, Florida to supplement crews at specific kinds of fires. This allows regular crews and equipment to stay in their firehouses to provide coverage in case additional fires occur. This is similar to the Scottsdale fire wrangler approach, but it utilizes regular fire department personnel.

Mobile crews do not have to be restricted to emergency service. Honolulu, Hawaii changed its deployment pattern for parks personnel to include mobile crews. Prior to the change, groundskeepers were assigned to each park. Afterward, a groundskeeper was responsible for routine maintenance at more than one facility while mobile crews with responsibility for mowing and gardening tasks for a particular group of parks circulated as needed. As a result of the rescheduling and use of mobile crews, the district reduced its staff (through attrition) by nine employees.[25]

Other goals of rescheduling may be to conserve resources such as fuel or to reduce the amount of unproductive time employees spend on traveling, waiting, and so on. Relocation of facilities for building inspectors in Fairfax County, Virginia was undertaken for these reasons. Prior to relocation, all inspectors reported to a central facility where morning preparation tasks such as planning and submitting daily inspection routes were done. After this, they would leave for their first inspection site, which could be a number of miles away.

Fuel shortages and rising costs resulting from the Middle East oil embargo led to development of a plan to redeploy inspectors to reduce fuel consumption. Field office sites were relocated to areas of expected high population growth. Instead of building new facilities, spare classrooms in schools were utilized. The plan resulted in less fuel savings than anticipated, however, largely because economic factors hurt the construction industry, reducing the demand for inspections and increasing the distance between inspection sites, which offset the fuel savings from redeployment.[26]

IMPLEMENTING RESOURCE REALLOCATION

As is true of other improvement methods, implementing change in resource allocation really involves two separate issues: gaining acceptance for the change, and planning and carrying it out. The latter aspect of implementation primarily requires use of various types of analysis. Most changes in scheduling or facility location are related to demands for service, which mean that analysis of patterns of demand will be required. The complexity of analysis needed will vary with the magnitude of change involved and the methodology used. Relatively simple kinds of analysis can be performed, such as preparing graphs or tables of demand data (e.g., calls for service by time of day and/or area). These can be compared to staff deployment or facility location to determine if there is an adequate match; if not, reallocation can be used to improve it. This kind of analysis could be used, for example, to increase the number of police officers on duty during peak crime hours or to place more firefighters in neighborhoods with larger numbers of fires. Work measurement or predetermined time standards can also be used to help schedule employees performing repetitive tasks.

Computer models for staff deployment or facility location are clearly a far more sophisticated approach to demand analysis. They require larger amounts of staff time to compile the appropriate data and set up the model, as well as experienced personnel to run the program. Staff time needed varies according to the model used, and can range from about two person-weeks to about two person-years.[27] Thus this approach is likely to be more time consuming and expensive, but has the advantage of providing better demand analysis and more sophisticated recommendations for allocation of resources.

An additional cost associated with relocation of facilities is the cost of the facility. This can become quite significant if some old facilities are closed and new ones built in different locations. However, such costs may be offset in the long run if fewer facilities are needed and, as a result, staff and equipment levels also decline.

Putting new schedules into effect is not generally problematic as long as sufficient advance notice is provided and new schedules are made clear. There can be some on-going communication problems if the new schedule involves a change from centralization to decentralization. A number of office routines had to be changed to accommodate decentralization of building inspectors in Fairfax County, Virginia, for example. Communication problems also arose, necessitating a weekly staff meeting to make up for the loss of contact among staff members and supervisors.[28]

Gaining acceptance for a change in resource allocation may be more difficult than actually implementing the change. However, the degree of resistance is likely to vary considerably by locality because it is influenced by factors such as the service or facility involved, the impact on personnel, and the scope of change. If the change is a minor one, it is unlikely to meet with internal or external resistance. Changes that have more noticeable effects, however, could find a number of barriers to implementation.

Not surprisingly, employees affected by change may not welcome it. Facility relocations that are intended to reduce overall staff levels will obviously be unpopular, but if a reduction by attrition policy is followed the resistance should be minimized. Changes in scheduling or deployment are also likely to be a source of discontent. Working hours and locations are important to employees, meaning that changes viewed as worsening working conditions are likely to be strongly resisted. It is also possible that union agreements may necessitate bargaining over such changes. State or local laws or civil service regulations regarding service provision or employee work schedules might also affect the ability to make changes.

Some changes in staffing patterns involving reduction in crew size are perceived as hazardous to employees and are resisted on those grounds. The use of one-officer patrol cars has been controversial in many communities, especially New York City, for this reason. However, it may be acceptable to employees if use is limited to areas and/or times of day with lower rates of violent crime, while two-officer cars are used for more dangerous assignments. The issue of crew size and safety has also been brought up with respect to other services. It has been suggested that the mechanisms of newer refuse collection trucks that require small crews may pose a danger. Reductions in firefighting crew size are also considered hazardous.

In addition to the possibility that employees will resist reallocation of resources, citizens might also act as a source of resistance. They may protest because of their own perceptions of the situation, or they might be mobilized as supporters by employees who are trying to block the change. Citizens may protest staff redeployment that reduces coverage in their own neighborhood (or on a citywide basis), particularly if safety-related services such as police or fire are affected. However, if reductions are minor, this type of reallocation may not create problems.

Relocation of facilities may also generate resistance. Facilities located within a particular area often take on symbolic importance in addition to their service provision functions. Closing such a facility is likely to generate stronger protest than would be associated with service reduction. For example, the decision to close a city hospital that had long served a low-income black community in St. Louis, Missouri, sparked considerable outcry from citizens in the affected area and ultimately became a major issue in the city's 1981 mayorality election. The symbolic importance of the facility seemed more significant than the actual impact its closing would have on health care. Removing a facility, particularly in low-income and/or minority communities, may be perceived as a withdrawal of municipal support for the affected group. Thus caution should be exercised in selecting facilities for relocation and in the way such decisions are publicized. Offering some form of replacement facility or service may be helpful if strong resistance to an allocation decision is encountered.

Adverse employee and/or citizen reactions to resource reallocation is generally the major barrier to implementation. If this barrier is not present, this type of change is not particularly difficult to implement and thus could be adopted fairly easily by communities whose service allocation systems could benefit from revision.

SUMMARY

This chapter has reviewed three improvement methods that are basically unrelated in terms of how they operate. However, they are related in the sense that they are all concerned with more efficient use of resources and/or cost reduction. These are summarized in Table 13-1.

New technology is most commonly associated historically with growth in productivity, particularly in the private sector. There are still many opportunities to utilize new equipment and/or computer technology in the public sector, either of which may entail changing work methods to suit the technology. Technology usually has a very direct effect on productivity by either substituting equipment for labor, or by increasing the amount of employee output. The primary drawbacks to this approach in the public sector are the high cost of many forms of capital equipment and the potentially negative reaction to displacement of employees if this results from adoption of technology.

Table 13-1. Summary of Methods Involving More Efficient Resource Use

METHOD	HOW THE METHOD WORKS
New Technology	Uses equipment to replace labor, or to increase the amount of output each employee can produce. Is applicable to a wide variety of jobs. Computers can be used to help plan and manage work that does not use equipment itself.
Organizational Restructuring	
Internal reorganization	Usually centralization of work to reduce duplication of effort and/or benefit from scale economies.
Contracting for services	Removes service provision responsibilities from government unit entirely. Cost-cutting measure.
Intergovernmental agreements	Arrangements between nearby jurisdictions to share facilities, major pieces of equipment, and/or personnel, or to jointly provide services, to reduce costs.
Reallocation of Resources	Relocation of facilities, changes in deployment or staffing of personnel. Leads to more efficient use of resources, and possibly overall cost reductions.

Organizational restructuring incorporates several kinds of change. Internal reorganization primarily involves centralization of functions or consolidation of units performing similar activities. This reduces duplication of effort and/or underutilization of capacity, and may lead to cost reduction due to economies associated with larger volume operations. Contracting for services means purchasing actual production or delivery of service from a private organization or another unit of government. This is done when third parties can provide the service at a lower cost. Intergovernmental agreements involve some form of cooperation between jurisdictions to purchase and operate equipment or facilities, to share personnel (particularly specialized personnel that are used infrequently), and/or to deliver services. This type of arrangement is similar to internal centralization or contracting in that it captures cost savings associated with larger scale activities and reduces underutilized personnel and/or facilities.

Changes in resource allocation, primarily the location of facilities or the distribution and/or level of personnel, is sometimes associated with productivity improvement. It is often related to more effective service delivery, but can result in reduced need for staffing or facilities as they are allocated to more appropriately correspond to needs or demand for service. Thus it can also lead to more efficient resource use and, potentially, to reduced costs.

The three methods discussed in this chapter are similar in that they are intended to increase efficiency of resources. New technology is most directly associated with productivity improvement. It increases staff efficiency by supplementing labor with technology of some kind (e.g., equipment, computers), thus increasing the amount of work that can be performed. The various forms of reorganization and resource reallocation seek to arrange work functions and resources in a way that will increase the efficiency of resource use. At the extreme, this can lead to arranging for other parties to perform particular functions (i.e., contracting for service provision). Resource reallocation and reorganization are not likely to have as strong an effect on productivity/efficiency as new technology, but they can be helpful additions to a PIP. All of these methods can be used in conjunction with most other improvement efforts in the PIP context.

NOTES

1. Kenneth L. Kraemer and John Leslie King, "Productivity and Computers" in ed. George J. Washnis *Productivity Improvement Handbook for State & Local Government* (New York: John Wiley & Sons, 1980), pp. 348-349, and Kenneth L. Kraemer et al., *Integrated Municipal Information Systems* (New York: Praeger Publishers, 1974), p. 55.
2. Peter L. Szanton, "Urban Public Services: Ten Case Studies" in ed. Richard R. Nelson and Douglas Yates, *Innovation and Implementation in Public Organizations,* (Lexington, Mass.: Lexington Books, 1978), pp. 128-129.
3. P. W. Park, "Rear-View Camera vs. Flagman on Garbage Trucks," *Public Productivity Review* 7 (September 1983): 294-295.
4. Probeye® is a registered trademark of the Hughes Aircraft Company.
5. Frederick O'R. Hayes, *Productivity in Local Government* (Lexington, Mass.: Lexington Books, 1977), pp. 62, 83.
6. Ibid., pp. 21, 83.
7. Albert J. Rigoni, "Automatic Water Meter Readings and Billings—By Computer," *Public Productivity Review 8* (Spring 1984): 91.
8. Kraemer and King, "Productivity and Computers," p. 346.
9. Hayes, *Productivity in Local Government*, pp. 268-269.
10. Ibid., pp. 172-187.
11. For a listing of these centers, see: Marion T. Bentley and Gary B. Hansen, "Improving Productivity Via QWL Centers," *Training and Development Journal* (March 1980):35-37.
12. Clyde Haberman, "Computer Network Aiding City,"*New York Times,* 13 July 1981, p. B3.
13. Damon Stetson, "$11 A Shift Extra Is Recommended for 2 Man Truck," *New York Times,* 12 December 1980, p. B1.
14. Norman Steisel, "Productivity in the Sanitation Department—The Two-Man Truck Story," *City Almanac* 16 (May 1982): 12.
15. Barbara J. Nelson, "Purchase of Services" in: ed. George J. Washnis, *Productivity Improvement Handbook for State & Local Government* (New York: John Wiley & Sons, 1980), pp. 433-435.
16. Ibid., p. 429.
17. Fred S. Knight, "Fire Service Productivity: The Scottsdale Approach," Municipal Management Innovation Series, No. 16, (Washington, D.C.: International City Management Association, March 1977).

18. For a full discussion of the Los Angeles County plan, see: Sidney Sonenblum, John J. Kirlin, and John C. Ries, *How Cities Provide Services: An Evaluation of Alternative Delivery Structures* (Cambridge, Mass.: Ballinger Publishing Company, 1977), pp. 71-115.
19. U.S. Department of Housing and Urban Development, Office of Policy Development and Research, *Practical Ideas on Ways for Governments to Work Together* (Washington, D.C.: U.S. Government Printing Office, May 1979), p. 6.
20. For a more complete discussion of service contracts, see Nelson, "Purchase of Services," pp. 437-441, which is the basis for the overview in this section.
21. John S. Thomas, "Operations Management: Planning, Scheduling, and Control" in: ed. George J. Washnis *Productivity Improvement Handbook for State & Local Government,* (New York: John Wiley & Sons, 1980), p. 182.
22. Ibid., pp. 175-182.
23. Edward K. Hamilton, "Productivity: The New York City Approach," *Public Administration Review* 32 (November/December 1972): 790.
24. Bernard R. Sullivan, "Channeling Non-Emergency Services Away from Police Officers," *Public Productivity Review* 8 (Spring 1984): 86.
25. National Center for Productivity and Quality of Working Life, *Improving Governmental Productivity: Selected Case Studies* (Washington, D.C.: U.S. Government Printing Office, 1977), pp. 46-54.
26. Ibid., pp. 15-20.
27. U.S. Department of Housing and Urban Development, Office of Policy Development and Research, *Practical Ideas for Governments Facing Planning and Scheduling Problems* (Washington, D.C.: U.S. Government Printing Office, May 1979), pp. 21-28.
28. National Center for Productivity, *Improving Governmental Productivity,* pp. 18-19.

Section IV
Productivity Improvement Over the Long-Run

The purpose of the chapters in this section is to describe the final stages of the Productivity Improvement Program (PIP). A productivity improvement program can be logically viewed as consisting of three stages:

1. Introducing the PIP and analyzing existing conditions to plan for improvement.
2. Selecting and implementing improvement methods.
3. Maintaining the improvement methods and the entire program.

The first two steps have already been discussed. The final stage, maintaining the PIP, will be explained in the next chapter.

The final chapter in this section will put the entire PIP in perspective by summarizing the key concepts related to conducting a PIP and the various improvement methods that have been presented in this book. This can also be used as a checklist or guide to refer to while progressing through the various stages of the PIP.

14
MAINTAINING THE PRODUCTIVITY IMPROVEMENT PROGRAM

The Productivity Improvement Program (PIP) does not end after the program has been established and the various agency or departmental productivity improvement efforts have been put into effect. Steps must be taken to insure that the various productivity improvements and the central PIP unit itself will be maintained over time. This maintenance stage requires changing the role of the central PIP unit from introducing improvement methods to departments, to helping maintain these efforts.

One aspect of maintenance is often referred to as routinization.[1] This occurs when an innovation comes to be regarded as a normal part of an organization's routine. This makes it more likely that the innovation will be maintained in the future. Routinization refers to individual improvement efforts as well as the PIP itself and it does not necessarily happen automatically. The public sector experience of a succession of budgetary reform efforts that died out after a few years substantiates this. This chapter will describe steps that can be taken to see that successful productivity efforts are routinized.

This chapter will also describe how to move into the maintenance stage of the PIP. The maintenance functions of the central PIP unit will be explained first. Then steps that can be taken to facilitate routinization will be discussed, with distinctions between the central unit and departmental efforts noted.

THE MAINTENANCE FUNCTION OF THE PIP

Beginning the maintenance phase of the PIP requires changing the central unit's goals and activities. Instead of introducing improvement methods to the departments, it now will help maintain them. If the PIP has operated in a sequential fashion, the central unit might be performing maintenance functions for some departments while performing introductory functions for others. However, this kind of overlap should not last long, and will not affect the nature of its responsibilities in either area.

In some instances, the organization and size of the unit responsible for maintenance functions may differ from that of the original central PIP unit. If a substantial central unit was created and staffed, it will probably be found that this unit is larger than necessary for performing only maintenance functions. In these cases, either a smaller central unit could be created, or long-term maintenance could be made the responsibility of a related department, such as personnel or budget.

The maintenance responsibilities of the central unit are these:

1. Monitor and evaluate departmental efforts and encourage/facilitate corrective actions as needed.
2. Provide encouragement to departments to maintain and improve their productivity programs.
3. Keep informed of new developments in productivity improvement and help departments update their methods.

1. Monitoring and evaluating departmental productivity efforts involves processing and/or reviewing the productivity measures collected by the department (unless other data collection responsibilities were originally designed). The measures will be evaluated to determine whether productivity is improving or being maintained at a satisfactory level, or if it is decreasing. Service quality will also be monitored. (Evaluation and quality control were discussed in detail in chapter 6.) Declines in performance will be investigated to discover their cause and help the department determine and implement the appropriate corrective action. The central unit will also transmit progress reports to the mayor and/or other higher level officials associated with the PIP.

2.The encouragement function of the central unit involves sustaining or renewing interest, effort, and enthusiasm after productivity improvement ceases to be a "new" program. At this time, it is important to emphasize to departments that the central PIP unit and the administration is committed to productivity *improvement* , not to a specific improvement *method*.[2] Thus, if one approach doesn't work, another will be tried. This is encouraging to departments because it reduces apprehension and helps create a more cooperative, optimistic atmosphere. This also makes it easier for departments to honestly report problems and negative productivity data.

One way to operationalize encouragement is through regular meetings with various groups involved in the PIP. Meetings could be held for the following groups:

Department heads and PIP staff from each department.

Department heads and PIP staff from different departments.

PIP staff and selected employees from different departments.

Meetings with each department administrator and the department's PIP staff are part of the normal process of evaluating the department's efforts to improve productivity. An effort should be made to keep the tone of these meetings supportive, which will help encourage departments to maintain improvement efforts. Departmental progress should be praised. Problems and poor performance should be discussed, but emphasis should be placed on helping departments determine corrective actions that can be taken.

Another way to provide encouragement and keep the PIP "fresh" is through periodic meetings between those responsible for productivity improvement in several different departments and the central unit staff.[3] The mayor (or someone representing him/her), should also attend at least some of these meetings. These meetings serve a variety of purposes. They provide a public forum for praise for departmental efforts. As department leaders discuss their own efforts and experiences, they may give new insights or ideas to others that can help them solve problems in their own departments, and may help revive their interest in productivity. Group meetings that include people from different departments provide encouragement by demonstrating to participants that they are part of a larger effort. This kind of meeting also provides an opportunity for the central PIP unit to present new ideas or methods for discussion and feedback. Of course, it also allows department personnel to air complaints or bring up questions or problems for general discussion.

A variation on this theme is to hold similar periodic meetings that include a representative group of lower-level employees. This also serves multiple purposes. It is supportive in showing the administration's continued interest in the needs and feelings of *all* employees, as well as acknowledgement of their importance in the productivity effort. It can be used for public recognition and encouragement, and to present employee awards (if they are used). It allows employees to recognize that productivity improvement is a group effort to which they are contributing. Finally, it provides a good opportunity for the central unit to get feedback from the employees most directly involved in carrying out the improvement methods.

3.The final maintenance step is to keep informed of new methods and help departments update their programs. Updating is needed because "old" methods will not continually produce improvements. Additional techniques will eventually have to be added to produce additional productivity gains. This is a continuation of the central unit's role in introducing the PIP, but on a smaller scale. This step utilizes the unit's knowledge of different sources of productivity improvement information. Part of this function may involve travel to other cities or to conferences to keep abreast of new developments and get a better understanding of methods that are being tried elsewhere.

The unit will act as an information clearinghouse for departments and help them install new improvement methods, as it did in the introductory stages.

The maintenance role of the central PIP unit involves a combination of evaluation, public relations, and expertise in improvement methods. These are functions it performed all along, but they are the dominant activities in the maintenance stage.

ROUTINIZING THE PIP

Routinization means that a program or change in operations is no longer regarded as "new," "experimental," or "a special project," but is considered a normal part of the organization's routine. This is important because normal aspects of the organization are far more likely to be maintained over time than "experiments" or "innovations." Routinization can be viewed as a psychological state of acceptance that promotes continuation of improvement methods.

Facilitating Routinization. Given the significance of routinization for program maintenance, steps to *facilitate* routinization should be included among the PIP's maintenance activities. Recent research on public sector innovations has identified several conditions that increase the likelihood that a new program or practice will become routinized.[4] For example, a practice or innovation is more likely to become routinized if need for it exists; it performs successfully; and practitioners accept it. These conditions are strongly influenced by the improvement method selected and the nature of its introduction, events which occur in earlier stages of the PIP. These factors are associated more with overall program success than with maintenance alone, and reinforce the common sense notion that successful programs are more likely to become permanent than unsuccessful ones.

However, one should not assume that a successful productivity improvement or the PIP itself will automatically become routinized. Steps can be taken to help facilitate the routinization of programs that are found to be successful. These steps are primarily related to resources that support the innovation, namely:

1. The budget
2. Personnel
3. Supplies and maintenance
4. Organizational rules
5. Rewards

These will be discussed in turn, with references to distinctions between the central PIP unit and improvement methods.

1. One aspect of routinization relates to the way an innovation is budgeted, namely whether its funding is soft, that is, from external (federal or state) funds or is locally generated.[5] The use of local funds, hard money, increases the likelihood of maintenance since soft money is usually allocated only for limited time periods. Projects financed by soft money are likely to disappear when their funding is withdrawn. Thus a transition from soft to hard money facilitates routinization, as does the initial use of hard money. However, this approach to routinization may become something of a moot point in the future as fewer external funds are available to local governments.

Not all improvement methods require significant additional funding of an on-going nature. Therefore, budgeting is most relevant for facilitating the central PIP unit and for those improvement methods that require additional funds (e.g., for purchasing new equipment or paying incentives). The best way to insure that the PIP unit remains in existance and that methods needing on-going funding are retained is to insure that they are initially funded with hard money.

2. Another way of facilitating routinization is to make supplies and maintenance related to an innovation part of the city's normal supplies/maintenance function.[6] This is only relevant for improvement methods using new equipment. During the introductory phase, supplies might be handled by special order to outside vendors and maintenance might be performed by the vendor. Stocking supplies in the city's own supply department and having city personnel perform maintenance on the equipment (which may involve additional training for them) indicates that the city is committed to continued use of the equipment. This will help employees accept its use as standard practice rather than as an experiment.

3. Personnel-related actions are a major focus in routinization. There are three areas where facilitating steps can be taken: job descriptions, training, and evaluation and rewards.[7] In instances where specific improvement methods have proved themselves, incorporating the new method into basic personnel documents and practices helps insure that they will be maintained not only by present employees but by future employees as well. Facilitating this aspect of routinization requires changes to be made for each job affected by an improvement method.

For example, if the method in question involves a new type of equipment, the job descriptions for positions using that equipment should be updated to specify that its use is required in the job. Training programs and/or manuals for employees in those jobs should be expanded to include operation of the new equipment. Similarly, job evaluations should be revised to include specific mention of the new equipment (unless it is used for a portion of the job that is too minor to warrant this degree of emphasis).

If the city formally evaluates employees, including the innovations among evaluation criteria facilitates routinization in two important ways. First, it automatically links innovation use to reward systems, for example, salary increases and promotions that may be based on evaluations. Second, it means there will be regular checks on whether or not the innovation continues to be used over time. Of course, all productivity improvement techniques are not equally easy or appropriate to include in all of these personnel related areas. Organizationwide changes like flextime, for example, are not appropriate for the techniques discussed here.

Routinization of the central productivity unit can also be facilitated through personnel related actions. Since it is likely that new positions were created or substantial changes made to existing positions, the task involved is not to change job descriptions, training programs, and evaluation criteria, but to create new ones. This is particularly important because it emphasizes commitment to the citywide improvement effort and its continuation. Similarly, personnel documents affecting agency and/or departmental heads and other supervisory positions responsible for decentralized aspects of the PIP should also be modified to make these responsibilities "official" and permanent.

4. Organizational rules play a similar role to personnel documents in routinizing productivity improvement.[8] Changing the rules or regulations that formalize the way an organization operates is a significant step that indicates the improvement method will be maintained in the future. A variety of documents might need modification to reflect different types of changes in organization practice. These could include: regulations that describe agency procedures and/or organizational structure; operating manuals; ordinances related to work practices; collective bargaining agreements or similar contracts. Most types of improvement methods, as well as the operations of the central PIP unit, could be reflected in one or more of these documents.

5. Another way to help facilitate routinization is to insure that former practices that are replaced by the new ones are terminated.[9] In some cases, "old" methods or equipment are maintained while "new" ones are employed on a trial basis. While this makes sense during the introductory stage, the continued possibility of reverting to the former method makes it more difficult for the new one to be routinized. Thus old equipment should be removed and former work methods prohibited. Replacing former practices can also be facilitated by changing rules and regulations and job descriptions related to them.

6. A final way to facilitate routinization is to provide rewards for using an improvement method. As noted earlier, rewards are often associated with

job evaluation. Productivity improvement and/or cooperation in using improvement methods can be specified as evaluation criteria. Thus, rewards usually linked with employee evaluation, generally wage increases and promotions, will encourage individuals to continue using and/or cooperating with improvement methods. The same logic applies to personnel in the central unit, whose evaluation will be based on successful introduction and maintenance of the overall PIP. Of course, if evaluations are not done, or if rewards are not really linked to them, this approach will not be useful.

Another type of reward can be offered to departments or agencies in addition to individual rewards. In exchange for participating in the PIP and for actual improvements in productivity, the department itself can be rewarded with increased resources and/or greater flexibility in using resources.[10] In effect, this represents sharing some (or all) of the monetary or personnel savings generated by the department. Thus, if a department reduces the number of labor hours necessary to perform a specific job, it could be "rewarded" by keeping the personnel hours or dollars saved and being allowed to use them in accordance with their own priorities. This will encourage department heads to improve productivity. Reducing personnel lines and/or budgets because of productivity improvement would seem more like a punishment and would not encourage agency cooperation.

Of course, in an era of fiscal constraint it is not possible to carry this philosophy too far. However, making an effort to share at least some of the savings with departments that generate them will make their leadership view the PIP as beneficial to them. This will help routinization, since department leadership will be inclined to regard as permanent and maintain any program that provides rewards, especially in times of austerity.

SUMMARY

This chapter has described activities that take place after a productivity improvement program has been established and improvement methods have been put into operation. It has focused on explaining how to facilitate the long-run survival of productivity efforts and of the PIP unit. This includes a changed role for the central unit. Its primary functions will be to monitor and evaluate department efforts; encourage continued interest and involvement in productivity improvement; and help departments update their efforts as necessary.

One approach to promoting maintenance is to facilitate routinization. Routinization (accepting an innovation as part of "standard operating procedures"), occurs *during* the maintenance stage (after it is no longer new) but also *contributes* to its maintenance. Various steps that can be taken during the maintenance stage to facilitate routinization of both the

Table 14-1. Summary of Steps to Help Facilitate Routinization

1. Use "hard money" rather than soft
2. Service equipment through *regular* supply/maintenance departments
3. Incorporate improvements in personnel-related matters:
   job descriptions
   training
   employee evaluations/rewards
4. Modify rules and regulations to incorporate the change
5. Abolish old methods
6. Provide rewards to individuals and departments for cooperation in using/introducing improvements

central PIP unit and successful improvement methods are summarized in Table 14-1.

The maintenance stage represents a winding-down of activities. Improvement methods have been installed and are in operation. A scaled-down central unit monitors them and keeps them functioning smoothly. It also stays abreast of new developments in order to update methods as needed. By now, productivity has moved from being a center of attention to being an accepted part of the way things are done. Some attention must be given to seeing that it stays an *active* part of the way administrators and employees view their job responsibilities. The maintenance functions described in this chapter are designed to serve that purpose and sustain the role of productivity improvement in local government.

NOTES

1. Robert K. Yin, *Changing Urban Bureaucracies: How New Practices Become Routinized* (Santa Monica, Calif.: The Rand Corporation, 1978), p. 4.
2. Thomas G. Cummings and Edmond S. Molloy, *Improving Productivity and the Quality of Work Life* (New York: Praeger Publishers, 1977), p. 281.
3. Using meetings to help maintain change is discussed in Richard Beckhard and Reuben T. Harris, *Organizational Transitions: Managing Compley Change* (Reading, Mass.: Addison-Wesley Publishing Company, 1977), pp. 101-103.
4. The discussion of routinization in this section relies heavily on Yin, *Changing Urban Bureaucracies,* pp. 46-56.
5. Ibid., pp. 46-47.
6. Ibid., p. 49.
7. Ibid., pp. 47-48.
8. Ibid., pp. 48-49.
9. Ibid., pp. 126-127.
10. Jacob B. Ukeles, *Doing More With Less: Turning Public Management Around* (New York: AMACOM, 1982) pp. 248-249.

15
SUMMARY: PUTTING IT ALL TOGETHER

This book has presented a comprehensive approach to public sector productivity improvement. It is recommended here that productivity improvement should be approached in the context of a comprehensive, centralized program. This framework places responsibility for the overall program in a central unit that helps departments and agencies implement their own improvement efforts. The improvement method(s) used in any department or unit should be selected to fit the organizational context and the jobs affected. This tailor-made approach to selecting improvement methods is more likely to successfully generate productivity gains than applying one improvement method on an across-the-board basis.

This chapter will summarize key points made about the productivity improvement program and the various improvement methods that can be used in it. This can be used as a checklist while going through the steps of the productivity improvement process.

WHY PRODUCTIVITY IMPROVEMENT IS NEEDED AND WHAT IT MEANS

The need for productivity improvement in the 1980s is related to the fiscal constraints most state and local governments are experiencing. Many government jurisdictions are facing declining tax bases, a problem compounded by years of poor economic performance at the national level, as well as inflation that has increased the cost of providing public services. The taxpayer revolt climate and the new federalism, which has reduced financial support for a variety of programs, have increased these problems.

Productivity improvement can help alleviate, but not eliminate these problems because its goal is to increase the amount of services produced by a specific quantity of resources. This book has defined productivity in terms of the *efficiency* with which inputs are converted into outputs. This emphasis is consistent with the need to use resources carefully due to fiscal limitations. The effectiveness of resource use is also important, but is viewed here as a different dimension of output that should be evaluated separately from productivity.

Productivity should be measured by a ratio of outputs to inputs. Outputs are measured in terms of completed service activities, such as streets cleaned, clients served, fires extinguished, and so on. Most departments or units require multiple output indicators to reflect different types of services provided and/or to reflect variations in work effort/skills within output categories (e.g., arrests could be classified by major types of crime). Inputs are measured in terms of labor hours used to perform the service.

ORGANIZING FOR PRODUCTIVITY IMPROVEMENT

A centralized form of organization should be used for the Productivity Improvement Program (PIP) for two reasons. It insures that efforts to improve productivity are not left to chance. It also provides a mechanism (the central PIP unit) for introducing and implementing improvement methods in various departments which might lack the information and/or skills to undertake an improvement effort on their own. The central PIP staff is responsible for introducing the program, helping departments select and implement improvement methods; and performing evaluation and maintenance activities after implementation.

The central PIP unit can be organized as a separate office under the mayor or city manager. Alternatively, it could be made part of another department, such as the budget office. There should also be decentralized PIP offices in each department to act as liaisons with the central unit and help it introduce, implement, and monitor productivity improvement in the departments.

INTRODUCING THE PIP

The introductory phase of the PIP is important because it helps generate support for the PIP as well as preparing for implementation of improvement methods. Table 15-1 summarizes key points relating to introductory strategies and methods as well as timing the introduction. In brief, the introductory strategy may be summarized as *telling* people about the program (providing information), and *selling* them on it (generating support and/or overcoming resistance). Specific strategies involve: demonstrating executive support for the program; initiating participation by affected managers and employees; implementing policies to build support (e.g., no layoffs); using persuasive communication to stress benefits of the program as well as provide information about it.

Various methods can be used to help introduce the PIP. Orientation meetings are particularly effective because all of the introductory strategies can be included in them. Other methods include informational materials, publicity, union involvement, and participation mechanisms (such as task

Table 15-1. Introducing the PIP

INTRODUCTORY STRATEGIES

• Executive support
• Participation of managers and employees
• Policies to build support
    No layoffs
    Share benefits
• Persuasive communication

INTRODUCTORY METHODS
• Orientation meetings • Informational materials • Participation mechanisms • Union involvement • Publicity
TIMING
• Introduction should be performed when working conditions are "normal" • Selective introduction should be used to build support

forces, surveys, and meetings). The timing of the introduction can also help generate support for the PIP. Managers and employees will be more receptive to a new program if it is introduced when working conditions are at normal levels, not during peak workload periods. A selective introduction approach can be used to help build support for the PIP. Improvement efforts can be introduced to departments one at a time so that initial successes generate greater acceptance for the PIP in remaining departments.

Another activity that is performed as part of the introductory stage of the PIP is establishing a measurement system. The main purpose of the measurement system is to provide feedback on the impacts the improvement methods have on productivity and service quality. This identifies areas needing corrective action and can be used to help motivate managers and employees by providing feedback and/or setting targets. Establishing a measurement system primarily involves:

- Identifying output measures that accurately reflect the work performed
- Identifying quality measures that reflect important aspects of service quality
- Establishing a system to collect and compile data on these indicators

The final step in the introductory stage of the PIP is determining which improvement methods can be used for particular jobs. This requires analyzing

Table 15-2. Characteristics of Jobs and Their Environment to Identify Before Selecting Improvement Methods

JOB CHARACTERISTICS
Employees: skills and attributes, number involved
Equipment: type, age, and condition
Production process: how work is performed
JOB ENVIRONMENT
Directly related jobs or services
Indirectly related jobs or services
Nature of contact with citizens
Rules and regulations limiting change
Organizational structure/management style

current conditions of jobs being considered for improvement. Analysis can be performed by developing profiles of the job and its environment. These identify features that can be used to help select improvement methods that are compatible with the job and its environment. These points are summarized in Table 15-2. Analyzing job characteristics identifies how the work is performed (including the equipment used), and who does it (including skills used and number of people involved).

Job environment analysis identifies factors external to the job that may influence choice of improvement methods. These include other jobs that are directly or indirectly related to the job being improved which might be adversely affected by changes in it. The nature of citizen contact is identified to determine how it might be affected by change. Rules and regulations that may restrict the kind of changes that can be made (e.g., civil service regulations affecting personnel use), are also identified. The final environmental factor is the structure of the organization and/or management style, which may not be compatible with certain kinds of change.

SELECTING IMPROVEMENT METHODS

Once job and environmental characteristics have been identified, the various improvement methods should be reviewed to determine which are compatible with it. The main features of methods that focus on improving productivity by increasing staff efficiency are summarized in Table 15-3. Limitations on the use of each method should also be reviewed at this time, since they may restrict use of a method in a particular situation. A final factor to consider is cost of the improvement method. All methods involve costs in the sense of time associated with preparation; for example analyzing current conditions,

Table 15-3. Summary of Improvement Methods

METHOD	HOW IT WORKS	LIMITATIONS ON USE	COST CONSIDERATIONS
Work Redesign	Changes work procedures (simplify work; eliminate steps, etc.)	1. Applicable to repetitive work 2. Regulations may limit ability to change methods/responsibilities	Cost of work analysis and redesign; possibly costs of training in new procedures.
Incentive Systems	Increases motivation by rewarding employees for increased output; better performance; or changed behavior	1. Output based incentives require quantifiable outputs 2. Regulations may prohibit pay variations associated with incentives	Costs associated with rewards; amount paid as monetary incentives or dollar value of other rewards (e.g., time off)
Job Enrichment (including job rotation and teams)	Increases motivation by filling higher level needs. Changes jobs to add diversity, responsibility	1. Useful only when employees need enrichment 2. Regulations may limit ability to change methods/responsibilities 3. Management may resist increased employee responsibility	Costs of analysis and redesign; possibly costs of training in new procedures. Employees may want higher pay for more work
Group Participation (including labor-management committees, task forces, and quality circles)	Increases motivation by filling higher level needs through employee participation. May lead to work changes more directly related to productivity	Management may resist increased employee responsibility	Work time lost while attending group meetings
Management by Objectives	Increase motivation because employee helps set own work goals. Targeting may help channel work efforts		Work time lost during objective setting and evaluation processes
Flextime	Increases motivation because employees participate in determining work hours	Impacts on related jobs and/or the public may limit use	Cost of time recording devices. Possible additional overhead costs

(continued)

Table 15-3. *(Continued)*

METHOD	HOW IT WORKS	LIMITATIONS ON USE	COST CONSIDERATIONS
New Technology	Equipment supplements or replaces labor. Computers used for better planning and/or to supplement or replace labor	1. Most applicable to jobs already using equipment 2. Employee/union resistance to reductions in labor force may limit use	Costs of equipment
Internal Organizational Restructuring	Reduces duplication and saves money by larger scale operations	More applicable for support-type services than those with direct client contact	Cost of designing reorganized structure
Contracting for services	Removes responsibility for service program; saves money	1. Politically sensitive services can't be contracted out 2. Provider must be available 3. Possible employee/public resistance	Cost of service provision; may increase in future
Intergovernmental agreements	Pool resources to share facilities/ equipment or provide services. Saves money	1. Nearby jurisdictions must be interested in cooperating 2. Politically sensitive services can't be provided this way 3. Possible employee/public resistance	Continuing portion of costs of services shared
Resource reallocation	Reallocate personnel/facilities to meet demand better; reduce excess	Possible employee/public resistance	Analytic costs (possibly including computer models). Cost of facilities, if built

selecting and designing the new method, and implementation. Some improvement methods have additional costs associated with them. In these cases, both start-up costs (e.g., purchase of new equipment) and on-going costs (e.g., operating and maintaining equipment, payments for incentive systems), should be included. Possible ways to finance costs should also be considered.

When selecting improvement methods, you are not restricted to applying only one method to a job or department. In fact, since most departments contain a variety of jobs, it is likely that more than one method will be applied in any department. It is also appropriate to use more than one method at a time for a particular job. Some improvement methods are frequently used together because they complement each other. Job redesign often accompanies new technology, job enrichment, and incentive systems, for example. Others can be used together because they do not conflict with each other. For example, a flextime system can be used in a department where some jobs have been redesigned and where others are under incentive systems.

The advantage of using multiple methods is that it enables productivity improvement to be approached from a variety of perspectives, and thus increases the potential impact on productivity. One method can use a direct approach, such as changing the way the job is performed, or using new technology. Another can be indirect, using one of the motivation-related techniques. A disadvantage of using multiple methods is uncertainty about how much each of them contributes to the resulting increase in productivity. If two methods are used on a given job, for example, and productivity increases 10%, it is difficult to determine whether the methods contributed equally to the increase, or whether one had a dominant effect on it. While knowing this may seem unnecessary, given that productivity improved, this kind of information is helpful when selecting improvement methods to use in other jobs. Another possible disadvantage to using multiple methods is that it may be confusing to employees to adjust to more than one improvement technique at a time.

If more than one method is to be applied to a given job, therefore, it may be better to introduce them sequentially, particularly if they are not complementary methods. This reduces the potential confusion to employees and can help in determining what kind of impact particular methods have on productivity. If methods are introduced to a given job sequentially, it is preferable to use methods with the strongest likelihood of improving productivity first. These include methods with the most direct relationship to output, namely job redesign, new technology, and output-related incentive systems. Methods with less direct links to output (such as those related to increasing motivation) can be added later. Applying additional improvement methods to a job over time makes sense because no method produces *continual* gains in productivity. Thus, after some period of time, a different method will have to be applied to generate additional improvement.

MAINTAINING PRODUCTIVITY IMPROVEMENT

Once improvement methods have been implemented, they should be monitored to be sure they are being used properly; are not having adverse side effects; and are, in fact, improving productivity. Continued monitoring of productivity and service quality is one of the major responsibilities of the central PIP unit after improvement methods have been implemented in all departments. This is the maintenance stage of the PIP (discussed in chapter 13). Other functions that should be performed in this stage are: encouraging departments to continue their improvement efforts; taking steps to facilitate routinization of improvement methods; helping departments update their efforts by keeping informed of new developments.

As this book has shown, there are many things to be considered while introducing productivity improvement in the public sector. The two most important points to help the PIP succeed can be summarized as follows:

Carefully plan and implement introduction of productivity improvement to facilitate acceptance.

Use the tailor-made approach to pick the method most suitable for each individual job and its work environment.

Following the guidelines presented here requires some time and effort on the part of those involved with the improvement effort. However, it will greatly increase the likelihood of achieving productivity improvement.

It is more important to focus on improving public sector productivity now than at any time in the past because of the fiscal realities of the 1980s. It is preferable to use resources as efficiently as possible—as Ukeles says, to do more with less[1]— than to cut back on needed public services as a response to fiscal constraints.

NOTES

1. Jacob B. Ukeles, *Doing More With Less* (New York: AMACOM, 1982), p. vi.

Appendix A
Productivity Questions and Answers

The Productivity Questions and Answers reproduced in this appendix were developed for use by communities involved in the Multi-Municipal Productivity Project in Nassau County, New York. It is presented here to provide a guide to how issues of concern to employees may be explained in a question and answer format as part of the Productivity Improvement Program introduction. If this format is adopted, questions and answers should be changed to accurately describe conditions related to the particular PIP, or to address concerns existing in a specific locality. For example, it might be pointed out that any reduction in force necessary will be accomplished through attrition, if this is the case.

PRODUCTIVITY QUESTIONS AND ANSWERS*

1. *What can I do to help the productivity program?*
   Employee cooperation is the key to the success of the productivity program.
   You can help by responding to surveys and by offering constructive advice to staff members when they begin a study of your department.
2. *Will I be required to work harder?*
   The theme of the productivity program is work smarter not harder.
3. *What is input?*
   Input is the number and amount of resources utilized.
4. *What is output?*
   Output is the result obtained.

*Source: Multi-Municipal Productivity Project, *An Approach to Productivity Improvement in the Public Sector: A Procedural Manual.* (Nassau County, N.Y.: 1975), pp. 17-29.

5. *How can you define productivity?*
   Productivity is comparing the amount of results (output) to the amount of resources (input).
   It is the achievement of increased service, with quality maintained by use of more effective work methods.
6. *What do you mean by productivity improvement?*
   Productivity improvement means changing procedures or using new technology to do each job in the best way possible. It can mean more effective and better quality service through rearranged work flow, changed work rules, or new equipment.
7. *How do you measure productivity?*
   Productivity is measured by comparing the amount of results (output) to the amount of resources (input). Resources include: (1) labor (2) capital (3) work system (4) equipment and supplies. Results (output) are the products manufactured or services performed.
8. *Will I be able to contribute ideas?*
   Yes, your ideas are vital. Employees will be asked by the staff to contribute advice and ideas.
9. *Will the productivity program cause any reduction in force?*
   The productivity program is a joint municipal-union effort and all parties have agreed that *no loss of jobs* will result from the operation of the productivity program.
10. *In what way will the productivity program affect my career ladder?*
    If productivity improvements are accomplished in your work, it could lead to a faster climb on the career ladder. Improved productivity has been demonstrated not to necessitate changes in job specifications. Your present career ladder will *not* be damaged.
11. *Will there be any ordered speed-ups?*
    No. The productivity program will not result in ordered speed-ups on the part of individual employees actually performing the service.
12. *Will my job responsibilities change?*
    Possibly, but not to require more work than is specified for your position, just better ways of doing your work.
13. *How does productivity affect my employer?*
    It enables the employer to respond to an increasing demand for services without increasing the tax burden on the citizen.
14. *If the productivity program recommends staff reorganization in my department will I be retained?*
    Yes. Increases in productivity *will not* result in loss of work.
15. *What is the productivity program?*
    It is a joint labor-management research and development program demonstrating the productivity of employer and employee in (*name of*

municipality). What we are actually trying to determine is the effectiveness of new methods for doing the same work *or* improving production as a result of using new technology. Our attention will be on the *work group* and productivity improvements will focus on this level of the work force, not at the *individual* level.

16. *How will the productivity program be conducted?*
The productivity program begins with several months of research and education by the staff in the field of public sector productivity improvement. The staff, with participating department heads, union representatives and employees, will select a few study areas where initial productivity improvements will be implemented. During the second stage, the staff will act as consultants to other departments engaged in Productivity Improvement Efforts (PIEs).
17. *How will I learn about the progress of the program?*
The labor and management liaisons in each department will keep their co-workers advised of the productivity program's progress through meetings and newsletters.
18. *Why should I as an employee actively support productivity improvement?*
There are four basic reasons:
    1. Salary or work benefit increases may be based on productivity increases.
    2. Participation in the productivity program will give you a say in the decision-making process.
    3. As a local resident and taxpayer, you may contribute to saving yourself and your neighbors taxes.
    4. Increased productivity is an important tool in fighting inflation.
19. *How will the productivity program effect my present position?*
The productivity program will not have any effect at all on some positions. For others it may entail a new procedure or method of doing the job. The productivity program may result in retraining so that you will be better prepared for another job, without any reduction in pay or seniority.
Depending on your position, the productivity program may improve and better define your level of responsibility, provide more training in your particular field, eliminate unrelated duties if they exist, or even result in an upgrading of your position.
20. *What effect will productivity improvement have on the taxpayer?*
Productivity improvement will help to slow the rate of growth of government costs at the local level and help keep taxes down. The benefits from improved productivity in local municipal government may also be passed on to the taxpayer in the form of additional services and better quality service for the same cost.

21. *What does productivity have to do with inflation?*
Productivity improvement is one way we can combat inflation. When wages go up faster than productivity, the item produced or service given is inflated by the extra cost of producing it. This makes the item or service more highly priced. As a result of the price increase, the wages earned and used to make purchases have the same or less *buying power.*
22. *How will the productivity program measure productivity improvement?*
In those areas where employees participate in attempts to achieve productivity improvements, measurements of input and output will be made before and after joint efforts begin. These measurements will be used to evaluate the success of the *total* unit effort to increase productivity; they will *not* be used as individual standards.
23. *Will safety standards be neglected as a result of improved productivity?*
No. A change may only result in an improvement of safety standards.
24. *If I produce more, will some people be laid off?*
No one will be laid off as a result of the productivity program. Productivity improvements will be used to meet the increased need for services.
25. *Will the productivity program have any affect upon the graded service salary plan?*
No effect is expected on the graded service salary plan.
26. *Can improved productivity result in a better contract for labor?*
Yes. Improved productivity can be used to achieve increases in salary or work benefits.
27. *What is productivity bargaining?*
Productivity bargaining is a method of negotiating increases for employees based on real increases in the productivity of government service. Productivity bargaining means that employees share directly in the savings realized through joint labor-management productivity efforts.
28. *Do you have any questions about the productivity program which you would want us to answer?*
Send your questions with your name and address to us for a response.

Appendix B Composite Productivity/ Quality Measures

Composite indicators usually include measures of one or more quality attributes in addition to output and input measures. It is not recommended that composite measures be part of the Productivity Improvement Program (PIP) measurement system for reasons to be explained below. However, since composite measures have some strong proponents and are often mentioned in productivity-related materials, it is worthwhile to understand what they involve.

One approach to composite measurement (using solid waste collection as an example), is presented in Table B-1.[1] The output measure is tons of waste collected. Cost is used as the input measure. Quality is reflected in two ways. The first is by use of a street cleanliness score ranging from 1 to 4, with 4 being the cleanest. The other quality indicator is the percentage of a survey population that was satisfied with collection services.

In this example, efficiency, as measured by tons collected per thousand dollars, increased 2.6%, while both quality measures decreased. The composite indicator shows a decline of 14%. Faced with *only* the composite figure, one would be at a loss to know exactly what had happened here. In this case, street cleanliness apparently declined as efficiency increased, causing citizen dissatisfaction. However, one has to go back to the original data to determine this so corrective action can be taken. The need to use original productivity and quality measures to find out what *really* happened (i.e., what increased, what decreased, and by how much) seems to negate the usefulness of the composite indicator.

An updated approach to composite measures is called $O \cdot K$ work.[2] The standard O (output indicator) in the productivity ratio is multiplied by a factor K that represents quality and/or effectiveness. This is then divided by the input measure, as in the previous example. One or more K variables must

Table B-1. Composite Measure for Solid Waste Collection Productivity*

BASIC DATA	YEAR 1	YEAR 2	RATIO
1. Tons collected	90,000	100,000	$\frac{100,000}{90,000} = 1.11$
2. Average street cleanliness rating	2.9	2.6	$\frac{2.6}{2.9} = .896$
3. Percent of survey satisfied with collection	85%	80%	$\frac{80}{85} = .94$
4. Costs (adjusted for inflation)	$1,200,000	$1,300,000	$\frac{1,300,000}{1,200,000} = 1.083$

PRODUCTIVITY RATIO:

Year 2 $\frac{100,000}{1,300,000}$ = 77 tons/thousand $

$$\frac{77}{75} = +2.6\%$$

Year 1 $\frac{90,000}{1,200,000}$ = 75 tons/thousand $

COMPOSITE MEASURE

To create the composite measure, multiply the ratio of the output measure by the ratios of the two quality measures, and divide these by the ratio of the input measure:

$$\frac{(1.11) \times (.896) \times (.94)}{(1.083)} = .86 = -14\%$$

*Source: Harry P. Hatry and Donald M. Fisk, *Improving Productivity and Productivity Measurement in Local Governments* (Washington, D.C.: National Commission on Productivity, 1971), p. 19.

be identified for each service analyzed. Each K represents the ratio of an achieved level of quality to a standard level of quality, not to prior year quality. This means a standard quality level must also be determined for each quality indicator. The K variables can be given weights to reflect their relative importance. K can be defined by the following equation:[3]

$$K = \frac{w_1k_1 + w_2k_2 + w_3k_3}{w_1 + w_2 + w_3}$$

To illustrate how the K variable works, assume that three quality variables have been identified for a particular service: speed, accuracy, and citizen satisfaction. Quality measures indicate the service reached 75% of its standard for speed of delivery; 99% of its accuracy standard; and 94% of its citizen satisfaction standard. It has been determined that speed is the most important quality criterion, accuracy is half as important as speed, and satisfaction is half as important as accuracy. The above information is expressed in the *K* equation as follows:

$$K = \frac{4(.75) + 2(.99) + 1(.94)}{7} = .85$$

Then:

$$\text{Productivity} = \frac{\text{O} \cdot \text{K}}{\text{I}} = \frac{\text{O}(.85)}{\text{I}}$$

Thus the quantity of output in the productivity ratio is reduced to 85% of its value to correct for the extent to which quality is not up to standard.[4]

Proponents of composite measures believe it is beneficial to emphasize the interrelationship between productivity (expressed in terms of efficiency) and service quality or effectiveness by adjusting the productivity ratio as described above. This approach is not recommended here because it complicates the process of measurement and analysis. If the composite measure indicates there is a problem, one must refer back to the individual productivity and quality measures to determine exactly what the problem is before taking corrective action. Thus it seems to impose an additional level of calculation without providing sufficient additional insight to justify its use. For the sake of clarity and simplicity, therefore, it seems preferable to use individual quality and productivity measures.

NOTES

1. Harry P. Hatry and Donald M. Fisk, *Improving Productivity and Productivity Measurement in Local Governments* (Washington, D.C.: National Commission on Productivity, 1971), pp. 18-19.
2. Ellen Doree Rosen, "O · K Work: Incorporating Quality into the Productivity Equation," *Public Productivity Review* 5 (September 1981): 207-217. For other examples of composite measures, see, for example: Everett E. Adam, Jr., James C. Hershauer and William A. Ruch, "Developing Quality Productivity Ratios for Public Sector Personnel Services, *Public Productivity Review* 5 (March 1981): 45-61; Robert J. Wallace, "Productivity Measurement in the Fire Service," *Public Productivity Review* 2 (Spring/Summer 1977): 12-36.
3. Rosen, "O · K Work," p. 215.
4. Ibid.

INDEX